Textual Connections in Acts

SOCIETY OF BIBLICAL LITERATURE
MONOGRAPH SERIES

Adela Yarbro Collins, Editor
P. Kyle McCarter, Jr., Associate Editor

Number 31
Textual Connections in Acts

by
Stephen H. Levinsohn

Stephen H. Levinsohn

Textual Connections in Acts

Scholars Press
Atlanta, Georgia

Textual Connections in Acts

by
Stephen H. Levinsohn

© 1987
Society of Biblical Literature

Library of Congress Cataloging-in-Publication Data

Levinsohn, Stephen.
  Textual connections in Acts.

  (Society of Biblical Literature monograph series ;
no. 31)
    Bibliography : p.
    1. Bible. N.T. Acts—Criticism, Textual.
I. Title. II. Series.
BS2625.2.L48   1987   226'.6048   86-20238
ISBN 1-55540-060-4 (alk. paper)
ISBN 1-55540-061-2 (pbk. : alk. paper)

Printed in the United States of America
on acid-free paper

CONTENTS

ABBREVIATIONS

AV	Authorized Version of King James
chap.	chapter
CU	continuing utterance (see Part One, sec. 1.251)
D	Codex Bezae
DU	development unit (see Part Two, sec. 1.1)
GA	genitive absolute (see Part One, sec. 4.2)
IU	initiating utterance (see Part One, sec. 1.251)
n.	note
NEB	New English Bible
NIV	New International Version
NPC	participial clause in the nominative case (see Part One, sec. 4.2)
NT	New Testament
q.v.	*quod vide*, which see
RSV	Revised Standard Version
RU	resolving utterance (see Part One, sec. 1.251)
sec.; secs.	section; sections
T	transitional temporal expression (see Part One, chap. 2)
v; vv	verse; verses
Ø	asyndeton

PREFACE

The author acknowledges the help given by Professor F. R. Palmer (University of Reading, England), Dr. J. Callow and Professor G. D. Kilpatrick. Professor Kilpatrick's extensive knowledge of the literature and of the different manuscripts of Acts eliminated many pitfalls, while his concern to identify the original text, whenever variants exist, was a spur to a careful examination of alternatives. Dr. Callow reviewed early drafts in great detail; many of his suggestions have been incorporated. Professor Palmer supervised the research on which the monograph is based and ensured that the conclusions reached were as objective as the subject matter permitted. A sincere thank you to each one!

INTRODUCTION

"What is said by one man in a conversation prehends what the other man has said before."[1] Most utterances relate in some way or other to their context, whether that context is linguistic (previous written sentences or past speeches), or non-linguistic (e.g., the scene before the speaker or his earlier experiences). Even the stereotyped "Once upon a time . . . " is the product at least of "Tell me a story!".

One problem faced by the linguist who seeks to identify "all the factors which, by virtue of their influence upon the participants in the language-event, systematically determine the form, the appropriateness or the meaning of utterances"[2] is that of selecting features to abstract, over against those which it is safe to ignore. This is what makes so attractive the analysis of a text written to inform someone of a series of events; to a large extent the non-linguistic context shared by writer and reader is eliminated. The two are in different places at different times; the reader is not able to observe the writer's gestures or hear his intonation patterns. Consequently, apart from "an assumed common ground of experience,"[3] the knowledge which is already available to the reader is limited to the immediate linguistic context.[4] The analyst of written stories can therefore work from the hypothesis that virtually all that is contextually of relevance to each sentence is to be found in the text itself.

This monograph considers how relating successive sentences of a narrative to their context affects the way in which sentences begin and the order in which their elements (words, phrases and clauses) occur. In particular, it is concerned with the range of choices open to the writer of Acts, as regards both the form taken by the initial phrase or clause of the sentence, and the conjunction employed. Because "meaningfulness implies choice,"[5] the signif-

---

[1] Firth, *Tongues of Men and Speech*, 110.
[2] Lyons, *Semantics*, 2, 572.
[3] Firth, *Tongues of Men and Speech*, 174.
[4] "In written language the context is entirely verbal" (Firth, *Tongues of Men and Speech*, 174).
[5] Lyons, *Introduction to Theoretical Linguistics*, 413.

icance is discussed of selecting one conjunction rather than another, and of beginning the sentence with one element in preference to some other.

To claim that the order of elements in a sentence is affected by its relationship to the context is not new. In 1924, Mathesius used the concept of "theme" in his "functional analysis of the utterance."[6] Vachek defines theme to be "the basis of the statement, . . . that part of the utterance which refers to a fact or facts already known from the preceding context, or to facts that may be taken for granted."[7] He continues, "the normal sequence of the two elements is such that the theme invariably precedes the rheme" (the rheme being a "comment" about the theme or "topic"). Other linguists have reached similar conclusions on the normal or unmarked order of theme and rheme.[8] Thus, "Philip (theme/topic) was found at Azotus (rheme/comment)" (Acts 8:40).

Firbas points out the need to modify Mathesius' scheme and criticizes the tendency to identify the first element of a clause with the theme.[9] Nevertheless, he concludes, "the first element *is* important, as the *basis* of a sentence," viz., "the sentence opening which . . . is directly linked to the context."[10]

Part One of this monograph develops the concept of the basis for relating a sentence to its context. The basis chosen affects the order of elements in the sentence and the form of the clause selected to begin a sentence in Acts. In particular, if a sentence begins with a basis, then the sentence is to be related to its context primarily by contrast with or *replacement* of a corresponding aspect of the last events described. The basis for the relationship may be temporal (e.g., *tē epaurion*, "the next day"; Acts 10:24), spatial (e.g., *en Ioppē*, "in Joppa"; 9:36) or thematic (e.g., *Philippos*, "Philip"; 8:40). In Acts, a thematic change usually concerns a switch of attention from one participant in the story to another.

If no such replacement basis occurs at the beginning of a sentence, this too is considered to be significant. "Continuity of situation" with the context is assumed. This means that, apart from any modifications stated in an initial participial clause, the cast of participants in the story remains unchanged, as does the spatio-temporal setting for the events. Consequently, the use of a parti-

---

[6] Mathesius, "On Some Problems of the Systematic Analysis of Grammar," 306–319.

[7] Vachek, *Linguistic School of Prague*, 18, 89.

[8] See, for example, Hockett, *Course in Modern Linguistics*, 201.

[9] Firbas, "On Defining the Theme," 268. See also Lyons, *Semantics*, 2, 507.

[10] Firbas, "On Defining the Theme," 268. For the term "basis," see Beneš, "Die Verbstellung," 5.6–19; Kirkwood, "Aspects of Word Order," 5.89.

cipial clause to begin a sentence, rather than a subordinated clause of time (a temporal basis), is meaningful; see Part One, sec. 4.2.

The scheme used in Acts for relating a sentence to its context is therefore very simple. Sentences may be related by means of a thematic, temporal or spatial replacement basis which begins the sentence. The absence of a basis implies continuity of situation with the context.

Elements are not placed at the beginning of a sentence only because they are replacement bases, however. It is generally recognized that "emphasis on an element in the sentence causes that element to be moved forward."[11]

In fact the subject of a clause precedes its verb for three distinct reasons. Emphasis accounts for little more than 10% of the examples, and concerns prominence given to the size or extent of the subject (Part One, sec. 1.3). The subject is the thematic replacement basis of the sentence in 30–40% of the examples (sec. 1.1). However, by far the largest number of cases (about 50%) involve "temporary focus" on the subject (sec. 1.2).

A subject may be in temporary focus for a number of reasons. For example, it may be to anticipate a switch of attention to another subject, through whose initiative the story will develop. Alternatively, particularly within the confines of a reported conversation, it may indicate that the event (speech) concerned is an "intermediate step," and the exchange has yet to be brought to a satisfactory conclusion.

In Part Two of the monograph, the distribution of *de* and *kai* in the narrative of Acts is explained in terms of a suprasentential "development unit" (DU) which reflects the author's purpose.[12] As a narrative unfolds, the author not only needs to show how the event he describes in a sentence relates to its context. He may also wish to indicate whether that event represents the next step in the development of his story or is concerned only with the step introduced in an earlier sentence.

For example, if an incident concerns primarily the interaction of two people, both may need to be introduced or reintroduced to the story before the interaction itself can be described. As far as the author's purpose is concerned, the first step in the incident may therefore be a combination of the two introductions. The first introduction is incomplete without the second, and the second is part of the same step as the first (see sec. 1.21).

[11]   Blass, Debrunner and Funk, *Greek Grammar*, sec. 472(2).
[12]   Gindin ("Contributions to Textlinguistics in the Soviet Union," 261–274) introduces a similar concept, which he calls a "suprasegmental entity" or "SE."

Alternatively, the author may record the departure of a participant to a different place, when subsequent events concern the activities of those who remain. Under such circumstances, the departure may well not represent the next step in the development of the story. It may simply be noted "to keep the record straight" (see sec. 1.22).

The scheme used in Acts for showing how each sentence relates to the development of the story is again very simple. *De* is an unmarked developmental particle, introducing new steps or DUs. Additional developmental conjunctions are *alla, gar, oun* and *tote*. Each of these conjunctions indicates a specific relationship with the previous DU (see chap. 5).

The elements (sentences) of DUs themselves are associated by *kai* or *te*, with *te* indicating a specific relationship between the sentences it links (chap. 2). Finally, prospective *men* associates the DU it introduces with a corresponding DU introduced by correlative *de* (sec. 3.22).

In the course of this monograph, various other concepts are introduced that are crucial to the understanding of the structure of narrative texts. These include the division of the cast of participants into the central character(s) of the story, major and minor participants (defined in Part One, sec. 1.2); and the distinction between the nuclear and preliminary events of an incident (Part Two, sec. 1.21). However, central to the monograph is (a) the distinction between the placement of an element at the beginning of a clause or sentence to emphasize it, bring it into temporary focus, or make it the replacement basis for relating the sentence to the context, together with the significance of the absence of a replacement basis (Part One); and (b) the identification of the DU as a meaningful suprasentential entity (Part Two).

The claims made in this monograph are also of significance to the interpretation of many passages in Acts. With a couple of exceptions, no *new* interpretation of any passage is offered. However, the conclusions presented frequently enable a choice to be made between interpretations offered by different commentators. In other words, based on the principles outlined in this volume, it is often possible to choose between widely accepted but different expositions of the same passage.

In this connection, it is important to note that the principles established for Acts are not necessarily of general application to Koine Greek. While the claims made for the replacement basis and for the existence of a suprasentential entity such as the DU should be of more general application, some of the details will be idiosyncratic. For example, a glance at John's Gospel reveals that *oun* has replaced *de* as the principal developmental marker. Wider studies of these phenomena will be needed, before it is known whether the use of *de* and *kai* in Acts is the norm for the Greek of the period or in part is idiosyncratic. What is claimed is that the author of Acts has systematic ways of indicating both how a sentence relates to its context, and how an event relates to the development of the story. Other authors may be expected to achieve the same ends in equally systematic ways.

Can the book of Acts be treated as a single homogeneous entity, for the purposes of linguistic analysis? The author probably combined several sets of notes and recollections, when producing his history (e.g., 1:1–15:35 or "I Acts", "II Acts" and the "we" sections of Acts).[13] Some analysts discern stylistic variations between the sources they propose. However, N. Turner concludes, after examining this question, "One thing is certain, whatever his sources may have been, and however extensive, there is a linguistic unity throughout his two books, and the final editor has been able to impose his own style upon all his material."[14] The present author also finds no evidence of changes in the principles on which the order of words or the distribution of conjunctions are based, as the book progresses. Rather, examples of most phenomena can generally be found, whichever part of the book is examined.

More problematic, particularly for the analysis of conjunctions in Part Two, has been the existence of variants in many passages. The text used for this monograph has been that of Nestle & Aland (1975, 25th edition), including the variants they record, supplemented on occasion by changes proposed by G. D. Kilpatrick.[15] The principles presented in this volume have been established solely from passages for which Nestle & Aland record no relevant variants. This means that, in general, the principles are based on the "Alexandrian" rather than the "Western" text.

Numerous reported speeches are found in the book of Acts, some short, others very extensive. The principles of this monograph have not been based on examples drawn from within them. Rather, they are grounded on the basically narrative framework in which the reported speeches are embedded. (The term "narrative" is used to refer in general to material whose overall framework is

---

[13] N. Turner, "Style," IV.45. For convenience, the author of Acts is referred to as "Luke" throughout this monograph.
[14] N. Turner, "Style," IV.57.
[15] Kilpatrick, "Proposed Changes."

chronological and which is concerned with actions performed by specific people.[16])

The main reason for excluding reported speeches as a primary source of exemplification is that successive sentences do not relate only to the immediately preceding sentences of the same speech. They relate to some extent to the context of the speech as a whole.

For example, Acts 22 records Paul's speech to a hostile Jewish crowd. Although the events recounted in the speech fit into a chronological framework, the structure of successive sentences is not always that which would be expected, were the immediately preceding sentences of the speech alone to be taken into consideration. However, the deviations are readily understood, if one takes into account why the crowd was hostile and recognizes that Paul was seeking to answer their criticisms. The structure of each sentence is still determined by reference to its context. However, it is necessary to refer both to the immediate linguistic context and also to the wider context which is the narrative in which the speech is embedded. This broadens the field from which factors judged to influence the structure of the sentence may be drawn, and the resulting analysis is consequently more subjective.

The term "sentence" is used in this monograph in a restricted sense to refer to a single independent clause, together with those clauses which are subordinated to it, whether by a preposed subordinative conjunction such as *hote*, or because the verb is in the form of a participle or infinitive. Independent clauses linked by some conjunction are viewed as separate sentences, for the application of the principles proposed, even if there are grounds for analyzing them as a complex of coordinated clauses.

A glossary of technical terms is found at the end of this volume.

When examples are cited, the pertinent material only is given in a transliteration of the Greek, and the expression which is under particular consideration is underlined. A free English translation follows (based on the RSV, but modified where appropriate, in order to reflect more closely the structure of the Greek). Any context quoted is also based on the RSV.

---

[16]   See Forster ("Narrative Folklore Discourse in Border Cuna," 3–6) on factors which distinguish text genres.

PART ONE. INITIAL ELEMENTS IN A CLAUSE OR SENTENCE

Part One of this volume is concerned with three factors which determine the order of elements at the beginning of a clause or sentence in the narrative sections of Acts.

(1) The majority of references to time or place which begin a sentence provide the basis for relating the sentence to its context. They not only establish the spatio-temporal setting for the next events to be described; they also replace the setting for the previous events. Similarly, nearly half of the subjects which precede their verb are replacement bases. The material is so organized that there is a switch of attention from one subject to another.

(2) About half of the subjects which precede their verb do so to indicate that the participant referred to is only temporarily in focus. This may be because attention immediately switches to a second participant who (rather than the first) determines the direction of development of the story. Alternatively, it may be that the first participant utters an "intermediate" speech of a reported conversation with another participant, and that that speech does not bring the conversation to a satisfactory conclusion.

(3) A minority of elements occur at the beginning of a clause or sentence to emphasize them. Emphasized elements include subjects whose extent or size is significant, the duration or frequency of an event, the goal of movement and a variety of adverbial expressions.[1]

It is accepted generally in the literature that emphasis is a determining factor on word order in Greek. One way to emphasize an element is to place it early in its clause, in violation of the natural order of elements.[2] Blass, Debrunner and Funk also note

---

[1] See Davies, "Position of Adverbs in Luke," 106–121.
[2] See, for example, Winer, *Treatise on the Grammar of NT Greek*, 684; Denniston, *Greek Prose Style*, 47; Blass, Debrunner and Funk, *Greek Grammar*, sec. 472(2).

the tendency to place "transitional temporal phrases"[3] at the beginning of a sentence (factor 1), though they do not explain the phenomenon. However, the present author knows of no work discussing temporary focus on a participant (factor 2).   The order of words on Greek boundary stones and other short inscriptions varies so much that one might conclude, "it is the fault, not of the enquirers after the truth, but of the truth itself, Greek word order being 'free,' 'arbitrary' or 'indeterminate'."[4] For the analyst who, like Dover, believes that word order is not so insignificant, "some, at least, of the determinants of order must be sought not inside the utterance itself, but outside it, in relation to its context."[5]

Dover begins his investigation of Greek word order by listing eight possible determining factors. They are: phonological (the length of the word might affect its position), morphological (one word class might prefer to precede another), syntactical (e.g., the subject might generally follow the predicate), semantic (e.g., verbs of motion might have a preferred position in the clause), lexical (e.g., a certain list of words might always come at the end of a clause), logical (a word which the hearer will not expect has a preferred position in the sentence), emotive (the focus of the speaker's emotion), and social or ceremonial (habits and styles in the language). Dover considers four of these factors to be important: (a) lexical and semantic; (b) syntactical; (c) logical; (d) stylistic.[6]

(a)   There are various lexical and semantic forms with limited mobility. For example, the position of postpositives (e.g., *de*) and prepositions is fairly fixed, as is that of demonstratives, interrogatives and negatives. In addition, the relative order of independent, subordinate, participial and infinitival clauses shows certain preferred patterns.

(b)   Certain syntactical preferences may be discerned, though there are numerous exceptions. However, "we find in fact that in the language of the New Testament, rules of order are much more easily defined in syntactical terms than they are in Classical Greek."[7]

(c)   Much of Dover's book is taken up with a discussion of "logical predicates" or nuclei, and "logical subjects" or "concomitants." Utterances may be analyzed into nuclei ("if it is indispens-

---

[3] Blass, Debrunner and Funk *Greek Grammar*, sec. 472(3).
[4] Dover, *Word Order*, 1.
[5] Dover, *Word Order*, 32.
[6] Dover, *Word Order*, 3, 4, 12.
[7] Dover, *Word Order*, 68.

able to the sense of the utterance, and cannot be predicated from the preceding elements") and concomitants ("in so far as it is deficient in either of those qualities").[8] Certain concomitants normally act like postpositives, others like prepositives. Under certain circumstances, they may be given preferential treatment.

(d) Finally, stylistic factors which affect the order of elements are chiasmus, when "two members of the same syntactical structure and similar content are in antithesis," and formulaic patterns (the tendency for a series of clauses to be of the form SV-SV-SV or VS-VS-VS (S = subject; V = verb).[9]

Each of these factors is now discussed.

(a) Any study of word order in Greek must recognize "lexical and semantic determinants" such as the position of postpositives and prepositions. In this monograph it is assumed that all conjunctions occur in their required positions, according to the rules stated in traditional grammars. When discussing what is initial in a clause or sentence, such elements are ignored. As for the preferred position of demonstratives, negatives and different types of clauses, these are all accounted for in the relevant chapter of Part One, or in Part Two, sec. 4.2 (demonstratives). The principles presented in these chapters explain, for instance, *why* a transitional temporal expression normally begins a sentence in narrative (sec. 2.1).

(b) Statistically, more clauses and sentences of the narrative in Acts begin with the verb than with the subject.[10] This conforms with Blass, Debrunner and Funk's statement concerning tendencies in the narrative of the NT: "The verb or nominal predicate with its copula stands immediately after the conjunction."[11] This verb-subject order is taken as the norm, and deviations from it are explained.

(c) An analysis of the clause into "nuclei" and "concomitants," or into theme (topic) and rheme (comment; see the Introduction) does contribute to a study of word order. This is because there is a tendency to proceed from the known to the unknown,

---

[8] Dover, *Word Order*, 40.

[9] Dover, *Word Order*, 53, 56.

[10] Out of 720 clauses whose subject or theme is different from that of the clause or sentence to which they relate:
  in a maximum of 264, the subject precedes the verb;
  the subject follows the verb in 310;
  no separate subject is present in 146.

[11] Blass, Debrunner and Funk, *Greek Grammar*, sec. 472(1).

from the theme to the rheme, from the topic to the comment.[12] These concepts explain the order of words in existential clauses (see chap. 1, n. 1).

Of much wider application at the beginning of a clause, however, is a modification of Beneš' *basis*, which, "serving as a point of departure for the communication, is directly linked to the context."[13] This concept is of particular value when discussing factor (1) above (see especially chap. 4).

(d)   Finally, while the existence of chiasmus as a stylistic determinant must be recognized, Denniston argues that it is usually restricted to situations where there is a repetition of some word or words, or when it is desired to sharpen the contrast between diametrically opposite ideas. He maintains that it is rarely found when the two contrasted ideas are merely complementary to each other.[14] Because of this restriction, chiasmus is never a relevant factor in the truly narrative sections of Acts. As for formulaic patterns, their relevance in Acts appears to be limited to the internal structure of elliptic sentences (e.g., 17:17).

This monograph therefore assumes that "logical" factors generally explain why a particular element begins a clause or sentence in the narrative of Acts. These factors are not those suggested by Dover. Rather, factor (1) concerns the "replacement basis" of a sentence, and in particular its relationship to the previous sentence in time (sec. 2.1), space (chap. 3) or theme (usually the subject in narrative; sec. 1.1). Factor (2) concerns the standing of the participant who performed the act, or of the act which he performed, relative to the development of the ongoing story (sec. 1.2).

Factor (3) accounts for a minority of examples and, since it is a generally recognised determinant of word order, little attention is devoted to it. Rather, in secs. 1.3, 2.2 and the Introduction to chap. 3, attention is given to establishing when an element precedes its verb because it is being given emphatic prominence, and when it is so placed because of some other factor. Examples of emphatic forefronting which do not involve subjects (themes), temporal, or spatial expressions, are not discussed.

The term "emphatic prominence" is here used to denote
two of K. Callow's aspects of prominence: emphasis and

---

[12] Moorhouse, *Studies in the Greek Negatives*, 70; Firbas, "On the Prosodic Features of the Modern English Finite Verb," 7.14; Kiefer, "On the Problem of Word Order," 127.

[13] Translation by Garvin, "Czechoslovakia," 1.508.

[14] Denniston, *Prose Style*, 75–76.

focus. Emphasis "highlights an item of information which will be surprising to the hearer." Focus highlights information which is "of particular interest or significance,"[15] perhaps because of the implications for some other event in the immediate context.

The term "forefronted" is used to refer to elements which precede the nuclear part of the clause or sentence. In connection with subjects, "forefronted" is synonymous with "precedes the verb." Consequently, a "forefronted" subject is not necessarily the first element in the sentence. It does occur before its verb, but some other element may precede it, e.g., an adverbial phrase functioning as the temporal basis.

When only part of a phrase precedes the verb and the rest follows it (e.g., *tis ēn mathētria onomati Tabitha*, "there was a disciple named Tabitha"; 9:36), the phrase is considered to be forefronted.

When a phrase occurs between two clauses and could pertain to either, it is considered to follow the first verb, rather than to be forefronted with respect to the second. See, for example, *idōn de ho Petros, apekrinato pros ton laon*, "and when Peter saw it, he addressed the people"; 3:12.

---

[15] K. Callow, *Discourse Considerations*, 52.

CHAPTER ONE

THE SUBJECT OR THEME PRECEDES ITS VERB

The subject of an independent or subordinate clause is placed before its verb for three basic reasons in the narrative Acts.

(a) When the events of two clauses or sentences are "not in sequence," the subject (or, more accurately, theme; see below) of the second is placed before its verb. In general, "not in sequence" means that the events concerned take place at the same time, and the second event is not a response to the first.

For example, in 9:7, after describing the conversation of vv 4–6 between Saul and the voice from heaven, Luke tells his readers what Saul's companions were doing. Because the events of v 7 took place at the same time as the conversation, its subject precedes the verb.

> (9:7) *hoi de andres hoi synodeuontes autō heistēkeisan eneoi, akouontes men tēs phōnēs, mēdena de theōrountes.*
>
> "Now the men who were travelling with him stood speechless, hearing the voice but seeing no one."

However, "not in sequence" also includes situations in which the second event is not related in time or space to the first. The "replacement basis" for relating the new event to the context is then a switch of attention from the subject (theme) of the first event to that of the second.

For example, in 9:1, following the description of Philip's activities as he travelled to Caesarea (8:40), attention switches to Saul. In other words, there is a change of theme. The chronological relationship of the two events is irrelevant. Because the basis for linking them is a switch of attention from one participant to another, for all intents and purposes they are not in sequence:

> (8:40) Philip was found at Azotus, and passing on he was preaching the gospel (*euēggelizeto*) to all the towns till he came to Caesarea.

(9:1) <u>Ho</u> de <u>Saulos</u> . . . proselthōn tō archierei, (2) ētēsato par' autou epistolas eis Damaskon pros tas synagōgas

"Now Saul . . . going to the high priest, asked him for letters to the synagogues at Damascus"

The exact rules determining the forefronting of a subject when two clauses or sentences are "not in sequence" are discussed in sec. 1.1. Consideration is also given to what constitutes being "in sequence," when the second sentence is introduced with gar or some other causal conjunction (sec. 1.112).

Although the majority of clauses or sentences which are "not in sequence" involve the forefronting of the subject, in a few clauses an element in an oblique case is the theme about which the comment is made:

(4:32) <u>Tou</u> de <u>plēthous</u> <u>tōn</u> <u>pisteusantōn</u> ēn kardia kai psychē mia.

"Now concerning the multitude of believers, their heart and soul was one."

Consequently, in general terms it is the theme, rather than the subject of a clause, which is or is not forefronted.

(In copulative sentences involving the dative of possession or quality, the theme is generally the element in the dative case, not the surface subject; e.g., 21:9.)[1]

(b)   When two clauses or sentences are in sequence, the subject of the second is still placed before its verb if it is in "temporary focus." This term covers a variety of situations, which are discussed in detail in secs. 1.21–6.

The following situation illustrates the concept of temporary focus. Suppose that an act is performed by a group of people. The next two sentences then contrast the actions of two sub-groups, and the subsequent story develops, not from the action(s) of the first

[1] Further evidence that the basis concerns the theme rather than the subject is provided by "existential-locative" sentences (Kahn, "The Greek Verb "To Be" and the Concept of Being," 2.245–265). When the existence of a person or object is stated as the subject of such a sentence, the reference generally follows the verb, even though the sentence is not in sequence with the last event described. See, for example, 9:10 (<u>Ēn</u> de <u>tis</u> <u>mathētēs</u> <u>en</u> <u>Damaskō</u> onomati <u>Hananias</u>, "Now there was a certain disciple in Damascus named Ananias"). Firbas (review of Dahl, Topic and Comment, 7.97) points out that the person whose existence is posited is not the theme of the sentence but the rheme. (See the use of the dummy subject "there" in English.) Consequently, the sentence cannot be related thematically to its context!

sub-group, but through those of the second. The first sub-group will have come only temporarily into focus (sec. 1.21).

In 13:13–14, for instance, the group *hoi peri Paulon*, "the ones around Paul," arrives in Perga. There, it divides into two: John, who returns to Jerusalem (v 13b), and the rest of the group, who continue their journey as planned (v 14). The story does not develop from what John did. Rather, it follows the activities of the rest of the group. Consequently, John is only temporarily in focus, because the story as it develops is not built upon the action he performs. (The reference to the rest of the group in v 14 is forefronted, since the two events are "not in sequence.")

(13:13a) The ones around Paul . . . came to Perga . . .

(v 13b) *Iōannēs de, apochōrēsas ap' autōn, hypestrepsen eis Hierosolyma.*

"And John, departing from them, returned to Jerusalem."

(v 14) *autoi de,* "And/But they" . . .

By far the most common manifestation of temporary focus, however, is that found in connection with reported conversations (sec. 1.25). Typically, the "intermediate steps" in conversational exchanges are introduced with forefronted subjects. See, for example, 10:3–6. In this reported conversation, v 4a is the "intermediate step" between the initial greeting of v 3 and the speech which brings the conversation to a satisfactory conclusion:

(10:3) (Cornelius) saw clearly in a vision an angel of God coming in and saying to him, 'Cornelius.'

(v 4a) *ho de . . . eipen*

"And he . . . said,
'What is it, Lord?' "

(v 4b) *eipen de autō*

"and he said to him,
' . . . (5) And now send men to Joppa . . . ' "

(The next sentence records that Cornelius did as the angel instructed him.)

More than half the examples of temporary focus occur in connection with intermediate steps in an exchange (see Table 1 below, and the figures of sec. 1.27).

(c) A third reason for placing the subject of a clause before its verb is to emphasize its extent or size. In 11:21b, for instance, Luke is not so much concerned with who it was that "turned to the Lord." Rather, he wishes to emphasize the size of the group that did so:

(11:20) ... some of them ... spoke to the Greeks also, preaching the Lord Jesus; (21a) and the hand of the Lord was with them.

(v 21b) *polys te arithmos ho pisteusas epestrepsen epi ton kyrion.*

"and a great number that believed turned to the Lord."

Clauses in which *hikanoi, polloi* or *polys* modifies a noun, or in which *pantes* alone is the subject, generally indicate its size or extent, rather than simply identifying it. In sec. 1.3 the forefronting of these and other subjects which are concerned with extent or size is discussed.

Table 1 indicates how often the subject is forefronted because of each of the above factors. The figures do not include five examples in which (*kai*) *idou* probably determines the position of the subject,[2] or five cases in which the subject is a temporal expression (see sec. 2.14). In addition, they exclude 24 instances in which more than one factor requires that the subject be placed before the verb, and four sentences in which there are significant variations in the word order between the manuscripts.

Table 1

factor:		
not in sequence ("basis"; sec. 1.1)		76
temporary focus (sec. 1.2)		131
intermediate step (secs. 1.25–6)	68	
other factors (secs. 1.21–4)	63	
emphasis on extent (sec. 1.3)		19
TOTAL		226

The above figures also exclude the following:
the forefronting of the subject within an articular clause or a clause which is the verbal object of another verb;

[2] When *idou* or *kai* (. . .) *idou* is used in connection with the introduction of a new participant (Bauer, Arndt and Gingrich, *Greek-English Lexicon*, 371b), the subject always precedes the independent verb of the sentence (e.g., 8:27b). This may reflect a restriction on the order of phrases imposed by the presence of *idou*, rather than the forefronting of a basis.

cases in which the demonstrative pronoun *houtos* is subject of its clause. (In the narrative of Acts it always begins its clause. This is because it is usually the equivalent of a relative pronoun. See discussion in Part Two, sec. 4.2.)

This chapter discusses only the two-way distinction of when a subject (theme) does or does not occur before a verb. No evidence has been found to suggest that the rules for forefronting subjects need to take account of the absence of a separate subject. In other words, for the purposes of this chapter, a clause such as *eipen de*, "and he said," functions like *eipen de ho Petros*, "and Peter said," rather than *ho de eipen*, "and he said."

1.1   Not in Sequence

In general, when two clauses or sentences are "not in sequence," but their subjects are different, the subject of the second is placed before its verb. Conversely, when they are in sequence, the subject of the second is forefronted only if factors other than those of this section require it.

There are three areas of exception to this rule: (a) when the first clause is ignored (e.g., because it is a background comment) and the second is deemed to be in sequence with an earlier event; see sec. 1.12; (b) when the second clause is existential; see n. 1; (c) when something new is introduced in connection with the formula *kai* (. . .) *idou* (the subject always precedes the main verb); see n. 2.

1.11   The Basic Principle

The basic principle of this section may be stated as follows:

> (1) When the theme of Event* Y is an animate** participant A who was not involved in the last Event* X, or any other element E which was not the theme of X, then reference to A/E is placed before its verb, provided that:
>
> X and Y are not in sequence.

The theme is usually the subject: see discussion above.

> *The term "Event" is used because this principle is applicable both inter- and intra-sententially. The term denotes any action, situation, parenthetical comment or explanation which is described in the clause or sentence concerned. Typically, the position of the initial subject (theme) in a sentence and/or the subject (theme) of an independent

clause is determined by its relation to the Event of the previous *sentence*. The position of the subject of a subordinated clause is determined by its relation to the Event of the *independent clause* to which it is subordinated.

**Animate participants are human beings, animals and supernatural beings (e.g., an angel, the Lord, the Holy Spirit). Elements which are not animate include not only concrete objects (e.g., the port), but also verbal nouns or abstract concepts (e.g., discord, the word). This distinction is made because the narrative of Acts is primarily concerned with interactions between animate participants, and the majority of rules are exemplified only when the subject is animate. The distinction is seldom significant for the application of the rules, however.

Sec. 1.111 considers the common situation in which "not in sequence" means that the second Event does not occur *after* the first. Sec. 1.112 deals with situations (mainly involving sentences linked by *gar*) in which "not in sequence" means that the second Event does not occur *prior* to the first.

1.111   Most commonly, "not in sequence" means that, if the events concerned are related in time, then the second (Y) does not occur after the first (X). So, for example, Y cannot be a response to X.

In 6:2, for example, the proviso to rule (1) (viz., "X and Y are not in sequence") is violated because the apostles act in response to the situation described in v 1:

(6:1) (X) . . . the Hellenists murmured against the Hebrews because their widows were neglected in the daily distribution.

(v 2) (Y) *proskalesamenoi de hoi dōdeka to plēthos tōn mathētōn, eipan*

"Having summoned the body of the disciples, the twelve said,
'It is not right that we should give up preaching the word of God to serve tables.'"

Conversely, when the second action takes place at the same time as the first, and is not a response to it, then the proviso to rule (1) is met, and the subject is forefronted.

In 12:16, for instance, Peter's action took place while the people inside were arguing over who could be at the door. His action is not in response to the last speech they made:

(12:15c) (X) They were saying (*elegon* [to the maid]), "It is his angel!"

(v 16a) (Y) *ho de Petros epemenen krouōn.*

"But Peter was continuing to knock."

(Most commonly, when two events occur simultaneously, one or both is in the imperfect. However, this is by no means mandatory. See, for example, 9:7 above and 21:7.)

As was noted earlier, "not in sequence" also includes situations in which no chronological relationship between the events concerned is indicated. In 12:25, for instance, the action of Barnabas and Saul is in no way a response to the situation described in the previous sentences. Rather, there is a switch of attention from one subject to the other. No chronological relationship between the sentences is expressed, and they are therefore "not in sequence":

(12:24) (X) the word of God was growing and multiplying.

(v 25) (Y) *Barnabas de kai Saulos hypestrepsan ex/eis Ierousalēm*

"Barnabas and Saul returned from/to Jerusalem"

In a number of passages in which the subject is forefronted, it is not clear from the context whether the events concerned are or are not in sequence. The principle of this section enables them to be interpreted as "not in sequence."

One important example is 6:7. Some editors consider it to record the result of the last incident (e.g., "(and) so"; Newman and Nida; NIV[3]). Others view it as transitional material, bridging the gap between incidents (e.g., "now"; NEB; de Zwaan[4]):

(6:1–6 describe the election of the seven deacons to take care of the temporal affairs of the growing number of Christians, and end:)

(6:6) (X) These (seven) the disciples set before the apostles, and they prayed and laid their hands upon them.

(v 7) (Y) *kai ho logos tou theou ēuxanen*

"and the word of God was increasing,"
and a great number of the priests were obedient to the faith.

---

[3] Newman and Nida, *Translator's Handbook*, 133.
[4] de Zwaan, *Harvard Theological Review*, 17.106.

(v 8 takes up the story of what happened to one of the
deacons, Stephen.)

The forefronting of the subject of v 7 indicates, according to the
principle of this section, that v 7 is *not* in sequence with v 6. Such
a position is consistent with de Zwaan's view that v 7 is a
transitional summary, linking two separate incidents, and does not
belong particularly to either of them.[5]

Other passages in which the subject is forefronted, but the
context does not make it clear whether the events concerned are or
are not in sequence, include 12:7b and 13:50. The principle of this
section enables them to be interpreted as not being in sequence.

In a few cases, it seems likely that the events in focus
technically are in sequence, but Luke preferred to relate them by
comparing or contrasting the actions of the different subjects. In
other words, Luke chose to relate the sentences on the basis of
contrasting subjects (themes), although he could have related them
chronologically.

A good example is provided by 27:42–43. When the ship
carrying Paul and other prisoners runs aground (v 41), the soldiers
want to kill them all, to prevent them escaping (v 42). The
centurion, desiring to save Paul, rules otherwise (v 43). The
centurion's action is in response to the soldiers' suggestion (see
"kept them from carrying out their purpose"). Nevertheless, the
forefronting of the reference to the centurion indicates that Luke
chose to contrast the desires of the two groups, thus downgrading
the sequential relationship:

> (27:42) (X) The desire of the soldiers was to kill the prison-
> ers, lest any should swim away and escape;
>
> (v 43) (Y) *ho de hekatontarchēs, boulomenos diasōsai ton
> Paulon*
>
> "But the centurion, wishing to save Paul,"
> kept them from carrying out their purpose, and ordered
> those who could swim to throw themselves overboard

In a number of cases in which the subject does not precede the
verb, it is again unclear from the context whether the events

---

[5] de Zwaan, *Harvard Theological Review*, 17.106. See also Bruce, *The Book of
Acts*, 131; Dibelius (according to Knowling, "Acts of the Apostles," 401 n. 1);
Jackson and Lake, *Beginnings of Christianity*, 4.66.

    De Zwaan's position on transitional summaries is adopted also in connection
with the function of *men oun*; see Part Two, sec. 3.22.

concerned are or are not in sequence. The principle of this section enables them to be interpreted as being in sequence.

One example of particular interest is 17:14b. A correct interpretation hinges on the meaning of *hypomenō*. The use of *te*, rather than *de*, indicates that the statement is not in contrast with v 14a (Part Two, sec. 2.2). The failure to place the subject before the verb confirms this, and suggests that v 14b is a result of (in sequence with) v 14a. This is an acceptable interpretation, because *hypomenō* indicates that Silas and Timothy remained *behind,* when Paul was sent away.[6] In other words, *hypomenō* focuses, not on them continuing to stay (*epimenō*; 10:48b, 21:10), but on the result of Paul leaving (see also Luke 2:43):

> (17:14a) (X) Then the brethren immediately sent Paul off on his way to the sea;

> (v 14b) (Y) *hypemeinan te ho te Silas kai ho Timotheos ekei.*

> "and both Silas and Timothy remained behind there."

1.112   The proviso to rule (1) is also violated if Event Y occurs *prior* to X. This happens when a participial clause, occurring after the independent clause to which it is subordinate, presents an event which occurred prior to that of the independent clause. See, for example, 24:10:

> (24:10) (X) Paul replied,

> (Y) *neusantos autō tou hēgemonos legein*

> "when the governor had motioned to him to speak"

The proviso to rule (1) is also violated in this way when a sentence introduced by *gar* presents the efficient cause of the last event described. The cause of the event and the event itself are in sequence.

In 21:35–36, for instance, the soldiers are forced to carry Paul (v 35), specifically because the crowd is jostling behind. The soldiers' action (X) is in response to the crowd's violence (Y). Consequently, the proviso is violated:

> (21:35) (X) When Paul came to the steps, he was actually carried by the soldiers because of the violence of the crowd;

> (v 36) (Y) *ēkolouthei gar to plēthos tou laou krazontes, aire auton.*

[6] Bauer, Arndt and Gingrich, *Greek-English Lexicon,* 835.

"for the mob of the people were following, crying, 'Away with him.' "

However, *gar* may introduce an explanation or exposition of an assertion, in which no direct "cause-and-effect" relationship exists between the sentences linked by *gar*. Under such circumstances, the events concerned are not in sequence, and the proviso to rule (1) is not violated.

In 19:23–27, for instance, the statements of v 24 which introduce Demetrius do not stand in a direct cause-and-effect relationship to v 23, even though Demetrius' speech in vv 25–27 was the inciting event which eventually produced "no little stir concerning the Way." Rather, the whole of vv 24–41 is a detailed expansion on this initial assertion:

> (19:23) (X) About that time there arose no little stir concerning the way.

> (v 24) (Y) *Dēmētrios gar tis onomati argyrokopos, poiōn naous argyrous Artemidos, pareicheto tois technitais ouk oligēn ergasian*

> "For a man named Demetrius, a silversmith, who made silver shrines of Artemis, used to bring no little business to the craftsmen"

1.12   In Sequence with an Earlier Sentence

In a number of passages, Event Y is preceded by a parenthetical comment or other Event X which is not in sequence either with Y or with the previous Event W. If Event Y is in sequence with W, however, then the subject of Y is not forefronted.

In 17:19–23, for instance, the philosophers ask Paul to address them (vv 19–20; W). Luke then inserts a comment about the interests of Athenians in general (v 21; X). This comment is in sequence neither with W nor the following Event Y in which Paul responds to the philosophers' invitation (vv 22–31). However, Y is in sequence with W. The subject of Y is therefore not forefronted:

> (17:19) (W) The philosophers took hold of Paul and brought him to the Areopagus, saying, "May we know what this new teaching is which you present? . . . "

> (v 21) (X) *Athēnaioi de pantes . . . eis ouden heteron ēukairoun*

> "Now all Athenians . . . spend their time in nothing"
> except telling or hearing something new.

(v 22) (Y) *Statheis de (ho) Paulos en mesō tou Areiou-pagou ephē*

"So Paul, standing in the middle of the Areopagus, said"

The same principle applies if X is a parenthetical comment employing *einai*, or an explanatory comment introduced by *gar* or *hoti*. In 19:13–15, for instance, v 15 (Y) is in sequence with v 13 (W), and v 14 (X) is a parenthetical comment:

(19:13) (W) Some of the itinerant Jewish exorcists undertook to pronounce the name of Jesus over those who had evil spirits, saying, "I adjure you by the Jesus whom Paul preaches."

(v 14) (X) There were (*ēsan de*) seven sons of a Jewish high priest named Sceva doing this.

(v 15) (Y) *apokrithen de to pneuma to ponēron*

"But the evil spirit answered them"

In 5:5–6, the event X which separates v 5a (W) and v 6 (Y) is itself in sequence with v 5a:

(5:5a) (W) On hearing these words, Ananias fell down and died.

(v 5b) (X) *kai egeneto phobos megas epi pantas tous akouontas.*

"and great fear came upon all who heard of it."

(v 6) (Y) *anastantes de hoi neōteroi, synesteilan auton*

"The young men rose and wrapped him up"

As noted in Part Two, sec. 1.222a, the use of *kai* in v 5b indicates that that response is not built upon by the subsequent events. In other words, v 5b in some sense is parenthetical to the overall story. It appears that this is sufficient motivation for Luke to ignore v 5b, and indicate that v 6 is in sequence with v 5a. See also 16:6 (*men oun* introduces v 5; v 6 is in sequence with v 4).

1.13   Summary

The principle at work in the examples of sec. 1.12 may be summarized in a note on the rule of sec. 1.11. This now reads as follows:

(1) When the theme of Event Y is an animate participant A

who was not involved in the last Event X, or any other element E which was not the theme of X, then reference to A/E is placed before its verb, provided that:

X and Y are not in sequence.

Note: If Y is in sequence with the previous Event W, this constitutes a violation of the proviso to rule (1), if Event X is a background comment about W, is not in sequence with W, or does not provide a foundation for the further development of the story (see Part Two, sec. 1.22).

The above rule accounts for at least 31% and possibly as much as 40% of the forefronting of the subject or theme in the narrative sections of Acts. In addition, it is a particular manifestation of a much wider principle, viz., that the "basis" of a sentence is forefronted, whenever its primary relationship with the context is that the previous theme, temporal setting (sec. 2.1) or spatial setting (chap. 3) is replaced by a new one (see chap. 4). Subjects (themes) are forefronted in accordance with rule (1) to indicate that the primary basis for relating the clause to its context is thematic, not chronological. One theme has been replaced by another, and any chronological relationship between the events concerned is downgraded.

1.2   Temporary Focus

Half the forefronted subjects in the narrative of Acts precede their verbs because they are only temporarily in focus. By forefronting the subject, Luke anticipates a further change of subject (secs. 1.21–4), or indicates that the event (speech) concerned is an intermediate step in an exchange with some other participant (secs. 1.25–6).

The clearest examples of forefronting because the subject is only temporarily in focus occur when a group divides into two sub-groups. Typically, the references to both sub-groups are forefronted. Reference to the second sub-group is forefronted in accordance with rule (1); see sec. 1.11. Reference to the first sub-group also precedes the verb, this time because it comes only temporarily into focus (sec. 1.21).

Temporary focus manifests itself in several other ways, too. When the intention of a subject is frustrated by the intervention of some other participant, reference to him is forefronted (sec. 1.22). When a participant appears temporarily to perform a significant action, and then disappears from the scene, reference to him is forefronted (sec. 1.23). Even the reference to a "major participant" (see below) may be forefronted, in anticipation of a switch of attention to some other major participant (sec. 1.24).   An interesting manifestation of temporary focus, and one which accounts for half the examples of this section, occurs almost exclusively within the confines of the reporting of conversational exchanges (sec. 1.25). The forefronting of such a subject indicates that the speech concerned is an intermediate step in the exchange. A few examples of this phenomenon are found when the event concerned is not a reported speech. These are discussed in sec. 1.26.

In this section a distinction is made between "major" and "minor" participants. Various linguists divide the cast of characters in a narrative into "(major) participants" and "minor participants" or "props".[7] Typically, major participants are involved in a series of events. Minor participants, in contrast, "disappear from the stage as soon as a predication involving them has been made."[8]

In the narrative of Acts, individual major participants are introduced by name and usually are identified further, e.g., by means of an appositional phrase or relative clause. Thus, *tis mathētēs en Damaskō onomati Hananias*, "a certain disciple in Damascus called Ananias" (9:10) is a major participant. However, the messenger in 5:25 identified only as *tis* "someone" is not. Similarly, some external identification of a group (e.g., its origin) is given, if the people concerned are major participants. For example, *tines katelthontes apo tēs Ioudaias*, "certain people who had come down from Judaea" (15:1). However, detailed identification of an individual or group is unnecessary, if it is assumed that he is already known to the reader (e.g., Jesus [1:1], king Herod [12:1], the priests [4:1]).

Among the major participants of the narrative, one or more may be the "central character(s)." The term "central character" is used to refer to those participants about whom the narrative as a whole is primarily concerned. Acts is concerned primarily with the lives and acts of certain Christian leaders. These leaders are the "central characters" of the book.[9]   Finally, "supernatural participants" may be thought of as "external" to the central scenes of the narrative of Acts, as the interactions between human participants unfold. Like minor participants, supernatural beings often just appear and act, then disappear from the scene, leaving the human interactions   to

[7] See, for example, Grimes, *Thread of Discourse*, 43; Levinsohn, "Participant Reference," 75.

[8] Levinsohn, "Participant Reference," 76.

[9] K. Callow, *Discourse Considerations*, 49; Longacre and Levinsohn, "Field Analysis of Discourse," 106. See also Grimes, *Thread of Discourse*, 337.

continue. Supernatural participants include angels, the Lord, the Holy Spirit and actors in dreams or visions.

1.21   Temporary Focus on a Sub-Group

On various occasions in Acts, an event involving or directly affecting a group of participants is followed by reference to the actions of one or more sub-groups of the original group. If the original group G splits into two parts, and the actions of the two sub-groups G^1 and G^2 are compared or contrasted, it is common for the reference to both sub-groups to be forefronted.

Allusion has already been made (sec. 1.111) to 13:13–14, in which the group *hoi peri Paulon*, "the ones around Paul," arrives in Perga (Event W). There it divides into two sub-groups. John (G^1) returns to Jerusalem (X). The rest of the group (G^2; *autoi*, "they") continue their journey as planned (Y). References to both G^1 and G^2 are forefronted:

(13:13a) (W) The ones around Paul . . . came to Perga . . .

(v 13b) (X) *Iōannēs de . . . hypestrepsen eis Hierosolyma.*

"And John . . . returned to Jerusalem."

(v14) (Y) *autoi de*, "And/But they"

In the above passage, the reasons for placing the subjects of X and Y before their verbs are different. The subject of Y is placed before its verb because Y is not in sequence with X; "they" was not involved in X (rule 1; sec. 1.11). However, John (G^1) was part of the group involved in the previous Event W, and X is in sequence with W. The subject of X is forefronted because John is only temporarily in focus. Attention immediately switches from his action (over against that of the rest of the group) to that of G^2. The story then follows their activities, not his.

Reference to a sub-group is *not* forefronted, if the story develops from its initiative. In 11:28, for instance, Agabus is a member of the group of prophets (v 27). Verses 29–30 are in response to his message.

(11:27) (W) Now in those days prophets came down . . . to Antioch.

(v 28) (X) *anastas de heis ex autōn onomati Hagabos*

"And one of them named Agabus, rising up,"
foretold by the Spirit that there would be a great famine. . . .

(v 29) Then the disciples . . . determined to send relief

The principle illustrated above may be expressed as follows:

> (2) When a group of participants G is involved in Event W, and a sub-group G^1 is the subject of Event X, then reference to G^1 is forefronted, if the subsequent events develop, not through X, but through the action Y of some other participant.

The above principle holds, both when X is a response to W (e.g., 17:4 below), and when W and X are not in sequence (e.g., 19:32).

In 17:2–4, v 4 (X) is a response to v 2 (W). However, the story develops, not from X, but from the reaction Y of other people (v 5; see also the use of *kai* in v 4, discussed in Part Two, sec. 1.221):

> (17:2) (W) And Paul went in (to the synagogue) . . . and for three weeks he argued with them from the Scriptures. . . .
>
> (v 4) (X) *kai tines ex autōn epeisthēsan*
>
> "and some of them were persuaded"
>
> (v 5) (Y) But the Jews were jealous, and . . . gathered a crowd.

(In Codex Bezae, the subject of v 5 is "the unbelieving Jews"; i.e., sub-group G^2.)

In 19:32, v 32c (X) is not in sequence with v 32b (W). However, the story develops, not from their state of confusion, but from the course of action decided upon by other members of the assembly (Y; v 33):

> (19:32b) (W) For the assembly was in confusion,
>
> (v 32c) (X) *kai hoi pleious ouk ēdeisan tinos heneka synelēlytheisan.*
>
> "and the majority did not know why they had come together."
>
> (v 33) (Y) But some of the crowd prompted Alexander

1.22   The Intention of the Subject is Frustrated

An interesting case of "temporary focus" concerns a person who desires to perform some action, but his wish is frustrated by the act of some other participant. The principle involved may be expressed as follows:

> (3) When participant A attempts to perform Event X, reference to him is forefronted, if the subject B who performs

Event Y frustrates his intention, so that X is not fully realised.

This rule applies, both when Event X is in response to an Event W with a different subject (e.g., 5:33), and when both W and X have the same subject (27:30).

In 5:33, the people whom the apostles had addressed (A; vv 29–32) were wanting to kill them. In this they were frustrated, because Gamaliel (B) counseled otherwise (vv 34–39). The direction of development of the story follows, not their initial desires, but Gamaliel's counsel:

> (5:29–32 record the apostles' Speech W to the council.)
>
> (v 33) (X) *Hoi de akousantes dieprionto kai eboulonto anelein autous.*
>
> "The hearers were enraged and wanted to kill them."
>
> (v 34) (Y) But a Pharisee in the council named Gamaliel . . . stood up . . . (35) . . . and said to them, "Men of Israel, take care what you do with these men. . . " (40) So they took his advice.

In 27:30–32, Paul (B) frustrates the intention of the sailors (A; v 30), by his speech of v 31 to the centurion:

> (27:29) (W) And fearing that we might run on the rocks, having let out four anchors from the stern, they (the sailors) were praying for day to come.
>
> (v 30) (X) *tōn de nautōn zētountōn phygein ek tou ploiou*
>
> "Now as the sailors were seeking to escape from the ship," and had lowered the boat into the sea . . .
>
> (v 31) (Y) Paul said to the centurion, . . . "Unless these men stay in the ship, you cannot be saved." (32) Then the soldiers cut away the ropes of the boat, and let it go.

Further clear examples of forefronting, anticipating the frustration of an intention, are found in 9:29b, 14:13, 19:30 (GA), 19:33b, 21:26, 25:9, 26:21, 27:12.

1.23   Temporary Interest in a Minor or Supernatural Participant

Sometimes, in the middle of an incident which concerns central character C, a human or supernatural being appears without previous introduction. He performs an action which affects C, then is mentioned no more. The presence of this person is of interest only insofar as his act affects C. Consequently, he comes only temporarily into focus, and the reference to him is forefronted.

This is seen in 17:15. The Christians of Beroea send Paul away (v 14a). It is clear from the context that Luke's primary interest is in Paul, and v 16 begins a new incident in which he is involved. Prior to this, however, his previously unintroduced guides take the initiative by taking him to Athens.[10] Luke's only interest in these people is in the effect their initiative has on Paul. The forefronted reference to them indicates that they come only temporarily into focus:

> (17:14) (W) Then the brethren immediately sent Paul off on his way to the sea. . . .

> (v 15) (X) *hoi de kathistanontes ton Paulon ēgagon heōs Athēnōn*

> "Those who were conducting Paul brought him as far as Athens" . . .

> (v 16) (Y) Now while Paul was awaiting Silas and Timothy at Athens

The principle involved in the examples of this section may be stated as follows:

> (4) If minor or supernatural participant M is the subject of Event X, which is a response to the last Event W, and C was the last central character involved in the story, then the reference to M is forefronted if:
>
> (a) C is the undergoer or benefactor of X;
> (b) the following Events Y develop from X in a way that affects C; and
> (c) M is not involved in W or Y.

Rule (4) is applicable to the following passages, among others: 5:19 (an angel [M]; the apostles [C]), 8:39 (the Spirit [M]; Philip [C]; see vv 40b,c), 9:38 (the disciples [M]; Peter [C]), 16:9 (a vision [M]; Paul/we [C]), 16:14b (the Lord [M]; Paul/we [C]), 16:26 (an earthquake [M]; Paul and Silas [C]), 17:10 (the brothers [M]; Paul and Silas [C]), 28:3 (a snake [M]; Paul/we [C]).

Condition (c) above is necessary in order to exclude passages

---

[10] See Lenski, *Interpretation of Acts.* 705. If D is followed, it is still true that the brothers took the initiative in taking Paul on from Thessaly to Athens.

in which a supernatural participant is involved in a series of events. In such passages, he is not functioning as a minor participant who makes a single appearance and then disappears from the scene.

In 16:6–7, for instance, the repeated reference to "the Spirit" implies that He was the guiding force, throughout the journey described:

> (16:6) And they went through the region of Phrygia and Galatia, having been forbidden *by the Spirit* to speak the word in Asia.

> (v 7a) And when they had come opposite Mysia, they attempted to go into Bithynia,

> (v 7b) *kai ouk eiasen autous to pneuma* (*Iēsou*).

> "and the Spirit (of Jesus) did not allow them."

1.24   Temporary Focus on a Major Participant

Forefronted references to a major participant as subject occur in a number of passages which do not meet the conditions of rules (1)–(4). The situations are varied (see below), and the number of examples of each very limited. The feature which they have in common is that a switch of attention to another subject immediately follows. This suggests that the forefronting indicates temporary focus on the major participant.

Sometimes, following the departure of the central character to another location, a comment is made about participants still at the previous location (sec. 1.241). On occasion, a major participant is in the process of doing something, when a new development occurs, involving a previously unintroduced subject (sec. 1.242). In a couple of instances, the introductory reference to a major participant in an existential-locative clause is forefronted because he comes only temporarily into focus (sec. 1.243). Then there are passages in which *men* marks the event concerned as transitional. Attention immediately switches to a different initiator (sec. 1.244).

No all-inclusive rule can be proposed for the examples of forefronting discussed in this section, because of their variety and the limitation in their number. Rather, the reason that many of them are interpreted as cases of temporary focus, is because the general principle has already been established in other sections, and they are satisfactorily interpreted by the principle.

1.241   *The Central Character Leaves the Location of the Last Incident*   In a few passages, a central character responds to Event

W at location L by leaving L (Event X), and the reference to him is forefronted. Immediately following his departure, a statement Y is appended concerning participants who remain at L. It seems likely that the forefronting indicates that, until the story as it affects L has been completed, the central character comes only temporarily into focus.

In 13:50, for instance, Paul and Barnabas are the undergoers of actions W performed by the Jews at Antioch. They respond by going to Iconium (X; v 51). The next incident occurs at Iconium and follows their activities (14:1–5). Nevertheless, further reference is first made to the disciples back in Antioch (Y; 13:52). The forefronting of reference to Paul and Barnabas thus indicates that, as far as events at Antioch are concerned, they are only in temporary focus, as they leave the scene:

> (13:50) (W) But the Jews . . . stirred up persecution against Paul and Barnabas, and drove them out of their district.
>
> (v 51) (X) *hoi de ektinaxamenoi ton koniorton tōn podōn ep' autous, ēlthon eis Ikonion.*
>
> "But they, shaking off the dust of their feet against them, went to Iconium."
>
> (v 52) (Y) And the disciples were filled with joy and with the Holy Spirit.

In 17:14, the same principle applies, but Paul is the object and theme of the sentence. In response to activities W directed against him (v 13), he is sent from Beroea (X; v 14a). Verse 14b (Y) turns to Silas and Timothy, still in Beroea. (Luke returns to Paul in v 15.)

1.242 A New Development Occurs, Involving a Previously Unintroduced Subject In some passages, a major participant A is in the process of performing action X (the verb is in the imperfect), when Event Y occurs, involving a previously unintroduced subject B. The story develops from the new development involving B, not from the act performed by A. Participant A is therefore only temporarily in focus, and reference to him is forefronted.

In 16:25, for instance, Paul and Silas (A) are praying and singing hymns to God, when an earthquake (B) occurs (viewed as a supernatural intervention; see sec. 1.23). The story develops from the earthquake, not from Paul and Silas' singing:

> (16:25)   Now about midnight
>
>   (X) *Paulos kai Silas proseuchomenoi hymnoun ton theon*

"Paul and Silas were praying and singing hymns to God" . . .

(v 26) (Y) Suddenly there was a great earthquake, so that the foundations of the prison were shaken; and immediately all the doors were opened . . . (27) When the jailor . . . saw that the prison doors were open

Other examples include:

12:21–23: Herod (A) was making an oration to the crowd (X; v 21) when an angel (B) smote him (Y; v 23);

20:7–9: Paul (A) was lecturing to the Christians in Troas (X; v 7) when a young man named Eutychus (B), who had gone to sleep while sitting in the window, fell to the ground (Y; v 9).

1.243 *The Introduction of a New Participant*   Rule (1) is not applicable to existential-locative clauses which introduce a participant, since the reference to him cannot be the theme of the sentence (see n. 1). Nevertheless, in a few passages, the subject of such a clause precedes its verb. This may be because Luke's primary interest is in the central character against the background of whose presence the new participant is introduced. The new participant thus comes only temporarily into focus.

In 9:36, for instance, the new participant is introduced in a different location from that of the previous events (vv 32–35 concerned Peter in Lydda):

(9:36) (X) *En Ioppē de* <u>tis</u> *ēn* <u>mathētria</u> *onomati* <u>Tabitha</u>.

"Now at Joppa there was a disciple named Tabitha (Dorcas)."

As the translation into English "there was" suggests, the new participant is not the theme of the sentence. Nevertheless, the subject is forefronted. It appears that this is because she is only temporarily in focus. Newman and Nida comment, "The two miracles performed by Peter in Lydda and Joppa seem to prepare the way for the even greater miracle of the giving of the Holy Spirit to Cornelius in Caesarea."[11] This view is confirmed by various linguistic hints (e.g., the use of *kai* throughout vv 34–35; see Part Two, sec. 1.223). Thus the importance of the incident involving Dorcas is that it brings *Peter* from Lydda to Joppa (see 10:5–6).

[11] Newman and Nida, *Translator's Handbook*, 199. See also Jamieson, Fausset and Brown, *Commentary on the Whole Bible*, 1095.

Dorcas herself is introduced against the background of Peter's presence in Lydda, and he is soon reintroduced into the story, ready to take the initiative (9:38–39). In other words, she comes only temporarily in focus, hence the forefronting of the introductory reference to her.

In contrast, reference to a major participant who is introduced in an existential-locative construction is not forefronted, when the reintroduction of the last central character in an initiating role is not anticipated. The clearest example of this is 11:20. Peter was the central character in vv 1–18, but does not appear in the new incident:

> (11:19) Now (*men oun*) those who were scattered because of the persecution that arose over Stephen travelled as far as . . . Antioch, speaking the word to none except Jews.

> (v 20) *ēsan de tines ex autōn andres Kyprioi kai Kyrēnaioi, hoitines elthontes eis Antiocheian elaloun kai pros tous Hellēnas.*

> "But there were some of them, men of Cyprus and Cyrene, who on coming to Antioch spoke to the Greeks also."

Thus, the forefronting of the introductory reference to a major participant is probably a further example of temporary focus. Its particular function is to indicate that the central character, against the background of whose presence the introduction is made, will shortly resume his initiating role.

1.244 *Temporary Focus on a Major Participant, in connection with men*   It is no coincidence that the subject is nearly always forefronted when *men* occurs. *Men* is always prospective (Part Two, sec. 3.22), and the event described in connection with it is "transitional."[12] Consequently, the subject of the sentence concerned is always in temporary focus. This may be because attention immediately switches to a fresh initiator (see below), or because his act is an intermediate step in some exchange (see sec. 1.26).

In 8:25, for instance, the final reference to Peter and John provides the transition from the incident in which they were involved (vv 14–24), to the incident which begins with the reintroduction of the deacon Philip (v 26). They thus are brought back temporarily into focus (*men*), following which attention immediately switches (*de*) to the angel (initiator) and Philip:

---

[12] Page, *Acts of the Apostles*, 94.

(8:25) *Hoi men oun diamartyramenoi kai lalēsantes ton logon tou kyriou hypestrephon eis Hierosolyma*

"Now when they had testified and spoken the word of the Lord (in Samaria), they returned to Jerusalem" . . .

(v 26) But (*de*) an angel of the Lord said to Philip (in Samaria)

Other examples, some of which anticipate a contrastive statement, include: 1:1, 8:4, 9:31.

1.25   Temporary Focus within a Closed Conversation

Consideration is now given to the forefronting of the subject within a "closed" conversation.

By a closed conversation is meant one in which each new speaker and addressee is drawn from the speakers and addressees of previous speeches, rather than being introduced to the scene prior to taking part.

For example, 9:10–15 form a closed conversation, because the only participants are the Lord and Ananias. Each in turn addresses his remarks to the other:

(9:10b) *kai eipen pros auton en horamati ho kyrios, Hanania.*

"And the Lord said to him in a vision, 'Ananias.' "

(v 10c) *ho de eipen, Idou egō, kyrie.*

"And he said, 'Here I am, Lord.' "

(v 11) *ho de kyrios pros auton, Anastas poreuthēti . . .*

"and the Lord said to him, 'Rise and go . . .' "

23:1–5 is also a closed conversation. In v 1 Paul addresses the Jewish council in general. In v 2 the high priest (as president of the council) responds by telling the people standing beside Paul to strike him. In v 3 Paul himself responds to the high priest's order. In v 4 the addressees of v 2 rebuke Paul. In v 5 he replies to them. All the new speakers were involved, prior to speaking, as addressees.

In contrast, Peter's speech in 2:14–39 is not part of the same closed conversation as that of vv 7–13, even though Peter is responding to the last remark made about the apostles in v 13. This is because the previous conversation involved only members of the crowd which heard the apostles speaking in different languages (v 6). Peter intervenes from outside that group:

(2:13) *heteroi de diachleuazontes elegon hoti, Gleukous memestōmenoi eisin.*

"But others mocking said, 'They are filled with new wine.'"

(v 14) *Statheis de ho Petros . . . epēren tēn phōnēn autou kai apephthegxato autois*

"But Peter, standing . . . , lifted up his voice and addressed them, '. . .
(15) . . . these men are not drunk, . . .'"

23:16–17 is not a closed conversation, because the addressee of v 17 (the centurion) has to be called over, prior to being addressed:

(23:16) Paul's nephew went and entered the barracks and told Paul (about the ambush).

(v 17) *proskalesamenos de ho Paulos hena tōn hekatontarchōn, ephē*

"And Paul called one of the centurions and said"

This section is not concerned about references to the subjects of such responses as 2:14 and 23:17, because the response involves other than a member of the closed group of participants in the conversation to date (speakers and addressees). Any forefronting of the subject of such sentences is determined by the rules which deal with a subject who was not involved in the previous event (sec. 1.11), a member of a group (sec. 1.21), or non-verbal responses (secs. 1.22–4).

In addition, the rule concerning a closed conversation is not generally valid, if the verbal response of the previous addressee is preceded by a sentence describing a non-verbal response (but see sec. 1.26). For example, in 2:37, the initial response by the addressees of Peter's speech of vv 14–36 is non-verbal. Consequently, their speech of v 37b is separated from the speech which induced it:

(2:37a) *Akousantes de katenygēsan tēn kardian,*

"On hearing this they were cut to the heart,"

(v 37b) *eipon te pros ton Petron*

"and said to Peter"

If a closed conversation consists of three or more speeches (direct or indirect), reference to the speaker of a *non-final* speech is forefronted 85% of the time (33 cases out of 38; furthermore, in two of the remaining cases, the sentence in question has the same subject as that of the previous sentence [sec. 1.253a]). However, reference to the speaker of the *final* speech of a closed conversation is forefronted only 52% of the time (25 cases out of 48).[13]

The following rule accounts for the above variations in the relative frequency of forefronting, both within closed conversations, and also within other closed exchanges in which the same participants interact in successive steps of the exchange (sec. 1.26):

> (5) When participant A addresses Speech W to participant B, who responds with Event (Speech) X, reference to B is forefronted if X is an intermediate step in a closed exchange, and fails to resolve it.

The concept of "temporary focus" is therefore manifested within a closed conversation, when the speaker in question performs only an intermediate act in the exchange. The logic behind rule (5) is examined in sec. 1.254.

If Speech X resolves an exchange, this generally means that X clinches the argument. This may be because B thereby persuades A to respond by performing the Event Y which B was desiring. Alternatively, the exchange is resolved because, by X, B acquiesces to A, and thereby concedes the point at dispute between them. Sometimes, X itself is the goal of the conversation.

Sec. 1.251 discusses closed conversations in which the final speech does resolve the exchange. Some closed conversations are not resolved by the final speech of the exchange; see sec. 1.252. Occasionally, the first speech of a conversation is introduced in connection with a verb of perception (particularly *akouō*, "hear"), and the response to that speech may occur in a sentence which has the same subject as its predecessor; see sec. 1.253a. Finally, *apokrinomai*, "answer," or a similar verb may introduce a complicating factor in a closed conversation, and destroy its "tight-knit" nature; see sec. 1.253b.

1.251   *The Exchange is Resolved*   One of the functions of conversation in general is to persuade the other party to perform a particular action or to adopt a certain attitude. In the reporting of

---

[13] The passages concerned are 1:6–7; 2:12–13, 37–38; 4:7–8, 18–21; 5:8–9, 27b–29; 7:1–2, 26–27; 8:18–24, 30–31, 34–35; 9:4–6, 10b–15; 10:3–4, 13–16, 21–23a, 28–34; 11:3–4, 7–9; 12:14–15, 21–22; 13:15–16, 45–47; 15:36–38; 16:30–31, 36–37; 17:18; 18:12–14; 19:2–4; 21:12–13, 33–34, 37–39; 22:7–8, 10, 18–21, 27–29; 23:1–5, 19–20; 25:2–4, 7–12, 14–22; 25:20–21; 25:24–26:29; 26:14–18, 30–31; 27:9–11; 28:17–21. In 19:3a, the forefronted reading is taken to be correct; see n. 15.

closed conversations in Acts, speeches which achieve this goal
("Resolving Utterances" [RUs]) are introduced without forefronting any reference to their speakers.

The position of any reference to the speaker of the first or
"Initiating Utterance" (IU) of a closed conversation depends on its
relation to the previous non-verbal context, and is determined by
applying the rules of the appropriate section. Any speeches of the
conversation which follow the IU but do not resolve the conversation ("Continuing Utterances" [CUs]) are introduced with
forefronted references to their speakers (exceptions are discussed
in sec. 1.253).

In 10:3–4, for instance, an angel appears and speaks to
Cornelius (v 3; IU). Cornelius responds by inviting the angel to
deliver his message (v 4a; CU). The angel does so (vv 4b–6; RU),
then leaves Cornelius (v 7):

> (10:3) (IU) Cornelius saw clearly in a vision an angel of God
> coming in and saying to him, "Cornelius."

> (v 4a) (CU) *ho de atenisas autō kai emphobos genomenos,
> eipen*

> "And he stared at him in terror and said,
> 'What is it, Lord?' "

> (v 4b) (RU) *eipen de autō*

> "And he said to him,
> 'Your prayers and your alms have ascended as a memorial
> before God. (5) And now send men to Joppa . . . ' "

> (v 7) When the angel who spoke to him had departed, he
> called two of his servants . . . (8) and . . . sent them to Joppa.

In the above exchange, the goal of the angel's visit is to persuade
Cornelius to send men to Joppa to fetch Peter (v 5). This purpose
is achieved, because Cornelius complies with his instruction (vv
7–8). It is not achieved, however, by Cornelius' initial response of
v 4a. This is simply an intermediate step, continuing the conversation which the angel has started. Consequently, the subject of v
4a is forefronted. In contrast, the second speech by the angel (vv
4b–6) does achieve his goal. This is reflected in the absence of a
forefronted subject in the introduction to the speech.

If the overall intention of a conversation is not achieved
immediately because of an objection by the other party, then
reference to the speaker whose speech should have resolved the
conversation (but did not) is forefronted. However, any reference

to the speaker of a later speech which does resolve the conversation is not forefronted.

This is seen in 9:10–15. The equivalent speech to that of 10:4b–6 above begins with a forefronted reference to the speaker (v 11), because the other party first introduces an objection (vv 13–14; using *apokrinomai* [sec. 1.253b]). The speech which overrules this objection (vv 15–16) is not introduced with a forefronted reference to the speaker, because its addressee complies with its intention (Event Y):[14]

(9:10a) Now there was a disciple at Damascus named Ananias.

(v 10b) (IU) The Lord said to him in a vision, "Ananias."

(v 10c) (CU) *ho de eipen*

"and he said,
'Here I am, Lord.' "

(v 11) (CU) *ho de kyrios pros auton*

"and the Lord said to him,
'Rise and go to the street called Straight, and inquire in the house of Judas for a man of Tarsus named Saul . . . ' "

(v13) (CU) *apekrithē de Hananias*

"but Ananias answered,
'Lord, I have heard from many about this man, how much evil he has done . . . ' "

(v 15) (RU) *eipen de pros auton ho kyrios*

"But the Lord said to him,
'Go . . . ' "

(v 17) And Ananias departed

---

[14] "IU", "CU" and "RU" are terms used by Longacre (*Anatomy of Speech Notions*, 168–172). However, this monograph does not necessarily use the terms with the meaning which he attaches to them.

For example, Longacre uses "RU" to refer to any speech which answers a question, responds to a proposal, or evaluates a remark. He reserves "CU" for speeches which counter an initiating utterance.

It does not appear that Longacre's RUs are marked in any distinctive way in the clauses which introduce the speeches. In contrast a number of languages, including Greek, indicate either that a speech resolves a conversation in the sense in which "resolve" is used in this volume, or that it merely continues the exchange. For this reason, the terms "IU" and "RU" are here restricted respectively to a speech which opens a conversation, and to one which brings the conversation to a satisfactory conclusion. All intermediate speeches are referred to as "CUs."

Other examples of closed conversations which are resolved include: 1:6(IU)–7(RU), 10:21(IU)–22(CU)–23(RU), 11:3(IU)–4(RU), 13:45(IU)–46(RU), 19:2a(IU)–2b(CU)–3a(CU)[15]–3b(CU)–4(RU), 21:37a(IU)–37b–38(CU)–39(RU).

In each of the above examples, the conversation is resolved when one of the parties achieves his goal. However, a conversation may also be resolved when one of the parties concedes defeat in his effort to persuade the other to adopt a certain attitude or course of action.

This is illustrated in 23:1–5. When the bystanders object to Paul reviling the high priest (v 4; CU), Paul's reply, "I did not know, brethren, that he was the high priest . . . " (v 5) is virtually an apology. He effectively withdraws his earlier remark of v 3, and thus resolves the exchange by acquiescing.[16]

> (23:1) (IU) Looking intently at the council, Paul said, "Brethren, I have lived before God in all good conscience up to this day."
>
> (v2) (CU) *ho de* **archiereus** **Hananias**
>
> "and the high priest Ananias"
> commanded those who stood by him to strike him on the mouth.
>
> (v 3) (CU) *tote ho* **Paulos** *pros auton eipen*
>
> "Then Paul said to him,
> 'God shall strike you, you whitewashed wall . . . ' "
>
> (v 4) (CU) *hoi de* **parestōtes** *eipan*
>
> "Those who stood by said,
> 'Would you revile God's high priest?' "
>
> (v 5) (RU) *ephē te ho* **Paulos**

---

[15] The preferred reading in Nestle and Aland (1975) is *eipen te*. This may be a copyist's error, repeating v 2a, since the use of *te* does not correspond to the conclusions of Part Two, chap. 2. This monograph follows the UBS preferred reading (*ho de eipen*), since Paul's second question is only an intermediate speech (CU). (There are further variants.)

The addition to the text of 9:6 (Et tremens ac stupens dixit) is also contrary to rule (5), since the speech of v 6 does not resolve the conversation. The same applies to the addition to the text at 8:37; Philip's statement of v 37a was not a resolving utterance.

[16] Bruce, *The Book of Acts*, 452 comments that Paul abandons his initial tactic, prior to trying a different one in v 6.

"And Paul said,
'I did not know, brethren, that he was the high priest; for it
is written, "You shall not speak evil of a ruler of your
people." ' "

In some passages, a conversation consists simply of an invitation to deliver a speech plus compliance with the request. In such a situation, Speech X itself is the goal of the conversation and resolves the exchange. (This should not be confused with situations in which the invitation to speak is part of an extended exchange, and the response in no way resolves the matter; see especially 7:1b, 26:1; sec. 1.252a.)

In 13:15–41, for example, Paul's speech to the congregation in the synagogue at Antioch (vv 16b–41) resolves the conversation which the synagogue rulers open when they invite him to speak (v 15), because he complies with their request:

> (13:15) (IU) . . . the rulers of the synagogue sent to them, saying, "Brethren, if you have any word of exhortation for the people, say it."

> (v 16) (RU) *anastas de* Paulos, *kai kataseisas tē cheiri, eipen*

> "So Paul stood up, and motioning with his hand, said"

1.252   *The Exchange is Not Resolved* In all the passages considered in sec. 1.251, some resolution of the conversation was achieved by the last speech recorded. This was reflected in the absence of a forefronted subject in the introduction to that speech. In many of the closed conversations of Acts, however, the last speech of the exchange is introduced with a forefronted reference to the speaker. This is because the final speech recorded leaves the matter under discussion unresolved. (a) The parties involved in the conversation may still be at loggerheads at the end of the exchange. (b) Alternatively, although the parties are not actually in conflict, the *overall* goal of the exchange is not realized by the conversation.

(a) In the first examples considered, although the reported conversation comes to an end, the participants have failed to reach agreement, and the conversation remains unresolved.

In 12:14–15, an argument is recorded between Rhoda and other disciples as to who is at the gate. Since the argument is not resolved until the door is opened (v 16b), all the speeches which continue the conversation begin with a forefronted reference to the speaker:

(12:14a) Recognizing Peter's voice, in her joy she did not open the gate but ran in

(v 14b) (IU) and told that Peter was standing at the gate.

(v 15a) (CU) *hoi de pros autēn eipan*

"They said to her,
'You are mad.'"

(v 15b) (CU) *hē de diischyrizeto houtōs echein.*

"But she insisted that it was so."

(v 15c) (CU) *hoi de elegon*

"They were saying,
'It is his angel.'"

(v 16) But Peter continued knocking.

Among other examples of closed conversations which are unresolved because the participants fail to reach agreement, the extended exchange between governor Festus, king Agrippa and Paul (25:24–26:29) is of particular interest. Paul seeks to convince his audience to accept Christianity (v 29). Agrippa is at best "almost persuaded" (v 28).

A further example is 10:13–16, the conversation which took place when Peter had his vision of a sheet of unclean animals let down from heaven (vv 11–12). After Peter refuses (v 14) to comply with the original command to kill and eat (v 13), the rebuke which closes the exchange (v 15) does not result immediately in his acquiescence, since the whole exchange occurs three times (v 16).[17] Hence, the forefronted reference to the voice in v 15.

(b) In some passages, the final speech recorded does not necessarily leave the participants in conflict. Nevertheless, the overall goal of the passage is not realized in the exchange.

This is evident in 28:17–21. Paul's words to the Jews in Rome (vv 17–20; IU) lead the latter to express interest in his views on Christianity (vv 21–22; CU). However, the matter which he raises, and about which they comment, viz., Christianity and "the hope of Israel" (vv 20, 22), is not explored. Rather, the exchange leads to

---

[17] "Did Peter refuse a second and even a third time after that first forceful warning? It seems so" (Lenski, *Interpretation of Acts*, 405). See also Bruce, *The Book of Acts*, 218.

the arrangement of a *later* meeting to debate the whole issue. Consequently, the speech of vv 21–22 by the Jews, though a positive response to Paul's comments, is treated only as an intermediate act which does not conclude the matter he raises:

> (28:17) (IU) When they had gathered, he said to them, ". . . (19) I was compelled to appeal to Caesar; though I had no charge to bring against my nation. (20) For this reason therefore I have asked to see you and speak with you, since it is because of the hope of Israel that I am bound with this chain."
>
> (v 21) (CU) *hoi de pros auton eipan*
>
> "They said to him,
> ' . . . (22) we desire to hear from you what your views are. . . ' "
>
> (v 23) Having appointed a day for him, they came to him at his lodging in great numbers and he expounded the matter to them from morning till evening.

Another example is 25:2–4. When the Jews ask Festus to bring Paul to Jerusalem to be tried (vv 2–3; IU), Festus replies that they should accompany him to Caesarea and present their charges there (v 4; CU). His answer leaves unresolved the question of Paul being tried at Jerusalem, which is raised again in v 9.

Note: A speech may be an intermediate step because the *same* speaker has yet to make a further speech before the exchange is concluded. See, for instance, 16:31.

1.253 *Apparent Exceptions to Rule (5)* Occasionally, reference to the speaker of an intermediate step is not forefronted. This is for one of two reasons.

(a) The previous speech was given in connection with a verb of perception, and technically no change of subject occurs between the sentences. For example, see 9:4–5 (he heard a voice saying to him, . . . *eipen de*, "and he said"). (This does not always happen; e.g., 22:8.)

The following note must be added to rule (5), to cover such examples:

> Note: When W is introduced in connection with a verb of perception, sentences W and X may be considered to have the same subject, in which case no reference to B as subject occurs.

(b) The speech concerned is not in a "tight-knit" relationship to its predecessor. The speeches in a closed conversation usually enjoy a "tight-knit" relationship to each other. By this is meant that the new speaker takes up the same topic as that of the previous speech, and develops the conversation from the point at which the last speaker left off. In addition, he generally directs his speech to the previous speaker.

In a formal setting, such as a trial or council meeting, however, each speaker addresses himself, not to the last speaker, but to the president or to the council as a whole. See 15:6–21, 24:2–23. Furthermore, the speeches often are not a direct response to the contents of the last speech (see especially 15:13–21, which refers back, not to the speech of v 12, but to that of vv 7–11). Speeches given in a formal setting probably do not therefore enjoy a tight-knit relationship with each other.

The tight-knit relationship between successive speeches is also broken in 9:13 and 22:28 (each introduced by *apokrinomai*, "answer"). In both passages, previous speeches had developed the conversation in a single direction, and the matter in hand should have been resolved by the last one recorded. However, the addressee of this last speech now makes a "counter-assertion"[18] which takes the conversation off in a new direction. The effect is to break the tight-knit relationship characteristic of the previous speeches.

> (Note: Passages like 10:14 and 22:19 suggest that a counter-assertion breaks the tight-knit relationship only if a definite direction has been established over several speeches. In both cases, the counter-assertion immediately follows the opening speech of the exchange.)

The above examples must be handled as an exception to rule (5), which required that all references to the subjects of continuing utterances be forefronted. The wording of the exception is given in sec. 1.254 below.

1.254 *Conclusions*   The conclusions of this section may be summarized as follows:

> (5) When a participant A addresses Speech W to participant B, who responds with Event (Speech) X, reference to B is forefronted if X is an intermediate step in a closed exchange, and fails to resolve it.

---

[18] Longacre, *Anatomy of Speech Notions*, 172.

Note: When W is introduced in connection with a verb of perception, sentences W and X may be considered to have the same subject, in which case no reference to B as subject occurs.

Exception: Rule (5) does not apply when, following a conversation which extends over at least two speeches, Speech X does not stem directly from the major thrust of Speech W, and is not in line with the force of W.

The marking of speeches in a closed conversation as intermediate steps towards a goal suggests that a (tight-knit) reported conversation does not function like a series of non-verbal events in sequence. Rather, it is treated as a single event complex, consisting of a set of steps which together are the equivalent of a non-verbal event. (Elements which break the tight-knit nature of an exchange are treated like individual non-verbal events; see above.)

Confirmation for this view of reported conversations is found in other languages. To give just one example, in Inga (Quechuan), the enclitic *ca* which introduces each "distinctive" event as a narrative progresses (see Part Two, sec. 1.1), is generally absent when the second and subsequent speeches of an exchange are recorded.[19]

Reported conversations may well be viewed as the equivalent of single non-verbal events in all languages, when certain conditions are met. Many narratives are concerned primarily with the unfolding of a series of basically non-verbal events. Conversations fit into the development of such a narrative, only insofar as they produce non-verbal results, or else as a speech itself is the goal of the exchange (e.g., Acts 13:15–41).

1.26   The Intermediate Step is Non-verbal

The principle that the subject of intermediate steps towards the goal of a closed exchange is forefronted, applies not only to conversations (sec. 1.25), but also to a few passages in which part or all of the exchange is non-verbal.

9:40–41 illustrates a closed exchange in which both the response X to the initial speech W (IU) and the resolving action Y which completes the realization of the original intention are non-verbal. When Peter tells Dorcas to get up (v 40b), she only partly complies with his order (v 40c), so he has to complete the process himself (v 41a). Verse 40c is thus an intermediate step in the fulfillment of Peter's intention, and its subject is forefronted:

[19] Levinsohn, "Progression and Digression," 1.128–29.

(9:40b) (W[IU]) ... and turning to the body, he said, "Tabitha, rise (anastēthi)."

(v 40c) (X["CU"]) *hē de ēnoixen tous ophthalmous autēs, kai idousa ton Petron, anekathisen.*

"And she opened her eyes, and when she saw Peter, she sat up."

(v 41a) (Y["RU"]) *dous de autē cheira, anestēsen autēn.*

"And giving her his hand, he lifted her up."

For another example of a non-verbal intermediate step, see 3:5. (More commonly, however, in closed exchanges which include non-verbal responses, the subjects of potential intermediate steps are not forefronted; e.g., 12:7–10.)

In addition to the above closed exchanges to which rule (5) applies directly, the general principle that the subject of an intermediate step is forefronted appears to extend to other passages. In 21:39–40, for instance, Paul asks the tribune to let him speak to the people (v 39). On receiving permission, he achieves this goal in two stages. He first quietens the people by signalling to them (v 40a; the intermediate step X). Then, when they become quiet, he actually addresses them (vv 40b–41):

(21:39) (W) Paul replied (to the tribune), " ... I beg you, let me speak to the people."

(v 40a) (X) And when he had given him permission,

ho Paulos, hestōs epi tōn anabathmōn, kateseisen tē cheiri tō laō

"Paul, standing on the steps, motioned with his hand to the people;"

(v 40b) (Y) and when there was a great hush, he spoke to them... (22:1) "Brethren and fathers, hear the defense..."

Other examples of intermediate steps include 21:32b and, in connection with *men oun*, 23:18. Less straightforward is 4:24:

(4:23) (W) When they were released they went to their friends and reported what the chief priests and the elders had said to them.

(v 24) (X) *hoi de akousantes homothymadon ēran phōnēn pros ton theon kai eipan*

"And when they heard it, they lifted their voices together to God and said,
'...(29) grant to thy servants to speak thy word with all boldness...'"

(v 31) (Y) And when they had prayed, the place in which they were gathered together was shaken; and they were all filled with the Holy Spirit and spoke the word of God with boldness.

In this passage, Luke is concerned with how the apostles respond to the authorities' ban on their preaching (see also 5:41–42). The response is in two stages. First they pray for boldness (vv 24–30). Then, as a result of the supernatural answer of v 31a–b, they actually continue their preaching (v 31c). As far as the conflict with the authorities is concerned, this second act is the crucial one. Consequently, the prayer of vv 24–30 may be viewed as an intermediate step towards this goal.

Finally, a whole incident may be treated as an intermediate step. In 25:12–22, following Paul's appeal to Caesar in v 11, the subjects of a whole series of sentences are forefronted. The first is governor Festus' reply of v 12 (perhaps considered by Luke to be the first step towards the goal of sending Paul off to Caesar). The following sentence does not introduce the actual dispatch of Paul (this is not described until 27:1). Instead, it records the arrival of king Agrippa (v 13). The subsequent events in the exchange between Festus and Agrippa also have forefronted subjects, including, in many manuscripts, that of v 22b. Thus, it is not inconceivable that every event which occurs prior to Paul's next appearance in the story is described with a forefronted subject, implying that they are only intermediate steps:

(25:11) (W) (Paul said), "...I appeal to Caesar."

(v 12) (X^1) *tote ho Phēstos ... apekrithē*

"Then Festus ... answered,
'You have appealed to Caesar; to Caesar you shall go.'"

(v 13) (X^2) Now when some days had passed,

Agrippas ho basileus kai Bernikē katentēsan eis Kaisareian

"Agrippa the king and Bernice arrived at Caesarea" (to welcome Festus).

(v 14) (X^3) And as they stayed there many days,

ho Phēstos tō basilei anetheto ta kata ton Paulon, legōn

"Festus laid Paul's case before the king, saying," ...

(v 22a) (CU) _Agrippas de pros ton Phēston_

"And Agrippa said to Festus,
'I should like to hear the man myself.' "

(v 22b) (?CU) (_ho de_) _aurion, phēsin._ " 'Tomorrow,' said he,
'you shall hear him.' "

1.27   Summary

The manifestations of temporary focus are varied. Nevertheless, they have in common the implication that the forefronting of
the subject anticipates a change of subject and initiative.

In order of frequency, an element is forefronted to denote
temporary focus for the following specific reasons:

> when an act of an exchange is intermediate (non-final) (secs.
> 1.25–6; 68 examples);

> when the story does not develop from the action X per-
> formed by a sub-group G^1 of the previous group G (sec. 1.21;
> 20–24 examples);

> when a major participant is introduced against the back-
> ground of the presence of a central character, in anticipation
> that the latter is about to resume his initiating role (sec.
> 1.243; 6–16 examples);

> when the intention X of the subject is frustrated by the
> action Y of another participant (sec. 1.22; 11 examples);

> when a minor or supernatural participant appears without
> previous introduction, to perform a significant action and
> then disappear from the scene (sec. 1.23; 11 examples);

> cases involving _men_ (sec. 1.244; 6–9 examples);

> when a participant is in the process of performing an action,
> during which a new development occurs involving a dif-
> ferent subject (sec. 1.242; 4 examples);

> when a participant leaves the scene of the last incident, and
> attention immediately returns to participants left at that
> location (sec. 1.241; 3 examples).

1.3   The Extent of Reference of a Subject

It is generally accepted that one way to emphasize a phrase in
Greek is to place it early in its clause, in violation of the natural
order of constituents.[20] However, only a minority of the elements

---

[20] See, for example, Winer, _Treatise on the Grammar of NT Greek_, 684.

which occur at the beginning of a clause or sentence are placed there to emphasize them. In particular, not more than 11% of the subjects which precede their verb appear to do so because their size or extent is emphasized.

An element is often emphasized because it highlights information which is "of particular interest or significance"[21] for a subsequent development. For example, in 13:44, the subject precedes the verb because it was the size of the crowds which led to the Jews' jealousy (v 45):

> (13:44) *Tō de erchomenō sabbatō <u>schedon</u> <u>pasa</u> <u>hē</u> <u>polis</u> synēchthē akousai ton logon tou theou.*
>
> "The next sabbath almost the whole city gathered together to hear the word of God."

Alternatively, an element is given "emphatic prominence" because it "highlights an item of information which will be surprising to the hearer."[22] See, for example, 16:26c (*pantōn ta desma anethē*, "every one's fetters were unfastened"). Contrary to expectation, it was not just Paul and Silas whose fetters were unfastened (see further below).

Note: Negative subjects are always forefronted in the narrative of Acts (e.g., 18:17b). This may reflect a syntactic constraint on the order of constituents, rather than emphasis on the (negative) extent to which something is true.

Occasionally, a forefronted subject consists of a noun (phrase) governing a genitive, with the genitive initial. Since a genitive normally follows the noun which governs it,[23] the forefronting of the genitive must also be accounted for. Thus, in 16:26c (see above), the phrase as a whole is forefronted because it is the thematic basis (v 26c is not in sequence with v 26b; sec. 1.11). Within the phrase, *pantōn* is forefronted to underline the extent of those affected.

1.4   Contrastiveness, Emphasis and Temporary Focus

This section reviews the argument that contrastiveness (a particular aspect of temporary focus in Acts; sec. 1.21) is distinct from emphasis (sec. 1.3).

In his original analysis of what constituted given and new

---

[21] K. Callow, *Discourse Considerations*, 52.

[22] K. Callow, *Discourse Considerations*, 54.

[23] Winer, *Treatise on the Grammar of NT Greek*, 239.

information, Chafe concluded that contrastive themes convey new information.[24] So, if the reply to the question, "What did you (pl.) do in town?" were, "I went shopping, and/but John went to a museum," "I" would be new information. Since "I" is also the theme of the sentence and carries the high pitch characteristic of emphasis, it is therefore the "emphatic theme" of the sentence.

However, Chafe noted that, unlike emphasized elements, elements in contrast carry their own distinctive pitch in oral English.[25] This occurs, even when the second part of the contrast is left unstated (e.g., "I went shopping . . . ," implying "John did something else"). Chafe therefore notes, "Every item that carries contrastive pitch is distinguished by its own pitch drop, no matter what comes after."[26]

In his 1974 article, Chafe claims that, in many ways, contrastive items behave not like new but like given information (e.g., in the area of pronominalization). He concludes,

> "Both new information and contrastiveness lead to high pitches, but of different kinds. It is doubtless unfortunate that linguists have so often resorted to unmotivated terms like 'emphasis' . . . to refer indiscriminately to both items of new information and contrastive items."[27]

One aspect of contrastiveness that distinguishes it from emphasis is its anticipatory nature. As noted above, contrastive pitch occurs in oral English even when the second part of the contrast is left unstated. So, in the reply, "I went shopping," there is a definite implication that John did not go shopping. This is demonstrated by the need for John to respond, "And I did, too," if this is not the case.

This anticipatory aspect of contrastiveness is not necessarily present when an element is emphasized. It is true, as noted in sec. 1.3, that some elements in Acts are forefronted for emphasis because of their relevance for the next event, or because they contrast with the expected. However, this is neither a requirement, nor is a further contrastive statement anticipated. See, for instance, 5:15 (*kan hē skia episkiasē tini autōn*, "that at least his shadow might overshadow some of them").

---

[24] Chafe, *Meaning and Structure*, 224. See also Halliday, "Notes on Transitivity and Theme in English," 4.211.

[25] Chafe, *Meaning and Structure*, 226–227.

[26] Chafe, "Language and Consciousness," 119.

[27] Chafe, "Language and Consciousness," 119. Hutchins ("Subjects, Themes and Case Grammars," 35.101–133) reaches a similar conclusion. He distinguishes between "normal (unmarked)," "contrastive" and "emphatic thematization."

If contrastiveness is a distinctive feature in oral material, then it should not be surprising if languages have means of marking it in written texts. What sec. 1.2 suggests is that in fact the forefronting of the subject of a contrastive statement brings out its anticipatory nature, and this feature is found also in other situations, labelled "temporary focus." Just as contrastive pitch on sub-group G^1 anticipates a contrastive statement about G^2 (sec. 1.21), so the forefronting of the subject of a verb of desire or intention anticipates a contrastive statement indicating how the intention is frustrated (sec. 1.22), and the forefronting of the introductory reference to a major participant anticipates the reintroduction of the relevant central character (sec. 1.243).

CHAPTER TWO
TEMPORAL EXPRESSIONS

Temporal expressions are placed at the beginning of a sentence for two reasons.

(1) "Transitional temporal phrases" normally precede the other elements of a sentence.[1] This is because they commonly establish a new point of reference in time, which replaces the temporal setting of the last events presented. In other words, they indicate the replacement basis by which the forthcoming events are to be related to their context (factor 1; Introduction to Part One). Sec. 2.1 considers temporal replacement bases, and the reasons for not forefronting references to points in time.

(2) Expressions which refer to the duration or frequency of an action precede their verb in order to emphasize that aspect of the event (factor 3; Introduction to Part One). Examples of forefronted references to duration and frequency are discussed briefly in sec. 2.2.

2.1 References to a Point in Time

References to the point in time at which an event occurred are expressed in Acts by means of a variety of constructions. These include articular infinitives governed by the prepositions *en, meta, prin, pro*; clauses subordinated by *achris hou, heōs hou, kathōs* (7:17), *hotan, hote, hōs*; phrases governed by *apo, dia, ek, en, epi, heōs, kata, meta, peri, prin, pro, hypo*; and adverbial phrases without a preposition, which are found most commonly in the dative case. In addition, temporal words or phrases occur as the subject of verbs such as *ginomai*, "become" and the passive of *plēroō*, "fulfill," in both independent clauses (see Part Two, sec. 1.141) and genitives absolute. All the above constructions define a point in time as the temporal setting of one or more events.[2]

---

[1] Blass, Debrunner and Funk, *Greek Grammar*, sec. 472(3).

[2] Although *eutheōs*, "immediately," generally occurs at the beginning of a

Concerning expressions which establish a point of reference in time, Blass, Debrunner and Funk write,

> "Transitional temporal phrases tend to stand at the beginning; but sometimes as a result of the tendency to begin the sentence with a verb, a meaningless *egeneto* . . . may precede."[3]

Blass et al's first claim is borne out statistically in Acts. Eighty-one examples of "transitional temporal expressions" are found at the beginning of a sentence in the narrative sections of the book. Only 13 are not (1:3; 2:41b; 5:21; 8:1b,6; 10:3,9; 13:14b; 16:18b,33; 18:9; 20:6,7).

As for the presentation of events in an infinitival clause which is the subject of *egeneto*, its presence is certainly not meaningless.[4] Nevertheless, it may be ignored, as far as the classification of what occurs first in the sentence is concerned. So, if a transitional temporal expression occurs immediately after *egeneto*, it may be treated as though it were at the beginning of the sentence. See, for example, 28:17 (*Egeneto de meta hēmeras treis sygkalesasthai auton* . . ., "It happened that after three days he called together . . .").

The reason that transitional temporal expressions occur so often at the beginning of sentences is because replacement bases begin sentences, to indicate how the events described are to be related to their context. So, if a sentence begins with *tē epaurion*, "on the morrow" (e.g., 10:24), this both establishes the temporal setting for the following events, and replaces the previous one (the day before). The basis for relating the two sets of events is through their temporal settings.

Narrative is characterized by chronological progression. Consequently, when a change of temporal setting occurs, the basis for relating new events to their context is usually temporal. The event(s)* prior to the temporal expression occur at time T^1.** The event(s) described after it take place at the new time T^2 established by the temporal expression itself.

---

sentence, it does not appear to establish a new temporal setting which forms the basis for relating the new event to its context. Rather, its function is to indicate the close temporal relationship between a particular event and the last one described. See particularly 17:10 (following a subject in temporary focus; no basis occurs) and 16:10 (following the temporal basis). The tendency for it to occur at the beginning of a sentence probably reflects the fact that it is normally appropriate to emphasize this aspect of an event (see sec. 2.2).

The positioning of *parachrēma* is probably determined in the same way.

[3] Blass, Debrunner and Funk, *Greek Grammar*, sec. 472(3).

[4] See Levinsohn, "Initial Elements in a Clause or Sentence," 23–25.

* The term "event(s)" is used because a reference to a point in time establishes the temporal setting for an indefinite number of events. The scope of a temporal setting appears to be determined by the context. It is applicable either until replaced by a specific new point of reference in time (e.g., 27:27–33–39), or until the context makes it clear that the setting has changed.

For instance, following a temporal basis, if a subsequent subject or theme is forefronted, it must be determined by inspection whether the time of the next event described is the same as that of the previous events or not. See, for example, the uncertainty over the temporal relationship, within 9:30–31–32 and 12:23–24–25.

** Time T^1 may not have been established by means of a temporal expression. For example, *tē hetera*, "the next day" (27:3; T^2) relates back to the day when "we" embarked in the ship (v 2; T^1). It does not necessarily relate to the temporal expression which begins v 1 ("when it was decided that we should sail for Italy"). Nevertheless, "the next day" represents a change of temporal setting with respect to v 2.

Forefronted temporal expressions which establish a new point of reference in time generally replace an earlier time as setting. However, they are also used to define a specific point *within* the more extensive period of time which was the setting for the last event(s) described. The basis for relating the forthcoming events to the previous ones is still temporal, but the actual change of temporal setting is from a vague span of time to a specific point within that span.

In 16:13, for instance, "on the sabbath day" is a specific point within the period "some days" of v 12:

(16:12) We remained in this city some days,

(v 13) <u>tē</u> te <u>hēmera</u> <u>tōn</u> <u>sabbatōn</u> exēlthomen exō tēs pylēs

"and on the sabbath day we went outside the gate"

This same principle holds when a vague temporal phrase is used, such as *en tais hēmerais tautais*, "in these days." The expression as such refers to the period of the last event(s). Nevertheless, the use of the aorist following the phrase indicates that a particular point within that period is the new setting. See, for example, 1:15:

(1:14) All these with one accord were devoting themselves to prayer. . .

(v 15) *Kai en tais hēmerais tautais anastas Petros en mesō tōn adelphōn eipen*

"In those days Peter stood up among the brethren . . . and said"

Transitional temporal expressions are nearly always placed at the beginning of sentences. Consequently, the validity of the claim that they provide the basis for relating the following events to their context must be established primarily with reference to passages in which they do not begin the sentence.

Three reasons may be discerned for not beginning a sentence with a transitional temporal expression: the new temporal setting does not relate to the time of the last events described (sec. 2.11); the temporal setting has not changed (sec. 2.12); some other basis is preferred for relating the events to their context by replacement (sec. 2.13).

2.11   The New Temporal Setting Does Not Relate to the Time of the Last Events Described

The temporal setting of an event is not placed at the beginning of a sentence when there is no previous point of reference in time to which it may relate, or which it may replace.

For example, when Cornelius is introduced in chapter 10, the first reference to time is *hōsei peri hōran enatēn tēs hēmeras*, "about the ninth hour of the day" (v 3). This expression is not forefronted, because it cannot be related to any previous stated or implied temporal setting. The basis for relating the new incident to the last one is not temporal (see the forefronting of the subject in v 1). In addition, within the new incident to date, there is no given temporal setting to which to relate.

Another example is found in 18:9. *En nykti*, ("one night"; RSV) does not relate the Lord's appearance (v 9) to the time of the previous events. No indication is given, for instance, as to the relationship in time between when "Crispus . . . believed in the Lord" and the night of the vision. Consequently, the temporal phrase is not forefronted:

(18:7) And Paul left there and went to the house of Titius Justus, . . .

(v 8) Crispus, the ruler of the synagogue, believed in the Lord . . . ; and many of the Corinthians hearing Paul believed and were baptized (*episteuon kai ebaptizonto*).

(v 9) *eipen de ho kyrios en nykti di' horamatos tō Paulō*

"And the Lord said to Paul one night in a vision"

The above principle explains why expressions such as *dia nyktos*, "during the night," do not begin sentences in Acts. The context may even suggest that the occasion was the next night after the last event described. However, the purpose of the phrase is to establish the "period of time within which something occurs,"[5] not to provide the basis for relating the event to its context by replacement. See, for example, 16:9:

> (16:8) . . . they came down to Troas.
>
> (v 9) *kai horama dia nyktos tō Paulō ōphthē*
>
> "and a vision appeared to Paul in the night"

2.12   The Temporal Setting Has Not Changed

Temporal expressions which indicate only that the setting for the next events to be described is the same as that of the previous ones are not placed at the beginning of the sentence. In 2:41, for instance, the presence of *en tē hēmera ekeinē*, "on that day," indicates that the 3000 people added to the church resulted from the events of the particular single day concerned. No change of temporal setting is implied by the expression, however, and so it is not forefronted:

> (2:41a) So those who received Peter's word were baptized
>
> (v 41b) *kai prosetethēsan en tē hēmera ekeinē psychai hōsei trischiliai.*
>
> "and there were added that day about 3000 souls."

In addition, a temporal expression is not forefronted if it is only part of the background to the story, and therefore does not change the temporal setting of the narrative. In 20:7, for instance, the comment about what Paul planned to do the next day does not affect the setting for the actual events described in vv 7–8. Consequently, it is not forefronted within the NPC:

> (20:7a) On the first day of the week, when we were gathered together to break bread, Paul talked with them.
>
> *mellōn exienai tē epaurion*

5 Bauer, Arndt and Gingrich, *Greek-English Lexicon*, 178b.

"intending to depart on the morrow,"

(v 7b) and he prolonged his speech until midnight. (8) There were many lights in the upper chamber where we were gathered (that night, not "on the morrow")

2.13 Some Other Basis for Relating the Events to their Context is Preferred

In general, if Event X takes place at time T^1, and Event Y occurs at T^2, then the reference to T^2 begins the sentence, because the preferred basis for relating events in narrative is temporal. Occasionally, however, some other basis for relating them is more appropriate.

In 5:21, for instance, the event concerned is related to that of vv 19–20 primarily in that it is a compliance with the angel's command. Had the basis for relating the events been temporal, the relationship of command and fulfillment would have been weakened. (By not forefronting the phrase, the impression is also avoided that the apostles delayed going to the temple.)[6]

(5:19) An angel of the Lord . . . said, (20) "Go and stand in the temple and speak to the people . . ."

(v 21) *akousantes de eiselthon* *hypo* *ton* *orthron* *eis to* *hieron kai edidaskon.*

"and when they heard this, they entered the temple at daybreak and began to teach."

It has already been noted that Luke sometimes chooses to compare actions performed by different participants, even though they are actually in sequence (sec. 1.111). Under such circumstances, the comparative thematic relationship between the events is preferred to the temporal one, and any temporal expression which occurs is not forefronted.

This is illustrated in 20:5–6. Instead of relating the two events on the basis of time, Luke chooses to compare the actions of the two sub-groups of the overall group which divided at Philippi and reunited at Troas. (In addition, v 6 fulfills the expectation of v 5 that "we" would go to Troas, so that the relationship of expectation and fulfillment could be an influencing factor.)

---

[6] J. Callow (personal communication) points out that the temporal expression could not have preceded *akousantes*. If the expression had been placed between the clauses, it would not have been clear to which clause it pertained. If it had begun the sentence, *akousantes* would presumably have been omitted.

(20:5) These men (*houtoi*) went on and were awaiting us at Troas,

(v 6) *hēmeis de exepleusamen meta tas hēmeras tōn azymōn apo Philippōn*

"but we sailed away from Philippi after the days of Unleavened Bread,"

and came to them at Troas in five days

In the (non-narrative) prologue to Acts, a transitional temporal expression occurs in a relative clause. The use of a relative pronoun indicates that the events concerned are related through the referent which they have in common (see the RSV translation "*To them* he presented himself alive . . ."). This being the case, the events cannot be related primarily on the basis of time:

(1:2) . . . *tois apostolois . . . hous exelexato . . .*

(v 3) *hois kai parestēsen heauton zōnta meta to pathein auton*

"to the apostles whom he had chosen, to whom he also presented himself alive after his passion"

2.14   Conclusions

The number of passages in which transitional temporal expressions follow other elements is few. Nevertheless, the fact that they are not forefronted when the new temporal setting cannot be related to an earlier setting (sec. 2.11), or when the temporal setting is not changed (sec. 2.12), is consistent with the reason why there is a strong tendency to forefront temporal expressions. This is that, when the expression is forefronted, the basis for relating the events to their predecessors is temporal. In other words, the new setting replaces the setting for the last event(s) presented.

When successive events could have been related on the basis of time but are not, there is motivation for preferring some other basis to relate them, or otherwise playing down the temporal relationship between them (sec. 2.13).

Thus, the position of a transitional temporal expression in the sentence is determined primarily by the need to relate the events concerned.

There remains the interesting question as to why, within a transitional temporal expression or GA whose subject is a time, the subject sometimes precedes the verb (e.g., *hēmeras de genomenēs*, "when day came"; 16:35), and sometimes follows it (e.g., *genomenēs de hēmeras*; 28:12).

Whenever these subjects are forefronted in Acts, the temporal setting concerned is paralleled by another temporal setting, and the same participants are involved on both occasions. For example, both 25:13 and 14 begin with statements which establish new temporal settings, and both verses involve king Agrippa and governor Festus.

In contrast, although successive verses may both begin with temporal expressions, the participants involved on the two occasions are different when the subject is not forefronted. See, for example, 23:11–12. In v 11, the participants are the Lord and Paul. In v 12, they are the Jews and (v 14) their leaders.

It thus appears that, when the basis for relating events is temporal, in an otherwise unchanged situation, this induces the forefronting, not only of the overall temporal expression itself, but also of the subject of that expression, if it is a time.

2.2 References to the Duration, Extent or Frequency of an Action

Expressions which describe the duration of an action most commonly occur in the accusative case, in connection with verbs such as *menō*, "remain," or *diatribō*, "stay." Other periods of time are expressed in phrases which feature an adjective of quantity such as *polys*, "many," or *hikanos*, "considerable," these being governed generally by *epi*, and occasionally by *dia* or *en*.

Expressions which describe the extent of an action are governed by *achri* or *heōs*, or occasionally by *eis* or *mechri*. Those which indicate the frequency of an action feature *kata* (e.g., *kath' hēmeran*, "daily"), indicating that an event habitually took place with the frequency indicated.

References to the duration, extent or frequency of an action generally follow the verb. See, for example, 28:30 (*enemeinen de dietian holēn en idiō misthōmati*, "and he lived there two whole years in his own hired dwelling"). One reason for this is that sentences which describe the duration, extent or frequency of an event take as their point of reference or starting point the temporal setting of the sentence before. Consequently, the temporal expression itself does not provide the basis for relating the new event to its context by replacement (sec. 2.11). Rather, it is to be interpreted with respect to the given point of reference.

In a few passages, reference to the duration or frequency of an action precedes the verb because of its significance (see sec. 1.3). It may be that that particular aspect of the event influences the action to which it relates (e.g., 25:14). Alternatively, in view of past events, it may be a surprising development (14:3 below).

In 25:14, it was doubtless the duration of king Agrippa's stay which induced governor Festus to introduce the topic of Paul, as a further way of occupying the king's time. That aspect of the situation is therefore emphasized by forefronting it:

> (25:13) . . . Agrippa the king and Bernice arrived at Caesarea to welcome Festus.
>
> (v 14) *hōs de pleious hēmeras dietribon ekei*
>
> "And as they stayed there many days,"
> Festus laid Paul's case before the king

See also 9:43 (the fact that Peter remained a number of days in Joppa was crucial to the outcome of 10:5–23).

In 14:3, the duration of Paul and Barnabas' ministry is emphasized, because it was noteworthy and even surprising, in view of the prevailing circumstances (v 2):

> (14:2) But the unbelieving Jews stirred up the Gentiles and poisoned their minds against the brethren.
>
> (v 3) *hikanon men oun chronon dietripsan parrēsiazomenoi*
>
> "So they remained for a long time, speaking boldly"

See also 5:42.

Thus, a reason for emphasizing the duration or frequency of an action may often be found in the context. It therefore appears that the forefronting of a reference to duration or frequency is indeed to emphasize it.

CHAPTER THREE
REFERENCES TO PLACE

Adverbial expressions of place occur less frequently at the beginning of sentences in Acts than transitional temporal expressions (sec. 2.1). Nevertheless, the general condition for forefronting them is the same, viz., that they must establish a new point of reference (in space) for the events to be described, which replaces the setting of the last events presented.

So in 9:36 (*En Ioppē de tis ēn mathētria onomati Tabitha,* "Now there was at Joppa a disciple named Tabitha"), the adverbial phrase which establishes the new setting may begin the sentence because (a) the previous events occurred at a different place (Lydda; vv 32–35), and (b) the two incidents are to be related. The basis for relating the two incidents by replacement is spatial.[1]

References to place do not begin sentences if they refer to the location in which the last events occurred (i.e., the spatial point of reference has not changed; compare sec. 2.12). In 18:7, for instance (*kai metabas ekeithen,* "and, leaving there"), *ekeithen* could not begin the sentence because the events of vv 4–6 took place at the same location as that from which the journey begins (sec. 3.1).

In addition, references to place which do meet the basic condition above are not forefronted if Luke prefers the basis for relating the events concerned to be other than spatial. In 13:14, for instance (*autoi de dielthontes apo tēs Pergēs,* "but they, passing on from Perga"), the preferred basis is thematic. Luke chooses

---

[1] This monograph does not discuss the forefronting of spatial expressions within indirect speeches (e.g., *apo Ierosolymōn,* "from Jerusalem"; 1:4) and infinitival clauses. As noted in the Introduction to Part One, it is not clear whether such forefronting is to be explained with respect to the immediate linguistic context, or whether it is determined by the broader context.

(In fact, it can always be argued that the basic condition for forefronting the expression is met, because the point of reference of the indirect speech or infinitive is different from that of the clause in which it is embedded. See especially 9:27 [bis].)

In addition, examples of forefronting which occur within articular clauses (e.g., 25:7) are not considered here.

primarily to compare what "they" did (sub-group G^2) with what John did (G^1; v 13b), rather than bring out the spatial relationship between the journeys of v 13a and v 14 (sec. 3.2).

Like temporal expressions, references to place may be divided into those that can function as "settings" ("starting points" or "spatial points of reference"), and those that cannot. In the case of temporal expressions, the distinction was between references to a point in time (sec. 2.1) and references to the duration, extent or frequency of an action (sec. 2.2). A similar distinction is possible for adverbial expressions of place. Spatial expressions which function as settings or points of reference for one or more events in narrative are limited, when no movement is involved, to references to the place itself ("there," "at the house." "in Athens"), and, when movement is involved, to designations of the source of the movement ("thence," "from Miletus"). Other spatial expressions parallel the "extent" category in time. One goes "to," "towards," "into" or "as far as" a location which is the "goal" of the movement.[2]

The validity of the above distinction emerges on considering the circumstances under which a writer of narrative might wish to establish a spatial setting. Most often, it is in the context of travel. A participant has moved, say, from location L^1 to location L^2. If there is spatial continuity between this journey and the following events (i.e., if the following events can be related in space to the end of the journey), then the participant will either be involved in events "at L^2" (e.g., 14:7 below), or will be moving "from L^2" (e.g., 14:26):

Event(s)	Point of Reference	Content
X	location L^1	travel from L^1 to L^2
Y	location L^2	events at L^2 or
		travel from L^2 (to L^3)

14:7 illustrates the forefronting of a spatial expression, because the previous event X described travel from a different place (v 6),

---

[2] It is not possible to claim for Acts that, say, expressions governed by *eis* describe only the goal of a movement, and therefore fall outside the category which potentially establishes spatial points of reference. Phrases governed by *eis* indicate also the overall location or area within which events take place (Bauer, Arndt and Gingrich, *Greek-English Lexicon*, 229b; e.g., 2:5). A similar problem in reverse concerns phrases governed by *en*. For example, in 9:37b, *en hyperōō*, "in an upper room," is the goal of the action of placing.

In addition, adverbs of place such as *hōde*, "here, hither," and *ekeise*, "there, thither," seem to refer to locations which are at once the goal of previous movement and the scene of the event which is the purpose of that movement (see 9:21, 21:3).

In this chapter, when there is no doubt that the place to which reference is made is the goal of a motion verb, then it is discounted as a potential spatial setting. Doubtful cases are treated as potential spatial points of reference.

and the following events Y occur at the goal of the journey concerned:

> (14:1–5 are set in Iconium (L^1) and conclude with an effort to stone Barnabas and Paul.)
>
> (v 6) (X) On learning of the plan, they fled to Lystra and Derbe, cities of Lycaonia, and to the surrounding country (L^2);
>
> (v 7) (Y) _kakei euaggelizomenoi ēsan._
>
> "and there they were preaching the gospel."

14:26 illustrates the forefronting of a spatial expression, because the previous event X described travel from a different place (v 25), and the following journey Y has the new location as its starting point:

> (14:25) (X) . . . they went down to Attalia (L^2),
>
> (v 26) (Y) _kakeithen apepleusan eis Antiocheian._
>
> "and from there they sailed to Antioch (L^3)."

In 27:4–5, the goal of journey X is not stated, but the initial NPC of Y establishes a new spatial point of reference for the rest of the journey:

> (27:4) (X) And putting to sea from there we sailed under the lee of Cyprus, * because the winds were against us;
>
> (*and continued our journey beyond Cyprus)
>
> (v 5) (Y) _to te pelagos to kata tēn Kilikian kai Pamphylian diapleusantes_
>
> "and having sailed across the sea which is off Cilicia and Pamphylia,"
> we came to Myra in Lycia.

The other circumstance under which a writer establishes a spatial setting is if he switches his attention from events in location L^1 to events at L^2. In English, one may say, "Now turning our attention _to_ location L^2," but the setting thus established is always a point of reference at which or from which the following events take place:

Event(s)	Point of Reference	Content
X	location L^1	events at L^1
Y	location L^2	events at L^2

This is illustrated in 9:36 (discussed above).

In each of the examples so far noted, the spatial expression is forefronted because it establishes a point of reference which is different from and replaces that of the last events recorded. The following sections consider examples which violate this condition (sec. 3.1), or in which some other aspect is in focus (sec. 3.2).

It may be an accident of the data, but no reference to the *goal* of a journey occurs at the beginning of a sentence in Acts. In a few passages, however, the goal immediately follows the basis for relating the sentence to its context, or else precedes its verb in a later clause.

The goal is forefronted in this way when it is emphasized (factor 3; Introduction to Part One). In 17:19, for instance (*epi ton Areion pagon ēgagon*, "they brought (Paul) to the Aeropagus"), the goal is probably forefronted because it was "a venerable institution,"[3] and therefore a particularly auspicious place in which to present the Christian message. In 17:10 (*eis tēn synagōgēn tōn Ioudaiōn apēesan*, "they went into the Jewish synagogue"), the goal is surprising, considering the Jewish opposition experienced in the last town. In 8:3 (*kata tous oikous eisporeuomenos*, "entering house after house"), the extent and thoroughness of the persecution is emphasized.

It is not always obvious why the goal should be given prominence (e.g., *tē polei*; 10:9). However, a reason is clear in a sufficient number of passages to conclude that the forefronting of the goal of a journey is to give emphatic prominence to it.

3.1 The Spatial Setting Has Not Changed

If a spatial expression refers to the setting for the last event(s) described, then it is not forefronted, because there has been no change in the point of reference (compare sec. 2.11). In 18:7, for instance, *ekeithen* refers to the same location as that of the previous events:[4]

> (18:4–6 describe Paul's ministry in the synagogue (L¹), concluding with his announcement that he was going elsewhere.)
>
> (v 7) *kai metabas ekeithen*
> "and leaving there (L¹),"
> he went to the house of a man named Titius Justus

[3] Bruce, *The Book of Acts*, 351.
[4] If the same argument can be extended to Luke's Gospel, the generally preferred reading at the beginning of Luke 11:53 (*Kakeithen exelthontos autou*, "And as he went forth from there") would be rejected, in favour of the Textus Receptus *Legontos de autou tauta pros autous*, "And as he said these things to them." The forefronting of *kakeithen* would be inappropriate in this context; the movement is from the scene of the previous incident.

If participants come from location L^2 to the location L^1 of the previous events, and the following events take place at L^1, then the reference to L^2 is not forefronted, because it is not replacing L^1 as the spatial setting. In 11:27, for instance, *katēlthon <u>apo Ierosolymōn</u> prophētai eis Antiocheian*, "prophets came down from Jerusalem to Antioch." Since both v 26 and vv 28–30 take place in Antioch (L^1), the reference to Jerusalem (L^2) is not intended to change the setting, and so is not forefronted.

The above reasoning may also explain the word order in 13:1. If Luke's intended reading in 12:25 were *hypestrepsan ex Ierousalēm*, "they returned from Jerusalem,"[5] "to Antioch" being understood, this would suggest that Luke had already readopted Antioch as his spatial point of reference (L^1; see 11:30). The adverbial phrase of place would not then be forefronted in 13:1:

(12:24) But the word of God was growing and multiplying.

(v 25) And Barnabas and Saul returned from Jerusalem (L^2)
. . .

(13:1) *Ēsan de <u>en Antiocheia</u> kata tēn ousan ekklēsian prophētai kai didaskaloi*

"Now in Antioch there were prophets and teachers in the church"

With the above interpretation, the word order in 13:1 is consistent with that of 2:5 and 9:10, in both of which an existential clause is used to introduce new major participants to a *given* location. It also contrasts with 9:36 (see Introduction to chap. 3), in which the existential clause begins with a forefronted spatial expression and the location is different.

Let $L^{1'}$ represent a particular place within the given wider location L^1. If sentence Y specifies the location $L^{1'}$ of an event, and $L^{1'}$ does not contrast with any other specific place, then $L^{1'}$ does not replace any previous spatial setting. Consequently, reference to $L^{1'}$ is not forefronted. See, for example, 13:5:

(13:5) When they arrived at Salamis (L^1),

katēggellon ton logon . . . <u>en tais synagōgais</u> tōn Ioudaiōn .

"they proclaimed the word . . . in the synagogues of the Jews ($L^{1'}$)."

[5] Several variant readings exist for this verse. Maybe Luke actually wrote *hypestrepsan eis Ierousalēm*, but intended either *eis Antiocheian* or *ex/apo Ierousalēm*. (To read and punctuate *hypestrepsan, eis Ierousalēm plērōsantes tēn diakonian*, the editor would have to show why "at Jerusalem" would merit special prominence.)

"The synagogues of the Jews" does not contrast with or replace any other comparable location, and so reference to it is not forefronted.

In a few passages, the location specified (L^1) is not forefronted because it does not replace any location identifiable from the context. In other words, there is no spatial way of relating the event concerned to the context.

In 27:27, for instance (*diapheromenōn hēmōn en tō Adria*, "as we were drifting in the Adria"), no location is given for the events of vv 18–26, which occurred during an extended period of time while the storm at sea was raging. The last place mentioned was the island of Clauda in v 16, but that ceased to be the spatial point of reference after v 17 (see *houtōs epheronto*, "and so we were driven").

3.2 Some Other Basis for Relating the Events to their Context is Preferred

On occasion, Event Y takes place at a different location from Event X, but Luke chooses some basis other than the spatial one for relating them. (a) Most commonly, the preferred relationship is thematic, in particular, a switch of attention from one participant to another. (b) Alternatively, he chooses not to change his spatial point of reference, because the event at the new location is followed by movement back to the old location.

(a)   In 10:1, attention switches from events at Joppa (L^1; 9:36–43) to events at Caesarea (L^2). Instead of forefronting the new spatial setting (as in 9:36), the sentence begins with reference to Cornelius (*anēr de tis en Kaisareia onomati Kornēlios*, "(There was) a man at Caesarea named Cornelius"). The difference in word order on the two occasions reflects the difference in purpose between the incidents. The first is recorded to explain why Peter went to Joppa, and how he came to be staying there, ready for Cornelius to send for him. The second is concerned specifically with Cornelius (the first Gentile convert to Christianity), and the location of the incident is of secondary importance.

In the introduction to chap. 3, reference was made to the forefronting in 13:14 of *autoi* (sub-group G^2), in preference to the spatial expression, because "their" action is contrasted with that of John (G^1; v 13b). Another passage in which a potential spatial basis is ignored, and the activities of two participants contrasted, is 8:40. After recording the eunuch's response to Philip's disappearance (v 39b-c), Luke notes, *Philippos de heurethē eis Azōton*, "But Philip was found at Azotus."

The word order in 18:19b reflects a similar purpose. The reference to the sub-group G^1 is forefronted, as the ground for the contrasting statement about Paul (G^2), and *autou* (variant *ekei*) is not forefronted:

(18:19a) (X) And they came to Ephesus,

(v 19b) (Y) *kakeinous katelipen autou*
"and those he left there,"

(v 19c) *autos de*

"but he himself"
went into the synagogue

(b) Typically, when participants at location L^1 send to L^2 to bring people to L^1, no reference is made to any activities at L^2, and the spatial point of reference remains L^1 throughout. In 20:17–18, for instance, Miletus is the spatial point of reference L^1 both for Paul's act of sending to Ephesus (L^2) to summon the church elders (v 17), and for his speech to them, when they arrive (vv 18–22):

(20:17) and from Miletus (*apo de tēs Milētou*), sending to Ephesus, he called to him the elders of the church

(v 18) And when they came to him (in Miletus), he said to them

The word order in 5:22 suggests that the spatial point of reference at L^1 may remain unchanged, even when an intervening event at L^2 is recorded. The religious authorities at L^1 send to the prison (L^2) to have the apostles brought (v 21c). The officers come into temporary focus as they discover that the apostles are not in the prison (v 22a; see sec. 1.23). The next sentence records their report, on returning to L^1 (vv 22b–23). Although the prison was the goal of v 21, reference to it is not forefronted in v 22, because the spatial point of reference of the story remains the place from which the officers were sent, and to which they were to return:

(5:21b) Now the high priest . . . called together the council and all the senate of Israel, and sent to the prison to have them brought.

(v 22a) *hoi de paragenomenoi hypēretai ouch heuron autous en tē phylakē*

"But the officers who arrived did not find them in the prison,"

(v 22b) and having returned (to L^1), they reported

3.3 Summary

The forefronting of spatial expressions reflects the operation of the same principles as those which govern the position of temporal expressions in the sentence.

References to the goal of movement (equivalent to the duration, extent or frequency of an action) are forefronted to give emphatic prominence to the goal (factor 3; Introduction to Part One).

References to the location of an event (including movement from it) are forefronted only if the basis for relating the event to its context is spatial, i.e., if they establish a new point of reference which replaces the spatial setting of the previous events (factor 1). The majority of spatial expressions are not forefronted because their referent is the same place as that in which the previous events were performed. In a few passages, a spatial expression which could have been forefronted is not so treated, because the preferred basis for relating the events is thematic (a switch of attention from one participant to another).

CHAPTER FOUR
THE REPLACEMENT BASIS AND CONTINUITY
OF SITUATION

This chapter brings together the conclusions reached concerning the basis for relating a sentence to its context by replacement. Two claims are then made. Only one basis for relating any sentence to its context ever occurs (sec. 4.1). If no replacement basis occurs, there is "continuity of situation" with the context (as defined in sec. 4.2).

If a sentence is to relate to its context, an author not only makes a comment about the theme or topic of the sentence. He must also conform to various principles of cohesion.[1] One form of cohesion with the context is achieved by beginning the sentence with a basis. This indicates that the sentence is to be related to past sentences by the replacement of a corresponding element.

In the narrative of Acts, the most common reason for forefronting an element is to indicate the basis by which the new sentence is related to its context. The element so forefronted is thematic (sec. 1.1), temporal (sec. 2.1) or spatial (chap. 3).[2] The theme (subject) or spatio-temporal setting established by forefronting the element replaces the corresponding theme or setting which was applicable to the previous events (this last being either stated overtly or only implied).

This monograph follows Beneš and Kirkwood in treating the basis as distinct from the theme of the sentence (though the theme may also be the basis; see 8:40 below).[3]

[1] See Halliday and Hasan, *Cohesion in English*, for a detailed examination of cohesion in English.

[2] In reasoned argument, a further basis is *conditional*. For example, in 25:11, two statements based on opposing protases are linked by a *men . . . de* correlation. V 11b is related to v 11a on a conditional basis. The new condition (*ei ouden estin hōn houtoi katēgorousin mou*, "if there is nothing in their charges against me") replaces the previous one (*ei adikō kai axion thanatou pepracha ti*, "If I am a wrongdoer and have done anything for which I deserve to die").

[3] Beneš, "Die Verbstellung," 5.6–19; Kirkwood, "Aspects of Word Order," 5.89.

This is illustrated in 12:1. (A traditional analysis of this sentence into topic and comment classifies "Herod" as the topic or theme, about which the comment "laid violent hands . . . " is made:[4])

> (12:1) *Kat' ekeinon de ton kairon epebalen Hērōdēs ho basileus tas cheiras kakōsai tinas tōn apo tēs ekklēsias.*
>
> "About that time [basis] Herod the king [theme] laid violent hands upon some who belonged to the church."

8:40 is an example in which the subject is both the theme and the basis of the sentence (Luke is contrasting the final acts of the eunuch [v 39b-c] and of Philip):

> (8:39) the eunuch . . . went on his way rejoicing.
>
> (v 40) *Philippos de heurethē eis Azōton.*
>
> "But Philip (basis/theme) was found at Azotus."

When an element is forefronted for temporary focus (factor 2) or for emphasis (factor 3), and a replacement basis is also present, the basis precedes it. See, for instance, 13:44:

> (13:44) *tō de erchomenō sabbatō / schedon pasa hē polis synēchthē akousai ton logon tou theou.*
>
> "The next sabbath [basis], almost the whole city [emphasized theme] gathered together to hear the word of God."

See 27:39 for an example in which the basis (*hote hēmera egeneto,* "when it was day") precedes an element in temporary focus (*tēn gēn,* "the land"; *kolpon tina,* "a bay," is the replacement basis in the next clause).

4.1 A Sentence Has Only One Replacement Basis

In most sentences, various links with the context may be discerned. Out of the set of possible links, the basis of a sentence is the specific one which has been selected to show how that sentence is primarily to be related to what has gone before.

For example, in 12:1 above, "Herod the king" is introduced in a way that suggests that the reader should already know of his

---

[4] See, for instance, Hockett, *Course in Modern Linguistics,* 201. This analysis differs from that of Halliday, who would classify "about that time" as theme, the rest of the sentence being the rheme. See Halliday, "Language Structure and Language Function," 161.

existence (see sec. 1.2). The allusion to "some who belonged to the church" presupposes prior knowledge of "the church." Potential bases for relating 12:1 to its context include thematic (a switch of attention from activities involving Paul and Barnabas to those involving Herod), and spatial (a switch of attention from activities in Antioch to those in Jerusalem). In fact, however, Luke has chosen primarily to relate the incident concerning Herod to its context on a temporal basis.

If the basis for relating a sentence in narrative to its context is thematic, temporal or spatial, can a sentence have more than one basis? It is difficult to reach a definite conclusion, since to a large extent it is a matter of opinion whether a second potential basis is significant or not. However, it appears that Luke at least intends the element which begins the sentence to be the *primary* basis for relating it to its context by replacement.

Secs. 2.3 and 3.2 discussed various sentences in which the subject (theme) is the first element of the sentence, when a temporal or spatial expression could have opened it. In each case, motivation was found for a thematic basis for relating the sentence to its context. Luke was concerned primarily with comparing or contrasting the actions of the different subjects, rather than with the temporal or spatial relationship between the events. See particularly 20:6 (the time of the event is also expressed; sec. 2.3) and 8:40 (the place is also expressed; sec. 3.2). In these examples, the order "theme - time/place" implies that the change of theme is the primary if not the sole basis for relating the new sentence to its context.

If the basis of a sentence is temporal, no precise spatial point of reference is ever recorded in Acts in the same sentence. The reported speech of chapter 7 provides an example in which a spatial point of reference is followed immediately by a transitional temporal expression:

(7:4b) _kakeithen / meta to apothanein ton patera autou metōkisen auton eis tēn gēn tautēn_

"and from there, after his father died, God removed him into this land"

The speaker's concern in the above passage is more with the fulfillment of God's command in v 3 to "go into the land which I will show you" than with the temporal relationship between the two stages of the journey which together fulfil the command (see sec. 2.13). Consequently, the spatial basis for relating them is primary.

In no other passage in which the basis of a sentence is spatial does a transitional temporal expression occur. For example, when Luke describes a journey from location L^1 to location L^3 which is performed in stages with a break at L^2, he generally relates the stages either in time or space. Except for 7:4 above, he never relates them in both ways.[5] This suggests that only one is ever the basis for relating a sentence to its context.

The combination of a transitional temporal expression and a forefronted subject (theme) is possible only if the new sentence is not in sequence with the last one (see sec. 1.11). The only definite example in which the two concur is 19:1:

> (19:1) *Egeneto de en tō ton Apollō einai en Korinthō*
>
> "Now it happened that, while Apollos was at Corinth,"
>
> *Paulon dielthonta ta anōterika merē elthein eis Epheson*
>
> "Paul, having passed through the upper country, came to Ephesus"

In the above sentence Luke appears to have established both temporal and thematic bases for relating the sentence to its context. The forefronted transitional temporal expression indicates that the new incident is to be related in time to the previous one. However, the forefronting of the reference to Apollos in the

---

[5] Luke's basis for linking the stages is usually *temporal*, if the time of the second stage can be stated by means of a temporal expression which itself may be related to the time of the first stage, e.g., "the next day," "after three days":

(At time T^1) we went (from Location L^1) to Location L^2.
At time T^2 we went to location L^3.
(T^1 and L^1 often are implied only from the context.)

See, for example, 20:15 (preferred reading):

(20:15b) *tē de hetera parebalomen eis Samon*
"the next day (T^1) we touched at Samos (L^2),"

(v 15c) *tē de echomenē ēlthomen eis tēn Milēton.*
"and the day after that (T^2) we came to Miletus (L^3)."

Luke's basis for linking the stages is usually *spatial*, making the goal of the first stage the point of reference for the second, if the time of the second stage is immaterial or, as in 7:4b, if it is not defined by reference to the time of the first ("after the death of his father"):

(From location L^1) we went to location L^2.
From there (L^2) (at time T^2) we went to location L^3.

articular infinitival clause* suggests that the reference to Paul provides the basis only for relating the clause concerned to the immediately preceding *clause*.

tō Apollō is forefronted, according to the above reasoning, because Apollos is in temporary focus; see sec. 1.242.

Diagram 1

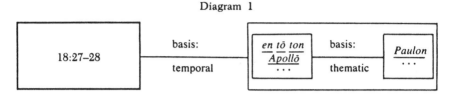

The combination of a forefronted spatial expression followed by a forefronted subject occurs only in the existential-locative clause of 9:36. However, the subject of such a clause is not the theme of the clause (see chap. 1, n. 1). In fact, the subject is forefronted because it is in temporary focus (see sec. 1.243).

There is therefore no clear evidence that a sentence can ever have more than one replacement basis for relating it to its context.

4.2   The Absence of a Replacement Basis Indicates Continuity of Situation

The forefronting of a thematic, temporal or spatial element indicates the nature of the basis for relating the sentence concerned to its context. The absence of a replacement basis means that there is "continuity of situation" with respect to the context (as defined below). The sentence may begin with a verb (independent or participial), with a temporarily focused element (factor 2; sec. 1.2), or with an emphasized element (factor 3; secs. 1.3, 2.2, chap. 3). As long as it does not begin with a subject forefronted in accordance with rule (1) of sec. 1.1, with a transitional temporal expression (sec. 2.1), or with an expression establishing a spatial setting (chap. 3), the situation applicable to the last events presented remains unchanged.

The most interesting aspect of this claim concerns sentences which begin with a participial clause. The specific circumstances of an event generally are expressed either with a participial clause, or with an adverbial clause of time subordinated by *hote* or *hōs* (hereafter, a "temporal clause"). If a circumstantial participial clause begins the sentence, there is "continuity of situation" between the independent clauses which are contiguous to it, viz., the independent clause X of the immediately previous sentence and the independent clause Y which follows the participial clause and to which it relates.[6]   No such claim can be made for temporal clauses. When they begin a sentence and the new temporal setting replaces the earlier one, no indication is given as to whether the previous situation otherwise remains unchanged or not (see further below).

Within narrative, "continuity of situation" between two independent clauses means the following. Apart from modifications described in any participial clause which precedes the second independent clause, the spatio-temporal setting of the events described in the independent clauses remains unchanged, as do the participants involved. So, for example, a new participant may be introduced to a scene in which other participants are interacting. If there is continuity of situation, then apart from the new arrival, the participants remain unchanged, as does the spatio-temporal situation and any other pertinent circumstances. (Under certain circumstances, the principle of continuity extends beyond the requirement that the participants and the spatio-temporal situation remain unchanged; see sec. 4.212a.)   An illustration of the principle of continuity is provided in 5:17. The reintroduction of the religious authorities follows a section which describes the habitual activities of the early church and the way the crowds flocked to the apostles (vv 12–16). By reintroducing the authorities in connection with a participial clause, it is understood that they are placed in the scene which has been set by the previous verses. Consequently, when the following independent clause indicates that "they were filled with jealousy," the reason for that jealousy is to be deduced from the immediate context:

(5:16) (X) The people also used to gather from the towns around Jerusalem, bringing the sick and those affected with unclean spirits, and they were all healed.

(v 17) *Anastas de ho archiereus*

"But the high priest, rising up," . . .
(Y) was filled with jealousy

[6] See sec. 4.212c for the circumstances under which this claim is modified.

Blass, Debrunner and Funk distinguish three categories of participle, "the *supplementary* participle (predicative completion of the idea of the main verb: *pauomai legōn*, etc.)", "the participle as *attributive* with or without the article, equivalent to a relative clause" and "the *adverbial* (circumstantial) participle" (*Greek Grammar*, secs. 411–23). Healey and Healey (*Genitive Absolute*, 12–14) discuss the problems that arise in distinguishing the circumstantial function of the participle from its other uses. For the purposes of this section, all participial clauses which being a sentence and are anarthrous are circumstantial.

It is recognized generally that the events described in circumstantial participial clauses and the independent clauses to which they are subordinate relate to one another in a variety of ways. For instance, Funk writes,

> "The circumstantial participle as the equivalent of an adverbial clause may be taken (i.e., inferred from the context) to denote time, cause, means, manner, purpose, condition, concession, or attendant circumstances."[7]

However, Robertson points out that

> ". . . there is a constant tendency to read into this circumstantial participle more than is there. In itself, it must be distinctly noted, the participle does not express time . . . These ideas are not in the participle, but are merely suggested by the context . . ."[8]

What, then, is the function of the circumstantial participle? It is not needed to express any of the relationships that Blass lists, for

> "Other more extended but more precise constructions are available for the same purpose: prepositional phrases, conditional, causal, temporal clauses, etc., and finally the grammatical coordination of two or more verbs."[9]

Robertson claims that "the circumstantial participle is an additional statement and does not form an essential part of the verbal notion of the principal verb."[10] In other words, if the independent clause expresses a main event in narrative, then the only role of circumstantial participial clauses is to express in an unmarked way that which is peripheral or additional to those events.

This section argues, however, that a circumstantial participial clause is not just a convenient means of expressing peripheral information without specifying its relation to the nuclear part of the sentence. Placed at the beginning of a sentence, it also indicates continuity of situation and even unity of topic between the independent clauses which are contiguous to it. Consequently, its function is not totally unmarked. Just as a temporal clause, apart from its general role of presenting peripheral information, has the specific function of expressing the temporal setting for the nuclear part of a sentence, so a circumstantial participial clause at the

---

[7] Funk, *Beginning-Intermediate Grammar*, 669.
[8] Robertson, *Grammar of the Greek NT*, 1124.
[9] Blass, Debrunner and Funk, *Greek Grammar*, sec. 417.
[10] Robertson, *Grammar of the Greek NT*, 1124.

beginning of a sentence has the specific function of indicating continuity.

For the purposes of this monograph, the term "circumstantial participial clause" refers both to participial clauses in the nominative case (NPCs) and to genitives absolute (GAs). Healey and Healey find that only 58% of the examples of GAs in the NT are truly "absolute" in the sense that the genitive subject has no coreferent in the rest of the sentence.[11] They conclude that the only characteristic of the GA that is statistically consistent is that its subject "is not identical with the subject of the leading verb."[12] Out of 313 NT occurrences of the GA, only five do not obey this rule.[13] Furthermore, NPCs almost always have the same subject as the verb to which they are subordinated. Healey and Healey therefore conclude that the GA is in complementary distribution with the NPC.[14]

If Healey and Healey's conclusions are correct, then all circumstantial participial clauses which begin sentences may be expected to behave alike and indicate continuity of situation between the independent clauses which are contiguous to them. This is indeed the case (secs. 4.21–22).

Sec. 4.21 discusses GAs and contrasts them with temporal clauses whose subjects are different from that of the following independent clause. Sec. 4.22 contrasts NPCs with temporal clauses whose subjects are the same as that of the following independent clause. Finally, sec. 4.23 extends the principle of continuity to sentences which begin with an independent verb, or with an element forefronted for temporary focus or emphasis.

> The functions of circumstantial participial clauses and temporal clauses may be contrasted, as long as they do not both occur in the same sentence. However, there are certain restrictions of concurrence.
> (1) When a transitional temporal expression is the basis of (begins) a sentence, other pertinent circumstances are ex-

---

[11] Healey and Healey, *Genitive Absolute*, 32.

[12] Healey and Healey, *Genitive Absolute*, 32. The quotation is from Smyth, *Greek Grammar*, sec. 2058.

[13] Matt 1:18, Mark 6:22, Acts 21:34, 22:17, 28:6. In 21:34 and 28:6, the GA is negative and expresses the failure of the subject to achieve his goal or see his expectation fulfilled. The following independent clause describes the alternative method or conclusion that he adopts. The change of direction implied in the adoption of this alternative may compensate for the failure to change the subject.

The GA of 22:17 is probably acceptable because the subject of the verb to which the GA is subordinated is in the accusative case in an infinitival construction following *egeneto*.

[14] Healey and Healey, *Genitive Absolute*, 31.

pressed only in participial form (1:10, 6:1, 10:9, 20:7, 25:23, 27:27, 28:13; see also 17:16, in which a spatial expression begins the sentence).

(If the basis is an adverbial phrase of time or location, it might be argued that the phrase is forefronted within the participial clause. However, in several of the above examples, a GA would not have been expected, according to the principles of sec. 4.21, had the adverbial phrase not been present. See especially 6:1, 10:9, 17:16. The adverbial phrase is therefore considered not to be part of the GA, and the GA is not initial in the sentence.)

(An adverbial phrase of time follows a participial clause only if the circumstances so expressed relate to an earlier temporal setting given within the same sentence. See, for example, 28:13b. A temporal phrase may follow a temporal clause [12:6, 27:27].)

(2) Similarly, following an NPC, a further circumstance whose subject is different from that of the NPC is expressed only with a GA (1:9; 20:3, 9; 27:7). This is true also when the circumstance separates *egeneto* from the infinitival clause which is its subject (16:16; contrast 10:25), and following a relative clause with a different subject (4:37).

None of the above examples are considered in the following sections, on the grounds that the form of the circumstantial clause could have been determined by its position in the sentence.

In the above introductory discussion, it has been assumed to be significant that the circumstantial participial clause precedes the independent clause to which it is subordinate. In other words, it is no accident that the participial clause is placed before the independent clause, rather than after it. In this connection, J.H. Greenlee observes that participial clauses which precede the verb generally describe events which are different from but "coordinate" with the independent verb (coordinate circumstances). Those that follow the verb, in contrast, are concerned usually with some aspect of the main event itself (they describe "a circumstance *accompanying* the leading verb").[15]

4.21   Genitives Absolute and Other Circumstantial Clauses Whose Subject is Different from the Independent Clause to Which They Relate

This section argues that, when a GA begins a sentence, the situation of the following independent clause is a continuation

---

[15] Greenlee, *A Concise Exegetical Grammar*, 66–67.

from that of the sentence preceding the GA, apart from any modifications expressed in the GA itself. This means that the participating cast and the spatio-temporal setting remain unchanged, apart from any changes described in the GA.

The examples of this section may conveniently be divided into two: those in which the subject of the GA is the same as that of the preceding independent clause (sec. 4.211); and those in which it is different from that of the preceding independent clause (sec. 4.212).

This distinction is made for two reasons. (a) Because of the nature of the GA, when its subject is the same as that of the preceding independent clause X, then the subject of the following independent clause Y is different from that of X. It usually follows that there is also a change of initiative between X and Y. This is not usually the case with the examples of sec. 4.212. (b) In the examples of sec. 4.212, the continuity between X and Y extends to far more than the participating cast and the spatio-temporal setting. If the same people interact with each other in both X and Y, then their roles vis-à-vis each other may not be reversed. Unity of thought and topic is also found, together with further development of the story in the same direction as before, features which do not apply to the examples of sec. 4.211.

Both sections cite examples of temporal clauses which occur in circumstances such that a GA would have been an unacceptable alternative. In many passages in which a temporal clause is found, a GA would probably have been acceptable, as far as the principle of continuity is concerned. Some, however, do not manifest the required continuity between X and Y. This point is developed in sec. 4.213.

4.211 *GAs Whose Subjects are the Same as Those of the Preceding Sentence* When Event X has subject A, and the next sentence begins with a GA whose subject also is A, then the following independent clause normally has a different subject B.

In every case in which the GA has the same subject as X, the continuity of situation between X and Y is pedantically obvious. The GA either refers back to X (e.g., 4:1 below), or else describes an action related to X which occurs at the same time as or immediately following X. In both cases, Y is then performed in the same spatio-temporal setting as X.

In the case of 4:1 (following Peter's sermon of 3:12–26), there is a shift of temporal setting from the end of Peter's speech back to some point prior to its completion. Apart from this, the arrival of the authorities is to the exact scene of the previous events, and with the same people present:

(4:1) *Lalountōn de autōn pros ton laon*

"And as they were speaking to the people,"
(Y) the priests . . . came upon them.

27:30 is a particularly interesting example. The activity described in the GA is related to the events of v 29 (X; see the italics), yet is itself a new development:

(27:29) (X) . . . the sailors *let out four anchors from the stern*, and prayed for day to come.

(v 30) *Tōn de nautōn zētountōn phygein ek tou ploiou, kai chalasantōn tēn skaphēn eis tēn thalassan prophasei hōs ek prōrēs agkyras mellontōn ekteinein*

"And as the sailors were seeking to escape from the ship, and had lowered the boat into the sea under pretence of *laying out anchors from the bow*,"
(v 31) (Y) Paul said"

In the above examples, the continuity of situation between X and Y is very obvious. It is therefore worth noting that Y does not have to occur in the same situation as X, just because the previous subordinate clause related back to X. In 19:1, for instance, the infinitival clause governed by *en (en tō ton Apollō einai en Korinthō*, "while Apollos was in Corinth") refers back to the events of the previous two verses, yet the following clause describes Paul arriving at Ephesus!

4.212 *GAs whose Subjects are Different from Those of the Preceding Sentence*   In the examples of sec. 4.211, the identity of the subjects of the GA and of the previous independent clause X means that a change of subject usually occurs in the following independent clause Y. It generally follows that there is a change also of initiator, and in the direction of development of the continuing story. When the subject of the GA is different from that of X, however, none of these changes are necessary. Rather, not only is there a continuity of situation between X and Y; the principle of continuity extends to other features as well; see (a), (b) below.

In a few passages, the activities immediately preceding the GA take place while some major participants are unaware of what is going on. The independent clause following the GA takes up the story, as it relates to those participants ([c] below).

(a) If the subject of the GA is different from that of the preceding independent clause X, then not only is there a continuity of situation between X and the following independent clause Y, but the principle of continuity extends to other features. For instance, when the same participants are involved in X and Y, then their roles vis-à-vis each other may not be reversed, if a GA occurs between them.

This may be seen by contrasting 18:5–6 (in which a GA occurs between X and Y) and 9:22–23 (in which a temporal clause separates X and Y).

In 18:5–6, Paul is subject of both independent clauses, and the Jews are undergoers. Even though these roles are temporarily reversed in the GA itself, between the independent clauses they remain unchanged:[16]

> (18:5) (X) When Silas and Timothy arrived from Macedonia, Paul occupied himself with preaching, testifying to the Jews that the Christ was Jesus.
>
> (v 6) *antitassomenōn de autōn*
>
> "But when they resisted," ...
> (Y) he shook out his garments and said to them

In contrast, in 9:22–23, Saul and the Jews change roles, between the independent clauses which are contiguous to the temporal clause:

> (9:22) (X) Saul ... confounded the Jews who lived in Damascus by proving that Jesus was the Christ.
>
> (v 23) *hōs de eplērounto hēmerai hikanai*
>
> "Now when many days had passed,"
> (Y) the Jews plotted to kill him

Independent clauses which are contiguous to a GA do not always involve the same participants. However, the principle of continuity requires that, insofar as it is relevant, the roles of the participants do not change.

For instance, the subjects of the independent clauses which are contiguous to the GA of 18:27 are different. The undergoer or benefactor of their actions remains the same, however:

---

[16] This principle implies that, in 15:2b, the unnamed "they" refers to the men from Judea (v 1), as in D, rather than to the Christians in Antioch ("the brethren"; Bruce, *The Book of Acts*, 302).

(18:26) (X) Priscilla and Aquila took Apollos and expounded to him the way of God more accurately.

(v 27) *boulomenou de autou dielthein eis tēn Achaian*

"And when he wished to cross to Achaia,"
        (Y) the brothers encouraged him, and wrote to the disciples to receive him.

The above example may be contrasted with 22:24–25, in which Paul is first an undergoer of the tribune's order (v 24), and then the initiator of a speech to the centurion (v 25). Because Paul's role vis-à-vis the other participants does not remain constant, a GA would have been an unacceptable alternative to the temporal clause of v 25:

(22:24) (X) . . . the tribune . . . ordered Paul to be examined by scourging . . .

(v 25) *hōs de proeteinan auton tois himasin*

"But when they had tied him up with the thongs,"
        (Y) Paul said to the centurion who was standing by,
"Is it lawful for you to scourge a man who is a Roman citizen . . . ?"

In a few passages, continuity of role is not a relevant factor. In such cases, the principle of continuity applies as far as it can.

For instance, the initiators of the event of 14:19 which was directed against Paul must have left the scene before that of v 20 occurred. Consequently, no continuity or reversal of roles between Paul and them is possible. The principle of continuity can therefore apply to vv 19–20 only as regards the situation:[17]

(14:19) (X) . . . having stoned Paul, they dragged (*esyron*) him out of the city, supposing that he was dead.

(v 20) *kyklōsantōn de tōn mathētōn auton*

"But when the disciples gathered about him,"
        (Y) he rose up and entered the city

In the above examples, the continuity of situation between the independent clauses that are contiguous to the GA is rather

---

[17] However, Lenski (*Interpretation of Acts*, 582) notes, "The imperfect *esyron* conveys the thought that this was not the end of the matter." If the use of the imperfect does create the expectation of "more to come," then a participial clause would be a particularly appropriate way of indicating that the following independent clause continued "the matter."

obvious, and a GA would scarcely be needed to perceive it. In a few passages, however, such continuity is not immediately apparent, and the GA has a meaningful role to play in indicating continuity of direction or unity of thought. 18:12 illustrates this. Having moved from the synagogue because of opposition from the Jews (v 7), Paul receives an assurance from the Lord that no one will harm him while he stays in Corinth (vv 9–10). He therefore remains there (v 11). However, the fresh initiative of the Jews in v 12 looks like changing the situation (see "but"; RSV):

> (18:11) (X) And he stayed a year and six months teaching the word of God among them.
>
> (v 12) *Galliōnos de anthypatou ontos tēs Achaias*
>
> "And when Gallio was proconsul of Achaia,"
>   (Y) the Jews made a united attack upon Paul and brought him before the tribunal

The use of a GA in v 12, rather than a temporal clause, implies continuity between vv 9-11 and the following events. Since Paul is involved in both sets of events, this must mean that there is no reversal in his fortunes. As the incident of vv 12–17 unfolds, it becomes clear that this is so. The charges against Paul are rejected by Gallio (vv 14–16), and it is this decision which makes it possible for him to remain for the eighteen months of v 11.[18] In other words, the incident explains how it was that Paul was able to remain so long, and the GA of v 12 has a significant role to play in indicating this continuity of topic and direction.

The above example may be contrasted with 14:5. In this passage, the intervention of the Jews does bring Paul's stay to an end (see v 3), and a temporal clause is used.

Another example is 7:30 (not D). The GA *plērōthentōn etōn tesserakonta*, "when forty years had passed" implies that the line of reasoning which Stephen is pursuing continues, notwithstanding the lapse of time. This becomes apparent in v 35 when he states, "This Moses whom they refused, saying, 'Who made you a ruler and a judge?'" (referring to the incident of vv 26–29 which precedes the GA), "God sent as both ruler and deliverer" (referring to the incident of vv 30–34 which follows the GA).

Similarly, the use of a GA in 23:12 implies a direct relationship between the Lord's promise to Paul that "you must bear witness also at Rome" (v 11) and the plot by the Jews to kill him. (On

[18] See Bruce, *The Book of Acts*, 377.

learning of the plot, the tribune immediately decides to send Paul to Caesarea [the first stage of his journey to Rome].)

(b)   In a few passages, the sentence following Event X begins with a GA which gives a previously unmentioned piece of relevant background information. This information helps to explain why the next event Y occurs. The continuity of situation and direction of development between the independent clauses which are contiguous to the GA is evident. If anything, this continuity is enhanced by the presentation of the reason for Y.

In 9:38, for instance, following the death of Dorcas, the information that Lydda was near Joppa explains why it would be natural for the disciples to think of sending for Peter to come (Y):

> (9:37b) (X) When they had washed her, they laid her in an upper room.
>
> (v 38) *eggys de ousēs Lyddas tē Ioppē*
>
> "Since Lydda was near Joppa,"
>   (Y) the disciples, hearing that Peter was there, sent two men to him

(When a GA presents background information which is not the reason for the independent clause with which it is is associated, the GA follows the independent clause. See 27:2, 5:2.)

(c)   On a couple of occasions, following Events W which involve participant A, a further set of Events X occurs, not involving A and of which he is unaware. Following a GA, the story as it involves A is resumed. Because A is unaware of the intervening events, for him there is continuity between the earlier Events W and the new Events Y, so that the GA is appropriate.

This is particularly clear in 16:35. The local authorities (A) had put Paul and Silas in prison (Event W; v 23). The next day they send to have them released (Y), quite unaware of the intervening events X of vv 25–34. The story as it affects them is resumed, just as though nothing had happened during the night.

(See also 5:21b, in which an NPC takes up the story as it concerns the authorities who last featured in v 18.)

In chapter 12, king Herod has Peter in prison, with soldiers guarding him (Events W; vv 4–6). Neither Herod nor the soliders are aware of the following Events X in which an angel releases him (vv 7–11). However, "when it became day" (GA; v 18), Luke refers again to the soldiers whom Peter had left behind (Events Y). The GA indicates that Luke is taking up the story at the point at which he had left off, as far as those whom Peter had left behind were concerned.

The above examples of participial clauses are thus interpreted as special cases in which the continuity of situation is between Events Y and earlier Events W, the major participants concerned being unaware of the intervening Events X.

4.213 A Comparison of GAs and Temporal Clauses In every passage involving a GA, a continuity of situation, thought or topic may be discerned. In the special cases of sec. 4.212c, the continuity is with earlier events, the participants concerned being unaware of intervening developments. Otherwise, the continuity is always between the events which are described immediately before and after the GA.

In some cases which employ a temporal clause subordinated by *hōs*, a GA could also have been used, as far as the principle of continuity is concerned (see 10:25; 18:9; 19:9; 20:14,18). However, sec. 4.212a has already referred to passages in which a GA would have been an unacceptable alternative, because the principle of continuity is violated (9:23, 14:5, 21:27, 22:25, 25:14). In addition to these passages, a GA could not have replaced a temporal clause in 27:1 (see below), and would probably have been inappropriate in 10:17.

27:1 begins a new section which deals, not with Paul's innocence in spite of his appeal to Caesar (the topic of chapters 25–26), but with his actual journey to Rome. In addition to this change of topic, there is no clear continuity in the cast of participants and their roles. (The vague "they" of 27:1 may include governor Festus, who was the addressee of king Agrippa's last remark [26:32]. Probably, however, having decided upon the course of action to be taken, he had delegated the details to subordinates.)

Thus, out of the 13 relevant occasions on which a temporal clause subordinated by *hōs* is the basis of a sentence, as far as the principle of continuity is concerned, a GA could have been used in five, it would have been inappropriate in six, and in a further two, its acceptability is open to doubt. Consequently, though there is overlap in the circumstances in which a GA and a temporal clause may be used, they are by no means identical.

This conclusion is very reasonable when one compares the functions of the GA and temporal clauses.

In Luke's writings, *hōs* has a recognised function as a "particle of time" or "temporal conjunction."[19] If the presence of a clause

---

[19] Winer, *Treatise on the Grammar of NT Greek*, 370; Blass, Debrunner and Funk, *Greek Grammar*, sec. 455(2).

subordinated by *hōs* therefore establishes the temporal setting of the following independent clause (the time or occasion when Y occurred), one would expect it to be found both when there is continuity of situation with the last event described (apart from the change of temporal setting), and also when such continuity is non-existent.

Similarly, "the logical relation of the circumstantial participle to the rest of the sentence is not expressed by the participle itself . . . but is to be deduced from the context."[20] The temporal relation is found among the range of relationships which are perceived between a circumstantial participle and the independent clause to which it is subordinate. Consequently, among the GAs which indicate a continuity of situation between the independent clauses which are contiguous to it, there are likely to be occasions when its relation to the rest of the sentence is most naturally interpreted as temporal.

The following diagram shows the overlap in the circumstances of use of participial and temporal clauses.

Diagram 2

Relation of Subordinate Cl. to Independent Cl:	+ Temporal (temporal clause)	− Temporal
Relation of Contiguous Independent Clauses		
+ Continuity (participial clause)		
− Continuity		

Diagram 2 indicates that, if there is continuity of situation between two events, and the intervening circumstance has a basically temporal relationship to the following independent clause, then either a participial or a temporal clause may be used. The type of clause actually chosen depends (all else being equal)

---

[20] Blass, Debrunner and Funk, *Greek Grammar*, sec. 417.

on whether Luke wishes to give prominence to the temporal relationship or to the continuity of situation.[21]

4.22 Participial Clauses in the Nominative Case and Other Circumstantial Clauses Whose Subject is the Same as That of the Independent Clause to Which They Relate

Out of the 212 NPCs (in the text of Nestle and Aland [1975]) which begin sentences in the narrative sections of Acts, 111 have the same subject as that of the preceding sentence. A further 84 introduce responses to the last event described (e.g., *Statheis de ho Petros*, "But Peter, standing up"; 2:14). In all these cases, continuity of situation with the last event presented before the NPC is pedantically obvious.

Even among the remaining 17 examples, continuity of situation is generally evident. They include ten passages in which an NPC follows a short background comment (e.g., *apolythentes*, "having been released" [4:23]; the NPC reiterates the last event before the comment of v 22). In these cases, continuity is with the situation of the last event presented before the comment. In one passage, the NPC records the arrival of participants last mentioned before a set of events of which they were unaware (5:21b; see sec. 4.212c). In just two passages is continuity of situation with the immediately preceding events less than clear.

One of these passages is 19:8. In the previous two sentences, the subject is the disciples, and Paul is not involved. However, by not making overt reference to Paul in v 8, Luke appears to have assumed continuity of situation with the last event in which Paul was involved, viz., v 6:

> (19:6) And when Paul had laid his hands upon them, the Holy Spirit came on them; and they spoke with tongues and prophesied. (v 7) There were about twelve men in all.
>
> (v 8) *Eiselthōn de eis tēn synagōgēn*
>
> "Now, having entered the synagogue"

A similar comment probably applies also to 13:13. This time the subject is named, but in the preceding sentence the participation of Paul is doubtless assumed, since the proconsul had originally summoned him and Barnabas "and sought to hear the word of God" (v 7). Furthermore, v 13 presents the resumption of the journey which was "interrupted" at Paphos by the opposition of the false prophet (vv 6b–12):

---

[21] The above comparison with GAs of temporal clauses subordinated by *hōs* applies equally to those subordinated by *hote*.

(13:12) Then the proconsul believed, when he saw what had occurred, for he was astonished *at the teaching of the Lord.*

(v 13) *Anachthentes de apo tēs Paphou hoi peri (ton) Paulon*

"Now, after Paul and his company set sail from Paphos"

Thus, with the above rather weak exceptions in which continuity of situation with earlier events is apparently assumed, NPCs begin sentences only if they take as their point of reference the spatio-temporal setting, participating cast and other circumstances as recorded in the immediately preceding sentences. In other words, apart from any modification described in or implied by the NPC itself, there is continuity of situation between the events which are contiguous to it.

There are only ten examples in Acts of temporal clauses with the same subject as that of the following independent clause. In some of them, continuity of situation with the last event presented is evident (see especially 1:13, 5:24, 21:12). In others, it is unlikely that an NPC could have replaced the temporal clause (see especially 16:4; other possible examples are 8:36, 16:15, 17:13, 21:1).

In a couple of cases, it is almost certain that an NPC would have been an unacceptable alternative to the temporal clause. In 8:12, the temporal setting is in contrast with that of the previous two verses, as is the attitude of the people. There is therefore no continuity of situation between the two verses which are contiguous to the temporal clause:

(8:11) (X) They used to give heed to Simon, because for a long time he had amazed them with his magic.

(v 12) *hote de episteusan tō Philippō euaggelizomenō*

"But when they believed Philip preaching," . . .
    (Y) they were baptized

As for 28:4 (*hōs de eidon hoi barbaroi*, "now when the natives saw"), the use of *idontes* would have implied that the incident continued with a switch of attention to the onlookers (see 16:19). In fact Luke keeps the two groups of participants apart (see Part Two, sec. 3.22 on the use of *men oun* in v 5), and v 5 is a continuation from v 3 but not from v 4.

Thus, the conclusions of sec. 4.21 concerning circumstantial clauses whose subjects are different from those of the following independent clause are equally applicable to those whose subjects remain the same. The use of a participial clause at the beginning of a sentence generally reflects continuity of situation between the independent clauses which are contiguous to it. Temporal clauses (and temporal expressions in general; see 12:1) establish the temporal setting or occasion of the following independent clause, regardless of whether otherwise there is continuity of situation with the previous independent clause. There are occasions in which either a circumstantial participial clause or a temporal clause would be an acceptable construction, as far as the principle of continuity and the relationship with the following independent clause are concerned. However, the reasons for beginning a sentence with a participial clause and with a temporal clause are different.

4.23   Other Sentences Which Do Not Begin with a Basis

In this section the principle of continuity which has been illustrated in secs. 4.21 and 4.22 is extended to sentences which begin with an element forefronted for temporary focus or for emphasis. The principle holds also for sentences which begin with an independent verb (with the possible exception of existential-locative clauses).

In general, events described in sentences which begin with an element forefronted for temporary focus show clear continuity of situation with that of the last event described. The forefronting of the reference to sub-group G^1, for instance (sec. 1.21), presupposes a continuity of situation at least with respect to the participating cast, since a sub-group is perceived as such only if reference to it occurs within a couple of sentences of the last appearance of the original group G. Virtually every other example of temporary focus concerns the subject of a response to the last event (secs. 1.22–1.242, 1.244–1.26), which presupposes a continuity of situation of the participants, and with the event which prompted the response. Finally, the forefronting of the introductory reference to a major participant indicates that he is being introduced against the background of the presence of the last Christian leader mentioned (sec. 1.243). This implies continuity of situation at least with respect to the central character involved.

Similarly, events described in sentences which begin with an element forefronted for emphasis always show clear continuity of situation with that of the last event recorded (e.g., 9:26b). The only examples which occur at a generally recognized paragraph break are those which are forefronted within an initial GA (see sec. 4.21 above).

In general, events described in sentences which begin with an independent verb are in sequence with the last event described, and often are direct responses to it (e.g., 9:17). (Following a background comment, continuity is with the situation of the last event presented before the comment; e.g., 9:8a.)

A special problem is posed by sentences which begin with an existential verb and introduce a major participant who is found in location L. The fact that L is the same general location as that of the immediately preceding events implies that the new participant is to be associated with them in some way. Nevertheless, his introduction is not related to the situation of those events, and further information has to be given to show how he "fits in." Apart from the general spatial setting, continuity of situation with the last sentence is therefore not assumed.

For example, the relationship to the events of vv 1–4 of the participants introduced in 2:5 is not known from the existential-locative clause itself. It is the GA of v 6 which indicates this:

(2:2) And suddenly a sound came from heaven . . .

(v 5) *ēsan de eis Ierousalēm katoikountes Ioudaioi*

"Now there were dwelling in Jerusalem Jews" . . .

(v 6) *genomenēs de tēs phōnēs tautēs*

"And when this sound happened"

See also 9:10a (the significance of the introduction of Ananias becomes apparent through the conversation of vv 10b–16), and 13:1 (no direct link to 12:25 is made, though 13:2–3 presuppose Barnabas and Saul's return to Antioch, which at least is implied in 12:25).

It therefore appears that, if a sentence begins with an existential-locative verb, any continuity of situation, other than the general spatial setting, can be determined only from an examination of the context.

4.3   Conclusions

The conclusions of secs. 4.21–3 may be summarized as follows:

(1)   Continuity of situation with the last event (or with respect to the central character of the last event(s); sec. 1.243) is to be assumed:

if a sentence begins with an independent verb, or an element forefronted for temporary focus or emphasis.

(2)   Continuity of situation with the last event is to be assumed, apart from any modifications expressed in the initial clause:

if a sentence begins with a participial clause.

(3)   Continuity only of spatial situation with the last event is to be assumed (other aspects of continuity must be determined from the context):

> if a sentence begins with an existential-locative verb.

(4)   Continuity of situation with the last event is not indicated (and must be determined from the context):

> if a sentence begins with a (thematic, temporal or spatial) replacement basis.

Thus, the absence of a basis always means that there is some continuity of situation between the sentence concerned and its context, unless the sentence begins with an existential-locative verb. The overall scheme for relating a sentence to its context is therefore the following:

Diagram 3: The Relationship of a Sentence to its Context

replacement basis	*implication*
theme (subject)	change of theme
transitional temporal expression	change of temporal setting
spatial expression	change of spatial setting
------------------	continuity of situation

The above diagram indicates that Luke uses a very straightforward scheme for relating each new piece of information to its context. He has the option of relating by replacement events which display a change of time, location or theme, by opening the sentence with the appropriate basis. This has the effect of replacing a corresponding point of reference which is applicable to the last events described.

If he selects none of these elements as the basis for the new sentence, then continuity of situation with the context is to be assumed.

The conclusion that new pieces of information may be related to their context on the basis of a change of time, location or theme is scarcely surprising. What is important, both for students of Acts, and also for text-linguistics in general, is that Luke has a *systematic* way of indicating to his reader which, if any, of these bases he has selected.

PART TWO. SENTENCE CONJUNCTIONS AND DEVELOPMENTAL UNITS

In the narrative sections of Acts, as "in all continuous writing, the connexion of sentences is the rule, the absence of connexion (asyndeton) the exception."[1] Of the conjunctions employed in the 779 sentences for which no conjunction variants are recognized,[2] *de* (408) and *kai* (274) are by far the most common (total 681 or 88%). Other conjunctions, in decreasing order of frequency, are *te* solitarium (47), simple *oun* and *men oun* (22), *tote* (15), forms of linkage connected with asyndeton (10) and *alla* (3). (See sec. 1.133 on the function of *gar*.)

Chapter 1 first describes the distribution of *de* and *kai*. Winer claims that *de* "subjoins something new, different and distinct from what precedes."[3] After demonstrating the validity of this claim, the nature of this "distinctive" factor is identified (sec. 1.1). (The word "distinctive" is used as a cover term for Winer's phrase "new, different and distinct".) The conditions under which *kai*, rather than *de*, links distinctive sentences are then established (sec. 1.2).

Kai itself has two basic functions. It is the normal means of linking information which is *not* distinctive. As such it is in contrast with *de* (sec. 1.1). In addition, it groups together distinctive information when the event it introduces does not represent a "new development," as far as the main story line (the nucleus of the story) is concerned (sec. 1.2).

If *de* indeed does introduce distinctive information, and elsewhere "in the narrative style, ... the several facts are in great measure strung together by *kai*, as simply following one another,"[4] the narrative of Acts may be viewed as consisting of a series of

---

[1] Winer, *Treatise on the Grammar of NT Greek*, 673.
[2] This total includes the examples of asyndeton discussed in secs. 4.2 and 4.3, but excludes instances of *gar*.
[3] Winer, *Treatise on the Grammar of NT Greek*, 552.
[4] Winer, *Treatise on the Grammar of NT Greek*, 543. J. Callow (Review of Levinsohn, "Four Narrative Connectives") highlights the associative function of *kai*. The idea of development units (Callow's "event-groups") is a product of this.

"development units" (DUs). Each DU presents something distinctive, and is introduced with *de*. The elements of the DU in turn are linked by *kai*.

The following diagram presents such a scheme. Each DU is represented by a box. The elements in the box are linked by *kai*:

de	
	Sentence 1
kai	Sentence 2
kai	Sentence 3

de	
	Sentence 4

de	
	Sentence 5
kai	Sentence 6

de	
	Sentence 7
kai	Sentence 8

For an example of such a scheme, see 5:1–6:

de	
5:1	A certain man called Ananias sold a property
v 2a	*kai* kept back part of the money
v 2b	*kai*, bringing the rest of the money, laid it at the apostles' feet.

de	
vv 3f	Peter condemned Ananias for seeking to deceive the Holy Spirit.

de	
v 5a	Ananias fell down and died
v 5b	*kai* fear came on all who heard.

de	
v 6a	The young men wrapped up the body
v 6b	*kai*, carrying it out, buried it.

Acts may be viewed as a series of such units. Each DU builds on earlier DUs, and each represents a new development of the story.

A new DU is introduced either by *de*, or by one of four conjunctions which have the dual role of presenting a new development and of conveying a specific relationship with the previous DU (see chap. 5). These developmental conjunctions are: *alla* (sec. 4.3d), *gar* (sec. 1.133), *oun* (sec. 3.1) and *tote* (sec. 4.1). In contrast with these conjunctions, *de* is an "unmarked" developmental conjunction. In other words, it simply introduces the next development in the story, without specifying its exact relationship to the previous DU.

te is the second member of the set of conjunctions which are not developmental, but rather link the internal elements of a DU (chap. 2). It indicates that the sentence it introduces is added or appended to the previous one. This generally implies that the two sentences are of unequal importance. An interesting corollary is that, if certain conditions are met, then *te* gives prominence to the sentence it introduces (sec. 2.31).

In connection with *oun*, *men* is always prospective, as in Classical Greek (chap. 3). When associated with correlative *de*, it usually groups together DUs which describe corresponding and sometimes conflicting events. As a corollary, when *men oun* introduces a transitional event or a summary, that summary is to be associated with the next incident to be described, rather than with the previous incident (sec. 3.22).

CHAPTER ONE

DE AND KAI

Some NT grammarians take the position that *de* is "usually . . . indistinguishable from *kai.*"[1] Others define the conditions under which *de* may be used without explaining why it often does not occur when those conditions are met. For instance, Winer correctly observes, "*De* is often used when the writer subjoins something new, different and distinct from what precedes. . . . "[2] However, at least a hundred times in Acts, *kai* introduces a sentence containing something distinctive.

This chapter maintains that Luke did discern "something new, different and distinct" whenever he employed *de.* Six factors of distinctiveness are identified in sec. 1.1.

De is not the appropriate conjunction to link two sentences when nothing distinctive is presented. *Kai* is the usual conjunction, when none of the six distinctive factors are present. A cursory glance at, say, the first chapter of Acts, however, reveals that *kai* sometimes does introduce distinctive information. Sec. 1.2 examines the circumstances under which it is used instead of *de.*

Funk observes that *kai* "links elements of the same grammatical order."[3] It does not link only sentences. It may also link two words or phrases within a clause, two subordinate clauses within a sentence, and even two paragraphs (e.g., 2:1). Since *de* is a "sentence connector,"[4] this chapter only considers examples of *kai* linking sentences or the larger elements of a text.[5]

[1] N. Turner, "Syntax," 331. See also Thrall, *Greek Particles in the NT*, 51.
[2] Winer, *Treatise on the Grammar of NT Greek*, 552. See also Robertson, *Grammar of the Greek NT*, 1184.
[3] Funk, *Beginning-Intermediate Grammar*, 485.
[4] Funk, *Beginning-Intermediate Grammar*, 487.
[5] The term "sentence" is defined in the Introduction. Within sentences such as *akousantes de anastasin nekrōn, hoi men echleuazon, hoi de eipan*, "On hearing of a resurrection of the dead, some scoffed and others said" (17:32), *de* is considered to occur in connection with an embedded sentence.

1.1 The Nature of *De*

If something distinctive is to be presented in a sentence, then *de* statistically is the normal conjunction employed in Acts to introduce it. Sentences which present something distinctive, yet are introduced by *kai*, do not constitute counter-examples, for the reasons to be presented in sec. 1.2. The only cases which, for the purposes of this section, might constitute counter-examples would be any in which *de* was employed without introducing distinctive information.

Two factors of distinctiveness account for more than 90% of the examples of *de*: a change of temporal setting (sec. 1.11) and a real change in the underlying subject (as defined in sec. 1.12). Further distinctive factors are identified in sec. 1.13.

Note: Column 3 of Appendix 2 indicates the section to which each sentence conjunction in the narrative of Acts pertains.

1.11 A Change of Temporal Setting

A change of temporal setting constitutes a sufficient change for *de* to be employed. In other words, a change of temporal setting constitutes something distinctive. This is evident from the relative frequency of *de* and *kai*, when introducing expressions conveying such a change.

When a change of temporal setting is expressed in a "transitional temporal phrase" or clause[6] occurring at the beginning of a sentence (e.g., 5:24), *de* occurs 58 times; *kai* only 6. A change of temporal setting is evident also in many sentences which begin with a genitive absolute (e.g., 12:18). In such sentences, *de* occurs 38 times; *kai* twice.

1.12 A Change of Subject Occurs Between Sentences

A real change in the underlying subject (as defined below) constitutes a sufficient change for *de* to be employed.[7] This is evident from the figures of Table 1. Sentences whose subjects change with respect to the previous sentence are compared with those whose subjects remain the same. (Sentences already covered in sec. 1.11, and those which begin with an adverbial expression of place [sec. 1.135] are excluded from these figures. Sentences in which *de* is accompanied in the same clause by *kai* introducing the new subject [see sec. 2.1] are counted as examples of *de*.)

[6] Blass, Debrunner and Funk, *Greek Grammar*, sec. 472(3).
[7] See also Goddard, *Some Thoughts on De and Kai*.

Table 1

	de	kai	(others)	Totals
change of subject	263	97*	(56)	360 (416)
same subject	44	155*	(28)	199 (227)

(*In 5:2b, it is assumed that no change of subject has occurred from v 2a, although a GA intervenes. In 2:41b, it is assumed that "about 3000 souls" refers to the same subject as that of v 41a.)

Various syntactic restrictions distort the numbers given in Table 1, particularly when the sentence begins with the subject. The figure for *de* includes up to 30 cases in which the subject is *ho/hē/hoi*, and *kai* is not possible (e.g., 3:5).[8] It also includes seven doubtful cases in which an initial pronoun (or article) is followed immediately by an NPC which may or may not be part of the subject (e.g., 4:21).

In addition to these cases, on up to a further ten occasions, the sentence concerned is the second part of a *men (oun)* . . . *de* correlation (e.g., 8:5). Again, *kai* is not possible.

To balance this, the figures for *kai* include three passages in which *men* is attached to an initial subject (e.g., 14:4b), and two in which the subject begins the sentence and is the negative *oude* (4:32b, 18:17b). In both of these situations, it is likely that *de* cannot occur.

Even after omitting these conditioning factors, the difference in the relative frequencies of *de* and *kai* is statistically significant:

Table 2

	de	kai
change of subject	71%	29%
same subject	22%	78%

The above figures indicate that *de* is the expected conjunction, whenever a change of subject occurs.

This is illustrated in 5:10. Peter tells Sapphira what will happen to her (v 9), and the next sentence records this event. The only change in the situation which occurs between the sentences is the shift from one subject to another, but *de* is the conjunction employed:

[8] Thrall, *Greek Particles*, 54.

de
> 5:9   Peter said to her, " . . . Hark, the feet of those that have buried your husband are at the door, and they will carry you out."

de
> v 10a–b   She fell immediately at his feet and died.

Nevertheless, there must be a *real* change in the underlying subject between the sentences, for *de* to occur. Several situations are found in which no such change is discerned.

On occasion, for instance, the person who experiences an event which is expressed with an impersonal element as subject himself becomes the subject of the next sentence. For example, "Immediately *his feet and ankles* were made strong, and (*kai*) leaping up *he* stood. . ." (3:7–8). *De* never occurs in such passages, because no real change in the underlying subject has taken place.

Another situation in which *de* is never found (unless some other factor requires its presence) is when an action by one participant in the presence of another immediately leads to an event performed by the two together. For example, in 8:38 the eunuch commands the chariot containing Philip and himself to stop, and (*kai*) the two of them get out. Again, in such passages, no real change in the underlying subject has taken place.[9]

When individuals have been united into a group, which then sub-divides in the same way, then *kai* occurs (e.g., 8:38c, involving Philip and the eunuch). Similarly, when there is a switch of attention from a group to a vaguely identified sub-group, then *kai* occurs (e.g., 13:48c, in which the switch is from "the Gentiles" to "those who were marked out for eternal life"). In such instances, insufficient change in the underlying subject has occurred for *de* to be warranted. (Contrast 11:28 ["one of them, Agabus by name"], in which a specific, previously unidentified member of a group is introduced, and *de* occurs. See also sec. 1.131.)

Thus, a *real* change in the underlying subject is necessary, if *de* is to be warranted. If there is such a change, however, this constitutes something distinctive.

1.13   Other Distinctive Factors

Tables 1 and 2 compared the relative frequency of *de* and *kai* for sentences in which a change of subject from the previous sentence did or did not occur. It was evident that *de* was used far

---

[9] In 8:8 "there was much joy in that city," *kai* is to be preferred to *de*, if v 7b marks a return to the main events of the story, following the comment of v 7c (factor 4 of sec. 1.15). This is because the participants are a general group which includes the subjects of v 7a,b.

less frequently when there was no change of subject than when there was a change.   Of the 44 examples of *de* which manifest no change of subject with respect to the previous sentence (Table 1), four involve a change of temporal setting (sec. 1.11; e.g., 25:6). Five significant factors may be identified to explain the presence of *de* in the remaining cases. Each in itself is enough to make distinctive the sentence in which it is present:

> a change in the cast of active participants (sec. 1.131);
>
> a switch back to the story line of the narrative, following a background comment (sec. 1.132);
>
> a switch from the story line to a background comment (sec. 1.133);
>
> a change in the circumstances, state or attitude of a participant, unless this change has been anticipated in the context (sec. 1.134);
>
> a change of spatial setting (sec. 1.135).

These factors are now considered in turn.

1.131   *A Change in the Participating Cast*   The introduction of a participant to the scene of a continuing incident changes the cast of participants who are interacting with each other. This change warrants the use of *de* (e.g., 9:41b below), unless it is anticipated from the context (e.g., 4:18b).

In 9:41b, new participants are introduced in an NPC, by means of a verb of calling:

---

de (variant *te*)
9:41a   Giving her his hand, he lifted her up.

---

de
v 41b   Calling the saints and widows, he presented her alive.

In contrast, the reintroduction of the apostles in 4:18b is anticipated in the previous speech, so *kai* is used:

---

de
4:15–17   Having commanded the apostles to go aside out of the council, they conferred with one another, saying, " . . . let us warn them to speak no more to anyone in this name."

v 18   *kai* calling them, they charged them not to speak . . . in the name of Jesus.

De also occurs when a *specific*, previously unidentified subgroup is introduced, with whom the subject then interacts (e.g., 14:23). Such an introduction is treated as a change in the participating cast (contrast sec. 1.12).

A change of cast also occurs when participants are excluded from a scene (e.g., 4:15).

1.132 *A Switch Back to the Story Line of the Narrative, Following a Background Comment* Following a background comment, a return to the main events of the story is introduced with *de* (e.g., 5:27 below),[10] provided that the sentence concerned takes the story beyond the last event described before the comment.

In 5:27, the initial NPC reiterates information given in v 26a, following the explanation of v 26b. The following independent clause records the next main event of the narrative, and *de* is used ("Having brought them, they set them before the council").

In contrast, following the comment of 7:58b, v 59 only refers back to and expands upon the main event described in v 58a. Consequently, *kai* is used.

1.133 *A Switch to a Background Comment* *De* is used also to introduce switches away from the main events, to make a background comment (e.g., 19:7).[11]

This use of *de* is distinct from the function of *gar*.[12] *Gar* introduces an explanation or exposition of the last assertion recorded. Most commonly, *de* introduces a background comment which is of relevance to some *following* event. If the comment concerns the previous event, it generally supplies parenthetical information such as the number of people present, not an explanation of the event itself.

1.134 *A Change of Circumstances* As the same subject performs a series of actions in sequence, any changes in his circumstances, state or attitude are most commonly part of the natural next step or consequence of the last events recorded, in which case *kai* is used (e.g., 3:7).

Occasionally, however, the change is not anticipated in the context, in which case it is new and distinctive information. Examples include: 10:10 (Peter became hungry); 20:38b (a complete change of activity from vv 37–38a); 23:6 (Paul changes his tactics).[13] Less obvious is 2:7; Luke may be conveying a change of

---

[10] Winer, *Treatise on the Grammar of NT Greek*, 553.
[11] N. Turner, "Syntax," 331.
[12] See Winer, *Treatise on the Grammar of NT Greek*, 566–67.
[13] See Bruce, *The Book of Acts*, 452.

attitude from the initial bewildered "excitement" (v 6) to the reaction of amazement and questioning that followed.[14]

1.135 *A Change of Spatial Setting*   In the context of travel (i.e., when the last sentence described a journey to location L^1), a further event performed by the same subject is perceived to be distinctive only if it takes place or starts at a different location L^2. An event performed at L^1 itself warrants the use of *de* only if some other distinctive factor comes into play.

Typically, when *de* is used, an initial NPC describes further travel from L^1 to a new and previously unstated goal L^2, or travel through a previously unreached area. The following independent clause then describes an event which took place at L^2, or further travel from L^2 (e.g., 16:7).

If the location mentioned in the NPC is only a particular place $L^{1'}$ within the larger area L^1 which was the goal of the previous sentence, then *kai* is used (e.g., 13:5). This is because the location of the event of the following independent clause is not totally different from that of the previous sentence.

Similarly, if a sentence begins with a further reference to L^1, employing the adverb *ekei* "there" (e.g., 14:7), then *de* is never used.

Thus, the location of an event must be different from that of the last sentence, if the information given is to be considered distinctive. In other words, a change of spatial setting warrants the use of *de* (cf. sec. 1.11).

1.14   Special Constructions

In all the examples considered to date, the distinctive information which warrants the use of *de* is found within the sentence which is introduced by *de*. However, this information may also be spread over two independent clauses linked by *kai*. In particular, the first clause may present information which simply sets the scene for the main event of the second. The first clause may describe the period of time before or during which the following main event occurred (sec. 1.141). Alternatively, it may present some preliminary event, and the second employ a historic present (sec. 1.142).

---

[14] Newman and Nida, *Translator's Handbook*, 37; Lenski, *Interpretation of Acts*, 65.

1.141 *A Period of Time and the Next Main Event* Grammarians have commented on the use of *kai* or *kai idou* introducing the apodosis, following a particle of time such as *hote* or *hōs*.[15] See, for example, 1:10:

> kai *hōs* atenizontes ēsan eis ton ouranon poreuomenou autou, *kai idou* andres duo pareistēkeisan autois
>
> "and while they were gazing into heaven as he went, (*and*) behold, two men stood by them"

This construction is paralleled by a special type of DU in which the first independent clause has a "temporal designation,"[16] describing an event which extended over a period of time, or which was repeated. A second independent clause, linked to this by *kai*, presents an event which took place at the end of the designated time (if both clauses are in the aorist), or during the period concerned (if at least the second is in the imperfect).

An example in which both clauses are in the aorist is 5:7:

de
5:7a   there was (*egeneto*) an interval of about 3 hours
v 7b   *kai* his wife came in . . .

28:30 illustrates the use of the imperfect in the second clause to present the main event which was taking place during the period described in the first:

de
28:30a   He remained there two whole years at his own expense
v 30b   *kai* habitually welcomed (*apedecheto*) all who came to him. . .

In the above passages, the DU consists of the description of an event in one independent clause, preceded by an independent clause which indirectly establishes its setting in time or space. As such, the DU parallels single sentences in which situational details are given in a transitional temporal expression or an NPC, and the main event is described in the following independent clause. It is therefore appropriate both that the unit as a whole be introduced with *de*, and that its elements be linked with *kai*.

---

[15] For example, Winer, *Treatise on the Grammar of NT Greek*, 546–47; N. Turner, "Syntax," 334.

[16] Blass, Debrunner and Funk, *Greek Grammar*, sec. 442(4).

1.142   *A Preliminary Action and a Historic Present*   The combination of *kai* and a historic present occurs up to eight times in Acts:
(*phēsin*—10:31, 22:2b, 23:18, 25:24; plus 8:36 [variant *eipen*];
legei—12:8c; *theōrei*—10:11; *heuriskei*—10:27 [variant *hēuren*]).[17]
In each case, the event described immediately before the historic
present may be viewed as preliminary to it, or as setting the scene
for it.

In some passages, a participant or inanimate element is introduced to the scene, and a speech is then made about him/it. In
8:36, for instance, Philip and the eunuch come to some water (the
new element), *kai phēsin* the eunuch, "See, here is water. What is
to prevent my being baptized?" In 25:23–24, Paul (the new
participant) was brought into the audience hall, *kai phēsin* Festus
(to king Agrippa), ". . . you see this man. . . . " In both cases, it is
not the introduction of the participant or object which is important
to the development of the following interaction, but what is said
about him/it.

The same sort of argument applies to 10:31. The answer to
Peter's question, "Why did you send for me?" (v 29) is not found
so much in the appearance of an angel to Cornelius (v 30; an act
which simply introduced him to the scene), but in his speech
(*phēsin*), ". . . Send . . . and ask for Simon who is called Peter . . . "
(v 31).

A parallel may be found between the above passages and the
use of the historic present in 10:11, 27. In 10:11 the key information for the development of the incident is not found in Peter
having a trance (v 10b) but in what he sees (*theōrei*). Likewise, in
10:27 it is not of great significance in itself that Peter entered the
house (v 27a), but that he finds (*heuriskei*) a large number of
Gentiles (the addressees of his speech of vv 28–29, and the reason
for him saying what he did). In both cases, the following speech is
based in particular on the contents of the clause described in the
historic present.

In both 12:8c and 22:2b, the historic present introduces the
final (key) speech which follows the non-verbal compliance of the
addressee with his last command or request. In neither case is the
compliance itself of any great significance. Indeed, in the case of
12:8b (*epoiēsen de houtōs*, "and he did so"), Luke could scarcely
have said less about Peter's response! (Contrast 3:5, in which the
compliance provides the point of contrast with the next speech.)

The pattern in 21:40–22:2 is as follows:

---

[17] Kilpatrick ("The Historic Present in the Gospels and Acts," 68.261) expresses
some doubt only in the case of 10:27.

de
21:40a When the tribune had given Paul permission to speak to the people (GA),
v 40b Paul . . . motioned with his hand to the people.

de
v 40c When there was a great hush (GA),
v 40d he spoke to them . . . , ". . . hear the defence which I now make before you."

de
22:2a On hearing that he addressed them in the Hebrew language, they grew the more quiet
v 2b *kai phēsin*. . .

In each of the above DUs, Paul's next action is dependent on the response given in the previous clause. In the first two DUs, this clause is a GA. In the third, however, it has an independent verb, and is linked to the key speech of the exchange by *kai*. (See sec. 1.211a on the orientation of an exchange with respect to a Christian leader, as exemplified in the above passage. In 12:7–9, however, a new initiative by the angel is described in each DU; see sec. 1.211b.)

Thus, when a historic present is introduced by *kai*, the event described is to be interpreted as the second and key part of a single DU. The first sentence of the DU describes the preliminary modifications in the setting and participating cast which set the scene for this event. Such structures closely parallel single sentences in which similar modifications are expressed in a participial clause, prior to a description of the main event in the following independent clause.

1.15 Conclusions

Whenever *de* is used in the narrative of Acts, it introduces something distinctive. This distinctive information is usually presented in the sentence which is introduced by *de*. On occasion, however, it is spread over two independent clauses linked by *kai*, the first setting the scene for the main event expressed in the second (sec. 1.14).

The following six factors of distinctiveness account for nearly every example of *de*:

1.   A change of temporal setting (sec. 1.11; see also sec. 1.141) or spatial setting (sec. 1.135).

2.   A change in the underlying subject (sec. 1.12).

3.   A change in the cast of active participants (this change must not be anticipated in the context) (sec. 1.131).

4.   A switch back to the main events of the story, following a background comment, provided that the sentence concerned takes the story beyond the last event described before the comment (sec. 1.132).

5.   A switch from the main events to a background comment (sec. 1.133).

6.   A change in the circumstances, state or attitude of a participant, unless this change has been anticipated in the context (sec. 1.134).

The presence of the majority of the above factors may be determined objectively (particularly 1, 2 and 3). The context, together with the verb forms and tenses used, generally makes it clear when a switch to or from a background comment has occurred (factors 4 and 5). The one factor which at times is very subjective is (6). Fortunately, however, a change of circumstances, etc., is often expressed at the beginning of a sentence in an NPC. Consequently, the number of cases in which there is no clue from the context as to the presence or otherwise of something distinctive is very small.

De is therefore used in Acts only when it introduces "something new, different and distinct," this distinctiveness usually taking the form of one of the above six changes. Passages may now be examined in which, judged by these criteria, something distinctive has been presented, yet the conjunction employed is *kai* rather than *de*.

1.2   The Association of Distinctive Elements Using *Kai*

Sec. 1.1 introduced the concept of DUs, each of which was introduced by *de* and presented something distinctive. The elements of the unit were linked by *kai*. The DU is a useful concept, because it helps to explain why two sentences are linked by *kai*, even though the second presents distinctive information.

The association by *kai* of distinctive elements at the beginning of an incident is considered in sec. 1.21. Sec. 1.22 considers the association by *kai* of distinctive elements elsewhere in an incident.

1.21   The Association of Distinctive Elements at the Beginning of an Incident

The book of Acts consists broadly of a series of incidents in which two or more participants interact. In the majority of these interactions, one of the participants is a Christian leader (Peter, Paul/Saul, Stephen, Philip, Barnabas), and the others are further major participants or groups of participants. Before any interaction can take place, the different people must be introduced or reintroduced to the story, if they are not already present. In addition, if they are in differing locations, they must be brought together into the same place. Sec. 1.211 discusses the circumstances under which *kai* is used to associate these preliminary events which bring together the participants who are to interact.

Kai is used also to group together the events which set the stage for an interaction between a Christian leader and another participant (sec. 1.212). Finally, sec. 1.213 examines the extended series of sentences introduced by *kai* which are found at the beginning of the book of Acts and in the first part of some reported speeches.

1.211 *The Association of Sentences Which Bring Two Participants Together* Incidents in which a Christian leader interacts with some other major participant or group may be divided into three basic categories. The characteristics of each are first described and exemplified. The reasons for the patterns which are found are then discussed.

In the first category fall examples in which the second protagonist (B) is introduced against the background of the presence of a Christian leader (A), and it is the latter who takes the initiative in the subsequent interaction. Typically, the introductory reference to B is forefronted (see Part One, sec. 1.243). This sentence is introduced with *kai*.

See, for example, 3:1–4:

---

de
  3:1 Peter and John (A) were en route to the temple

v 2 *kai* a certain lame man (B) was being carried there (3) who, on seeing them, asked for alms.

---

de
  v 4 Peter gazed at him and said. . .

See also 14:7(A)–8(B), 14:28(A)–15:1(B), 16:1a(A)–1b(B), 16:13(A)–14a(B).

In the second category fall examples which begin with Christian leader A active. Participant B is introduced as he reacts or responds to the Christian leader, and the initiative passes to him.

Typically, the introductory reference to B is *not* forefronted (see Part One, sec. 1.11). This sentence is introduced with *de*.
See, for example, 6:8–9:

---

de
  6:8 Stephen (A), full of grace and power, was doing great wonders and signs among the people.

---

de
  v 9 Some of those who belonged to the synagogue of the Freedmen (B) . . . arose, disputing with Stephen. . .

See also 14:15–18(A)–19(B), 15:4(A)–5(B).

In the third category fall examples in which the second protagonist B is a supernatural participant (i.e., an external participant; Part One, sec. 1.2) who introduces himself into the presence of Christian leader A. The introductory reference to B may or may not be forefronted (Part One, sec. 1.23). If the previous sentence made reference to the Christian leader, then the introductory reference to B is introduced with *kai*, even though it is B who takes the initiative.

See, for example, 12:6–7a:

---

de
  12:6 . . . Peter (A) was sleeping between two soldiers, bound with two chains. . .

  v 7a *kai idou* an angel of the Lord (B) appeared. . .

See also 9:10a (Ananias [A])–10b (the Lord [B]).

The first two categories are now contrasted. The characteristics of the third are then discussed.

(a) The key factor which determines the use of *kai* in connection with the first category, and *de* in the second, is the continuity of the role occupied by the Christian leader.[18]

In the first case, Christian leader(s) A (e.g., Peter and John [3:1]) are introduced in an active role. The forefronting of the

---

[18] The roles occupied by different participants in the story as a whole have been examined by a number of linguists. Van Dijk (*Some Aspects of Text Grammars*, 147) advocates an extended set of categories. Others, however, suggest that only three basic categories need to be recognized: initiator, undergoer, and "other" (participants in any other role).* This section employs these three categories.
*Hale, *Clause, Sentence and Discourse Patterns in selected Languages of Nepal*, 11; Longacre, *Discourse, Paragraph and Sentence Structure in Selected Philippine Languages*, 1.197; Levinsohn, "Participant Reference," 70.

introductory reference to the second participant B (e.g., the lame man [v 2]) anticipates an initiative on the part of A (v 4; see Part One, sec. 1.243). Consequently, A's active role is not affected by the introduction of B. The two events are then associated with *kai*, because together they set the scene for the following interaction in which A is the overall initiator.

In the second case, although A is introduced in an active role (e.g. Stephen [6:8]), the initiative shifts to B, when he/they appear (e.g. "some of those who belonged to the synagogue of the Freedmen" [v 9]), and A is the undergoer of their initiative. The introduction of B therefore represents a new development in the history of the Christian leader, and is described in a separate DU.

The general principle which is in operation in the above two sets of examples may be stated as follows:

> If a major participant B is introduced against the back-ground of the presence in the story of central character A*, then his introduction is not described in a new DU, if:
>
> (i) the role of A does not change, when B is introduced; and (ii) the introduction of B is into the same spatio-temporal setting as that of A.**
>
> *"A" is a Christian leader, or some other major participant, if no Christian leader is present.
> **The reason for condition (ii) emerges below.

This principle holds for other situations than those already described. In 28:8, for instance, Paul's role (A) changes from that of undergoer in v 7 to initiator in v 8b, as a result of the introduction of Publius' father (B). Paul was one of the group "us" who experienced the hospitality of Publius for three days. However, he takes the initiative, when Publius' father is sick. Consequently, the two events are presented in different DUs:

---

de
28:7   In the neighborhood of that place were lands belonging to the chief man of the island, named Publius, who received us (A) and entertained us hospitably for three days.

---

de
v 8   It happened that the father of Publius (B) lay sick with fever and dysentery; whom Paul visited. . .

In 15:30, the second participants B are introduced as a result of the continuing initiative of the Christian leaders A who were the subject of v 30a. Verse 30b forms part of the same DU as v 30a, because the Christian leaders' role has not changed:

men oun
15:30a   When they (A) were sent off, they went down to Antioch
v 30b   *kai* having gathered the congregation (B) together, they delivered the letter.

The above principle still applies when the Christian leaders were the undergoers of the last events in which they were involved and are the second of the protagonists to be reintroduced. In 4:5–7, the Jewish Council (B) first assembles (vv 5–6), *kai* sends for the apostles (A) (v 7) whom they had placed in prison (v 3). As the incident begins, these roles remain unchanged; the Council takes the initiative in commencing the questioning. Consequently, the two events are presented in the same DU:

de
4:5   On the morrow their rulers (B) . . . were gathered together in Jerusalem . . .
v 7   *kai*, having set the apostles (A) in the midst, they inquired. . .

Thus, *kai* is used to link events which bring the two protagonists together when the role of the Christian leader or other key participant has not changed. *De* is used when his role changes as a result of the introduction of the other protagonist.

Condition (ii) of the above principle states that a new participant must be introduced into the physical presence of a Christian leader, if *kai* is to be used in connection with the introduction of the new participant. This is illustrated in 10:1. The introduction of the new participant (Cornelius) occurs against the background of the last Christian leader mentioned (Peter), and so reference to him is forefronted (Part One, sec. 1.243). Nevertheless, the Christian leader is in a different location, so that *de* is used. Similarly, in 4:36 and 5:1, the introduction of the new participants occurs at the beginning of a repeated "cycle" of events (see 4:34b–35), and again they do not come into the presence of the Christian leaders until the end of the cycle (4:37b, 5:2b).

(b)   When a supernatural participant is introduced into the presence of a Christian leader, the situation is somewhat different. The supernatural participant always takes the initiative when he appears. Nevertheless, his intervention is always temporary. Unlike the overall initiator of an incident, he does not have a continuing part to play. Consequently, his role may be thought of as "causative," rather than that of a true initiator. In other words, he may cause a Christian leader to be the initiator in a subsequent interaction with other participants (e.g., 8:26–40, 9:10–19). Alternatively, within an ongoing incident he may cause a Christian leader *not* to be the undergoer of the initiative of the other major participant who is involved (e.g., 12:6–11).

The principle of the last sub-section cannot therefore be applied to the introduction of a supernatural participant. Instead, *kai* occurs as follows:

> If central character A features in sentence X, and supernatural participant B is introduced in the next sentence Y, then his introduction is not described in a new DU if:
>
> X and Y have the same spatio–temporal setting.

This means that the introduction of a supernatural participant is associated with the last reference to a Christian leader, provided that there has been no lapse of time or change of location with respect to the last sentence.

This principle is illustrated in 9:10. Ananias is the Christian leader involved, in the absence of any of the apostles or deacons:

de
9:10a   There was a disciple at Damascus named Ananias
v 10b   *kai* the Lord said to him. . .

13:2 illustrates the violation of the condition of the principle. The initial GA establishes the temporal setting for the supernatural intervention, and thus effectively separates v 2 from the existential sentence of v 1, which is unrelated to any temporal setting:

de
13:1   In the church at Antioch there were prophets and teachers. . .

de
v 2   While they were worshipping the Lord and fasting, the Holy Spirit said. . .

1.212 *The Association of Sentences Which Bring Together the Participants in the Nuclear Interaction of an Incident* This section describes two situations in which some preliminary events must take place before the two participants whose interaction is central to an incident in fact do so. (a) A Christian leader is not in the location of the other protagonist, and must journey there in order to interact with him. (b) A preliminary interaction between other participants must occur, before the nuclear interaction between Christian leader A and participant C is reached. In both situations, *kai* is used to group together the preliminary events.

(a) The nucleus of the incident of 8:26–40 is an interaction between the Christian leader Philip and an Ethiopian eunuch. Their meeting takes place in the desert. At the beginning of the incident, however, Philip is in Samaria, and he travels to the desert on the instruction of an angel (v 26a). This journey is only of a preliminary nature, in relation to the interaction with the eunuch, so *kai* introduces v 27a. (*Kai* is used in v 27b because Philip's active role is not affected by the introduction of the eunuch; see sec. 1.211a.)

---

de

  8:26   An angel told Philip to go south to the Jerusalem-Gaza road

  v 27a *kai* rising up, he went

  v 27b *kai idou* an Ethiopian eunuch (who)* had been to Jerusalem (28)* was returning. . .

---

*Some MSS omit *hos* in v 27c, which affects the need for a conjunction at the beginning of v 28, where the variants are *de*, *te* and asyndeton. Since v 28 only brings the eunuch to the scene of his interaction with Philip, the *de* variant is rejected.

In 28:11–15, the different stages of Paul's journey to Rome are also linked with *kai* (vv 12, 13b, 14b), as is the introduction of the Christians who come to meet "us" (*kakeithen*; v 15a). In this example also, the travel to the scene of the next interaction with other participants is preliminary to that interaction.

(b) On occasion, an incident may begin with a preliminary interaction between Christian leader A and another major participant (B), but the nuclear interaction is between the Christian leader and a third party (C). *Kai* groups the preliminary events together.

In 18:1–3, for instance, Paul (A) first meets Priscilla and Aquila (B) in Corinth (v 2). The introduction of the new participants constitutes something distinctive (sec. 1.131; see 9:33), so *de* would have been expected. However, the nuclear interchange in Corinth is between Paul and the Jews (C [vv 4–7]), so *kai* is used to introduce Priscilla and Aquila.

The little incident of 9:26–27 does not exactly fit into the present category, but it does illustrate the use of *kai* to associate events which together set the scene for an interaction. When Saul attempted to join the disciples (v 26a), the latter were afraid of him and did not let him come into contact with them (v 26b). There was thus no interaction between them. The events of v 26a and v 26b *together* form the basis for Barnabas' initiative on Saul's behalf (v 27), and so are linked by *kai*:

---

de
  9:26a   Saul was trying to join the disciples

  v 26b   *kai* all were afraid of him, believing that he was a disciple.

---

de
  v 27   Barnabas took Saul to the apostles. . .

In summary, before the nuclear interaction of an incident can take place, it may be necessary not only to introduce the main protagonists, but also to describe the movement of one of them to the location of the other, or otherwise to present events which bring them together. If this preliminary material is spread over more than one sentence, then *kai* is used to link the sentences, even though they may present information which, according to the principles of sec. 1.15, is distinctive.

1.213 *Extended Series of Sentences Which are Linked by Kai*
The above conclusion, that *kai* is used to associate distinctive elements together, when the information they convey is of a preliminary nature with respect to nuclear events, is applicable also to whole discourses, and even to the whole book of Acts.

    Paul's address of 13:16–41 illustrates this. Grammarians have noted the unusual sequence of sentences linked with *kai* which extends from v 17 to v 22. Blass, Debrunner and Funk refer to this very passage, for instance, when they comment, "The excessive and monotonous use of *kai* to string sentences together makes the narrative style of some New Testament authors . . . unpleasing and colloquial."[19]

    Distinctive information is presented in these verses at least in vv 18, 20b (changes of temporal setting; factor 1 of sec. 1.15) and vv 19, 22 (changes of circumstances, etc., expressed in NPCs; factor 6). The reason for the absence of *de* in the verses is that they are

---

[19] Blass, Debrunner and Funk, *Greek Grammar*, sec. 442.

preliminary to the nucleus of the address, which concerns Jesus and begins at v 23.[20] Consequently, *kai* is used.

In most of the other extensive speeches recorded in Acts, key assertions occur early in the address, so that this pattern does not occur; but see 15:8, 15.

The other long passage which is characterized by the predominance of *kai* is the opening chapter of the book, extending as far as 2:4. The passage generally is divided into five paragraphs: 1:1–5, 6–11, 12–14, 15–26 and 2:1–4. The conjunctions used to link the sentences of each paragraph are indicated in the following diagram (each box represents a sentence):

	1:1–3
kai	4–5

men oun	1:6	
Ø	7–8	
kai	9a	(variants *de*/*kai*)
kai	9b	
kai	10–11	

tote	1:12	
kai	13	(see sec. 4.2)
houtoi	14	

kai	1:15–26
(*kai* used throughout)	

kai	2:1–4
(*kai* used throughout; variant *te* in v 3b)	

Note: *Te* (variant *de*) introduces a parenthetical comment in 1:15b which interrupts the sentence that began in v 15a. Its domain is therefore confined to that sentence. The *de* of 1:5 is not relevant to the structure of the narrative, since it occurs within the confines of a reported speech.

---

[20] Lenski (*Interpretation of Acts*, 516) comments, "The theme is plainly marked in v 23." Bruce (*The Book of Acts*, 271) labels vv 17–22 "Preparation for Christ."

It is evident from the above diagram that, with the possible exception of 1:7,[21] the sentences of each of the five paragraphs are associated together, rather than being presented in separate DUs. This is in spite of the fact that distinctive information is presented in each paragraph. According to the principles of distinctiveness, *de* would have been expected in connection with the changes of temporal setting in 1:10, 13, 15; 2:1 (four of the seven examples of *kai* introducing transitional temporal expressions [sec. 1.11] occur in this passage). It would also have been expected in 1:4, 9a, 9b, 23, 24, 26b; 2:2, 3!

This absence of *de*, within and even at the beginning of each paragraph, suggests that the events described in them are viewed as being of a preliminary nature. Thus, because the ascension of Jesus (v 9) and the appearance of the angels (vv 10–11) are introduced by *kai*, they are not viewed themselves as nuclear events. Even the use of prospective *men* (*oun*) in v 6, which anticipates the fulfillment of Jesus' directive of vv 4–5, tends to make the material it introduces of secondary importance (see sec. 3.221).

In 1:12, *tote* has a similar function to that of *de* (see sec. 4.11). Nevertheless, the arrival of the apostles in Jerusalem (the scene of the events of the day of Pentecost) does not lead immediately to any nuclear interaction. Instead, the use of *kai*, first to introduce the group of vv 13–14, and then throughout the description of the election of a new apostle (vv 15–26), indicates that the nucleus has yet to be presented. *Kai* continues to be used even for the presentation of the initial events of the day of Pentecost. This suggests that the coming of the Holy Spirit is also viewed as a preliminary to some later nuclear interaction. *De* appears only with the introduction of the Jews who will form the congregation for the apostles' message (2:5).

[21] If correlative *de* were read in 1:7, this would mean that the events of vv 1–5 were preliminary to the nuclear interaction of vv 6–8. (The use of *men oun* in v 6 would have to form the background to the "key speech" of vv 7–8 [see Blood and Blood, "Overview of Acts," 74.4]. Such a function of *men oun* would not be paralleled exactly elsewhere in Acts; see sec. 3.22.) The presence of *kai* in vv 9–11 would then indicate that the next nuclear interaction does not develop from the remaining events (sec. 1.22).

One problem with such a reading is that *de* should then occur at 2:1, when the occasion of the next set of nuclear events is finally reached. Having encountered *de* in v 1, the absence of *de* in vv 2–4 would then indicate that the coming of the Holy Spirit was of a preliminary nature, with respect to the nuclear interaction which follows the introduction of the Jews in v 5. The absence of *de* in 2:1 suggests that in fact the whole of 1:1–2:4 should be viewed as preliminary. In turn, this implies that asyndeton (or even *kai*) was the original reading in 1:7.

If the first nuclear interaction of the book of Acts does not occur until the Jews of 2:5 have been introduced, it follows that the whole of 1:1–2:4 is to be viewed as preliminary material, setting the stage for the nucleus of the book. Such a view is consistent both with many analyses of the book of Acts, and with statements as to its purpose. Lenski, for example, says that Luke wrote "his Acts in order to enlighten (Theophilus) in regard to the course of the gospel from Jerusalem to Rome."[22] This statement of purpose does not feature the events of chapter 1.

To assert that chapter 1 is to be viewed as setting the stage for the book is not controversial.[23] What possibly is controversial is to view the coming of the Holy Spirit as an (albeit essential) preliminary incident, at least of the day of Pentecost. However, this is implicit in many analyses of Acts. For example, Lenski labels chapters 2–7 "the progress in Jerusalem,"[24] and Blood and Blood talk about the "spirit-empowered witness."[25] If Luke's interest is in the progress of the church in Jerusalem, then the coming of the Spirit, empowering the apostles to be witnesses to their future converts (1:8), is preliminary to and sets the stage for those interactions between the apostles and their audiences.

The absence of *de* in the different incidents of 1:1–2:4, and the use of *kai* to associate distinctive events, is therefore totally consistent with Luke treating those events as setting the stage for the nucleus of the book in which he describes "the progress of Christianity from Jerusalem to Rome." This passage thus further illustrates the principle of sec. 1.212, that *kai* is used to associate together events which are preliminary to a nuclear interaction.

To summarize sec. 1.21, *kai* groups distinctive elements together (a) when the sum total of the events so linked and the participants so introduced is necessary for the story to develop, as it affects the interaction of a central character with another participant; (b) when the events so linked set the stage for such interactions.

---

[22] Lenski, *Interpretation of Acts*, 8. See also Bruce, *The Book of Acts*, 20; Newman and Nida, *Translator's Handbook*, 2; Blood and Blood, "Overview of Acts," 4.

[23] See Lenski, *Interpretation of Acts*, 15; Bruce, *The Book of Acts*, 30. Although Blood and Blood's "Introductory Tie" extends only to v 11, they do classify vv 12–26 as "Preliminary Incidents" ("Overview of Acts," 4, 15).

[24] Lenski, *Interpretation of Acts*, 15.

[25] Blood and Blood, "Overview of Acts," 15. In fact, they classify 2:1–4 as "the Occasioning Incident for Division 1."

1.22 The Association of Distinctive Elements Elsewhere in an
      Incident

This section is concerned primarily with the presence of *kai*
introducing responses which, according to sec. 1.12, warrant the
use of *de*. *Kai* introduces a response when the immediately
subsequent events are concerned with the subject of the previous
event and a third party, rather than with the subject of the response
itself (sec. 1.221). *Kai* also introduces events which subsequent
events do not build on (sec. 1.222). Sec. 1.223 considers passages
in which the sentences which bring a sub-incident to a close are
associated together by *kai*, prior to the further development of a
larger incident. Residual examples are discussed in sec. 1.224.

1.221 *Orientation with Respect to a Third Party* When a Christian leader or other major participant A makes a speech or action
which produces a response, *kai* may introduce the response. This
occurs when attention is directed, not so much to the subject B of
the response, as to the effect that the response will eventually have
on the major participant.

In a number of passages, A speaks to B, recommending or
calling for a particular course of action, or even prophesying that a
particular event will happen to B. The next sentence describes B's
compliance, or the fulfillment of the prophecy in B.

Typically, when *de* introduces B's response, the following
events are concerned with B. (Whether or not A is also involved is
not relevant.)

For example, when the apostles are brought before the Council
(5:27–42), and the members of the Council wish to have them
killed (v 33), Gamaliel (A) intervenes and recommends that they
refrain from doing so (vv 34–39). The Council (B) follows his
advice (v 40a). The following sentences describe what they do to
the apostles (v 40b,c) and how the apostles in turn respond to them
(vv 41–42):

---

de
> 5:35 ... (Gamaliel) said to them, "Men of Israel, take care what
> you do with these men ... (38) ... keep away from these men and let
> them alone ... "

---

de
> v 40 They took his advice...

However, when *kai* introduces B's response, the immediately
subsequent events are concerned with A rather than B (e.g.,

11:24–25 below). Alternatively, they are concerned with the response of a third party C, which leads to an interaction between A and C in which B is not involved (e.g., 16:18–24 below).

11:23–24 describe the ministry of Barnabas (A) in Antioch, and the response of those who heard him (B). Verses 25–26 present Barnabas going to Tarsus to seek Saul and bring him to Antioch. The story is concerned with Saul, rather than Barnabas' hearers,[26] so *kai* introduces v 24b:

---

de

11:23 . . . (Barnabas) exhorted them all to remain faithful to the Lord with steadfast purpose. . .

v 24b   *kai* a large company was added to the Lord.

---

de

v 25   Barnabas went to Tarsus to look for Saul.

16:16–18 record the encounters that "we" used to have with a slave girl who had a spirit of divination (v 16) and who used to follow us, announcing our presence (v 17). Eventually, Paul (A) commands the spirit (B) to leave the girl (v 18b), and (*kai*) the spirit complies with this order (v 18c). The spirit features no further in the story. Instead, attention switches to the masters of the slave girl (C), and to what they do to Paul and Silas, on realizing the implications of what has happened (vv 19–21):

---

de

16:18b   Paul . . . said to the spirit, "I command you . . . to come out of her."

v 18c   *kai* it came out the same hour.

---

de (variants *kai/te*)

v 19   When her masters saw that the hope of their gain was gone, they caught Paul and Silas. . .

The same argument applies to 6:5. When dissatisfaction arises among the body of the disciples (v 1), the apostles (A) tell the disciples (B) to select seven men (C) whom they will appoint as deacons (v 3). Although the disciples' compliance with this recommendation stretches over vv 5–6a, the final event of v 6b concerns the apostles and the deacons, but not the disciples. Consequently, *kai* introduces v 5. (See sec. 1.223 on the use of *kai* throughout vv 5–7.)

[26] See Newman and Nida, *Translator's Handbook*, 226.

The principle illustrated in this section may be expressed as follows:

> When a speech or action performed by participant A leads to a response involving participant B, then *kai* introduces this response, if:

> the immediately subsequent events describe the reaction of a third party C, which leads to an interaction with A, and B is not involved.

1.222 *The Following Events Do Not Build Upon the Event Introduced by Kai* This section concerns the use of *kai* to introduce an event which does not provide the lead-in to subsequent events. For convenience, the examples are divided into two. Sub-section (b) discusses passages in which the sentence introduced by *kai* is followed by one introduced by *te*. Although these examples are considered separately, the presence of *kai* is due to the same principle throughout, viz., the fact that the subsequent events do not build upon the event introduced by *kai*.

(a) In the examples of this sub-section, *kai* introduces a sentence, because the event described does not provide the lead-in to subsequent events. There are two situations in which this is so. The event concerned may terminate the description of an incident, following which Luke introduces a different incident. Alternatively, the following events may relate back, not so much to the event itself, as to a preceding event.

The first situation is exemplified in 4:31. In response to the apostles' prayer to God for boldness (vv 24–30), the building is shaken and they are filled with the Holy Spirit (v 31). This event is introduced with *kai*. Verse 32 begins a completely new section, concerned particularly with the communism of the early Christians:

---

de

4:24 When they heard it, they lifted their voices together to God and said, ". . . (29) . . . grant to thy servants to speak thy word with all boldness. . ."

v 31 *kai* when they had prayed, the place in which they were gathered together was shaken and (*kai**) they were all filled with the Holy Spirit and spoke the word of God with boldness.

---

de

v 32 The company of those who believed were of one heart and soul. . .

(*See sec. 1.12.)

14:18 also is a concluding statement introduced by *kai*, because the next sentence begins a new incident. It records the limited success of Paul and Barnabas' speech of vv 15–17. The next sentence does not build on it, but begins the description of the incident which developed from the arrival of antagonistic Jews:

---

de

14:14 When the apostles Barnabas and Paul heard of it (the people's intention to sacrifice to them) they tore their garments and rushed out among the multitude, crying, . . .

v 18 *kai* with these words they scarcely restrained the people from offering sacrifice to them.

---

de

v 19 Jews came there from Antioch and Iconium. . .

Kai is used also when subsequent actions ignore the event it introduces, or else relate more to a prior act than to the event itself.

In 5:5b, for instance, *kai* introduces the reaction of those who heard about the incident between Peter and Ananias (vv 2–5). Attention immediately switches to the burial of Ananias by the young men (v 6). This action builds, not on v 5b, but on v 5a:

---

de

5:5a When Ananias heard these words, he fell down and died

v 5b *kai* fear came upon all who heard of it.

---

de

v 6 The young men rose and wrapped Ananias up. . .

A similar argument applies to the intervention of the widows (9:39c), when Peter arrives in connection with the death of Dorcas (vv 36–39b). In this case, the next sentence relates back to both the previous ones, since the "all" whom Peter puts outside includes the widows. However, as far as the development of the story as it involves the major participants Peter and Dorcas is concerned, v 39c makes no particular contribution. It is therefore associated by *kai* with v 39b, which had brought the Christian leader to the scene of his interaction with Dorcas (vv 40–41):

---

de

9:39 . . . When Peter had come, they took him to the upper room (where Dorcas' body had been laid)

v 39c *kai* all the widows stood beside him weeping, and showing coats and garments which Dorcas made while she was with them.

> *de*
> v 40   Having put them all outside, and having knelt down, Peter prayed; then turning to the body, he said, . . .

A further example is 16:26d. Verse 27 refers specifically to v 26c. The intervening statement is either ignored or else subsumed under v 26c. Consequently, it is introduced with *kai*:

> *de* (variant *te*)
> 16:26c   Immediately all the doors were opened
>
> v 26d   *kai* everyone's fetters were unfastened.

> *de*
> v 27   When the jailer woke and saw that the prison doors were open . . .

The above examples may be contrasted with the response of the bystanders in 13:48a to the exchange of vv 45–47 between the Jews and the apostles Paul and Barnabas. This event leads to the further results of vv 48b–49, and to the decision of the Jews to move against the apostles (v 50). In other words, it *is* built upon by the following events, and so *de* is used:

> *de*
> 13:46   Paul and Barnabas spoke out boldly (to the Jews),
> " . . . behold, we turn to the Gentiles. . . "

> *de*
> v 48a   On hearing this, the Gentiles were glad
>
> v 48b   *kai* glorified the word of God . . .
>
> v 48c   *kai* as many as were ordained to eternal life believed.

> *de*
> v 49   The word of the Lord was spreading throughout all the region.

> *de*
> v 50   The Jews incited the devout women of high standing . . . and stirred up persecution against Paul and Barnabas . . .

On occasion, although a Christian leader who performs the concluding act of an incident is not involved in the immediately following events, that act is an essential prerequisite to his involvement at a later stage in the incident. Under such circumstances, *de* is used.

One example of this is 9:43, which reads, "It came to pass

(*egeneto*) that he (Peter) stayed in Joppa for many days with one
Simon, a tanner." This verse occurs at the end of the incident in
which Peter is sent for because of the death of the disciple Dorcas.
The next incident begins with the appearance of an angel to the
centurion Cornelius in the town of Caesarea (10:1–7). Because
Peter is absent from this scene, *kai* might be expected to introduce
9:43. However, Peter's presence at the tanner's house in Joppa is
an essential prerequisite for the angel's instruction to Cornelius,
"Send men to Joppa, and bring one ... Peter ... " (10:5–6).[27]
Consequently, *de* is used, even though the new incident does not
build immediately upon Peter's concluding act in 9:43. This
indicates that the event is a new development in the story, and
therefore of relevance to the following events.

See also 11:18. The Christians in Jerusalem are now convinced
that the Christian message is also for Gentiles (contrast vv 2–3).
This is an essential prerequisite to their later sending Barnabas to
Antioch (v 22), even though they do not feature in the opening
events of the next incident (vv 20–21).

The above passages may be contrasted with the conclusion to
the incident in which Saul has a supernatural encounter, en route
to Damascus (9:3–9). Having been blinded by the light which
flashed about him (vv 3,8b), he was brought by his friends into
Damascus (v 8c), "*kai* for three days he was without sight, and
neither ate nor drank" (v 9). The next sentence begins the incident
between the Lord and Ananias, which eventually results in the
latter going to Saul "that you may regain your sight" (v 17). A
certain parallelism with the examples considered above may be
discerned. However, Saul does nothing in v 9 which might be
viewed as a new development providing an essential prerequisite
for the outworking of the next incident. On the contrary, he was
already en route to Damascus, the reader already knew that he was
without sight, and the fact that he was neither eating nor drinking
is taken up only *after* his encounter with Ananias, when he "took
food and was strengthened" (v 19a). *Kai* thus is used in v 9,
because the sentence does not describe any new development
which is built upon, either in the immediately following events, or
even when he is reintroduced to the story.

The principle illustrated in this sub-section may be expressed
as follows:

> *Kai* links sentences W and X if the following events Y* do
> not build upon the event described in X.

---

[27] On the use of *egeneto*, see Levinsohn, "Initial Elements in a Clause or
Sentence," 5–6.

(*If the subject of X is a Christian leader [central character] and his action is of relevance later in the next incident Y, then *de* is used. Otherwise, "the following events" mean "the immediately subsequent events.")

(b) On various occasions, a participant performs an action which may be viewed as the natural conclusion to the incident which has just been described. He then performs a further action which is the specific lead-in to the next incident. Alternatively, Luke refers to a particular aspect of the first action, which again is the specific lead-in to the following incident (see especially 9:29a below). Under such circumstances, the first sentence is introduced with *kai* and the second by *te*. (See sec. 2.31 for a discussion of the functions of *te* in these passages. The present section refers to its presence simply in order to show that the event introduced by *kai* is not the specific lead-in to the following incident.)

This principle is illustrated in 9:28–29. When Saul seeks to join the disciples in Jerusalem (v 26a), they will have nothing to do with him (v 26b). Consequently, Barnabas has to intervene, taking him to the apostles and assuring them that he has become a Christian (v 27). The natural consequence of this intervention is that Saul starts to go around with the disciples in Jerusalem (v 28). In particular, he begins to dispute with the Hellenists, an action which leads to the events of vv 29b–30. The first of these sentences (v 28) is introduced with *kai* and the second by *te*. This is because it is from the specific event of v 29a rather than from the general statement of v 28 that the subsequent events develop:[28]

---

de
   9:27   Barnabas, taking Saul, brought him to the apostles, and declared to them how . . . he had preached boldly in the name of Jesus.

   v 28   *kai* he was going in and out among them at Jerusalem, speaking boldly in the name of the Lord.

- -

te
   v 29a   He used to speak and dispute against the Hellenists.

---

de
   v 29b   They were seeking to kill him.

---

[28] In the following diagrams of DUs, the element introduced by *te* is separated from the preceding elements with a broken line. See chap. 2 for the place of *te* in DUs.

(See also the use of *kai* in 12:11, 19:29 and 3:9 [if *te* is read in 3:10[29]].)

An interesting variation on this pattern is found in 14:20–21. This follows the incident in which the Jews stone Paul (v 19). After the disciples surround him, he reenters the city of Lystra (v 20a) *kai* the next day leaves for Derbe with Barnabas (v 20b). The following sentences describe further actions which he and Barnabas perform back at Lystra and the other towns in which they had experienced opposition (vv 21–23). The first of these sentences is introduced with *te*, since the following events build, not on Paul's departure (v 20b), but on his return (v 21):

---

de

14:20a   When the disciples gathered about Paul, he rose up and entered the city

v 20b   *kai* on the next day he went on with Barnabas to Derbe

- -

te

v 21   having preached the gospel to that city and made many disciples, they returned to Lystra and to Iconium and to Antioch, (22) strengthening the souls of the disciples. . .

Thus, if subsequent events develop, not from the first sentence involving a particular participant, but rather from a later sentence involving him, then *kai* introduces the initial sentence and any further ones which precede the description of the key action. This last action is introduced with *te*.

The above conclusion is consistent with the principle stated in sec. 1.222a that *kai* links sentences W and X if the following events Y do not build upon the action described in X.

1.223   *Extended Series of Sentences Which Are Linked with Kai*
As an exchange between Christian leader A and another participant B draws to a close, *kai* (and *te*) sometimes introduce the concluding sentences. This series of sentences occurs when the exchange, though self-contained, is but part of a larger incident involving the Christian leader. The final events of the exchange are hurried through by grouping them together with *kai*. Attention then moves to the next stage of the larger incident, involving the Christian leader and some other participant C (compare sec. 1.222).

[29] Kilpatrick's preferred reading (see "Proposed Changes").

The interaction between Paul and Silas (A) and the jailer in Philippi (B) illustrates this (16:25–34). The final *de* in the interaction is in connection with their words, "Believe on the Lord Jesus, and you will be saved and your household" (v 31). The further exchanges between the two parties up to v 34 are all linked by *kai*, except that the final group of actions is introduced with *te*:

---

de

  16:31 They said, "Believe in the Lord Jesus . . . "

  v 32 *kai* they spoke the word of the Lord to him . . .

  v 33a *kai* taking them the same hour of the night, he washed their wounds

  v 33b *kai* he was baptized at once . . .

- -

*te**

  v 34 bringing them up into his house, he set food before them . . .

(*In this case, and also in 6:7c and 9:18b below, *te* does not set the scene for the next incident. See secs. 2.1 and 2.2 for the function of *te* in these passages.)

Luke associates together the final events of the exchange, because the outcome of the larger incident (the interaction between the apostles and the authorities which began in vv 20–24) is still to be described.

Further examples of a series of sentences linked with *kai* (and *te*), at the conclusion of an interaction between Christian leader A and participant B, and immediately prior to the next stage of the larger incident, include:

9:17–19a (Saul [A] and Ananias [B]; v 19b begins the description of Saul's activities as a Christian in Damascus)

9:33–35 (Peter [A] and people in Lydda [B]; v 36 begins the next incident in the series involving Peter which leads to the giving of the Holy Spirit to Cornelius in Caesarea)[30]

16:19–23[31] (Paul and Silas [A] and the authorities [B]; v 24 sets the scene for the interaction between Paul and Silas and the jailer).

[30] Newman and Nida (*Translator's Handbook*, 199) comment that the two miracles performed by Peter in Lydda (9:32–35) and Joppa (vv 36–43) "seem to prepare the way for the even greater miracle of the giving of the Holy Spirit to Cornelius in Caesarea."

[31] This is particularly clear if *te* is read in v 23.

This same phenomenon is found in 6:5–7. A series of sentences linked by *kai* follows the apostles' recommendation to the body of the disciples that they select seven men to be appointed as deacons (v 3). The series continues into the summary of v 7,[32] terminating with a sentence introduced with *te*:

---

de

  6:2 Having summoned the body of the disciples, the twelve said, "... (3) ... pick out from among you seven men of good repute ... "

  v 5a   *kai* what they said pleased the whole multitude

  v 5b   *kai* they chose Stephen ...

  v 6b   *kai* having prayed, they laid their hands upon them.

  v 7a   *kai* the word of God increased

  v 7b   *kai* the number of disciples multiplied greatly in Jerusalem

- -

te

  v 7c   a great many of the priests were obedient to the faith.

The above grouping of events by *kai* and *te* is again because they are part of a larger incident. In particular, they are preliminary (sec. 1.213) to the confrontation which ends with the martyrdom of the deacon Stephen.

Some commentators consider that the first major section of the book of Acts ends with the summary of 6:7. The heavy use of *kai* in vv 5–7 indicates that this is not so. An analysis which associates together the election of the deacons (vv 1–6) and the martyrdom of Stephen is to be preferred. A number of commentators offer such an analysis. For instance, Bruce's major unit "II. Persecution Leads to Expansion" begins at 6:1. His first sub-unit is "1. Stephen. (a) The Appointing of the Seven."[33]

Another passage in which the use of *kai* assists in the choice between conflicting analyses is 18:22–23. Both verses present distinctive information (factor 1 of sec. 1.15), yet *kai* is used:

[32] In itself, the presence of *kai* in v 7 is not surprising. It could indicate simply that vv 8–10 do not build upon the summary (sec. 1.222). However, since the series of sentences linked by *kai* begins in v 5, it seems appropriate to view the presence of *kai* in v 7 as being due to the same phenomenon. Also, the series terminates with the use of *te*, as in most of the examples discussed in sec. 1.223.

[33] Bruce, *The Book of Acts*, 127.

de
> 18:20 When they asked him to stay for a longer period, he de-
> clined; (21) but bidding them farewell and saying, "I will return to
> you if God wills," he set sail from Ephesus
>
> v 22 *kai* having landed at Caesarea, he . . . went down to Antioch
>
> v 23 *kai* having spent some time there, he departed . . .

de
> v 24 A Jew named Apollos . . . came to Ephesus . . .

The significance of *kai* in vv 22–23 emerges when it is recognized that the section as a whole is concerned with events at Ephesus.[34] Verses 18–21 occur in Ephesus, Apollos' activities are set primarily in Ephesus (vv 24–27), and Paul returns to Ephesus in 19:1. Once this pattern is discerned, Paul's travels away from Ephesus (18:22–23) can be seen not to further the development of the story as it concerns Ephesus (cf. 14:20b, discussed in sec. 1.221). Consequently, they are associated together by *kai*, so that Luke can move on quickly to the next events in Ephesus itself.

1.224 *Residue* There remain a few passages which illustrate the operation of the principles outlined in previous sections, but which do not fit neatly into the categories considered.

(a) In a couple of passages, the event introduced by *kai* is of little consequence in comparison with the key event that follows. Both occur towards the beginning of an incident. They are preliminary events, presented prior to the description of a nuclear interaction. A parallelism may therefore be discerned with the examples of sec. 1.212. The main difference between these passages and those of sec. 1.212b is that both the preliminary events and the following exchanges involve the same participants.

Cornelius' speech in 10:30–33 is given in reply to Peter's opening question, "Why did you send for me?" Both Peter and the reader already know the reason. Cornelius' encounter with the angel was recorded in vv 3–6, and the messengers gave some explanation to Peter when they met him (see v 22). Furthermore, the intention of Peter's visit was to be "to hear what you have to say" (v 22). Consequently, the opening exchange between Peter and Cornelius is no more than preliminary to the message which Peter has come to deliver (vv 34–43). (See sec. 2.31 on the use of

---

[34] Bruce, *The Book of Acts*, 13; Newman and Nida, *Translator's Handbook*, 354.

te in v 28, marking the actions which follow as those on which the nuclear events are based.)

> *te*
>   10:28   Peter said to them, "... (29) ... I ask then why you sent for me."
>
>   v 30   *kai* Cornelius said, " ... (33) ... we are all here present ... to hear all that you have been commanded by the Lord."

> *de*
>   v 34   Peter opened his mouth and said, ...

The presence of *kai* in 21:19 (not D) is for a similar reason. The passage as a whole explains how Paul came into the hands of the Jews and Romans, in line with the prophecy of v 11. This being the case, Paul's words about "the things that God had done among the Gentiles through his ministry" (v 19) are no more than preliminary to the response of the elders. Indeed, it is their recommendation (vv 20b–25) which leads eventually to his arrest:

> *de* (variant *te*)
>   21:18a   On the following day Paul went in with us to James
>
> *te*
>   v 18b   all the elders were present
>
>   v 19   *kai* having greeted them, he related ... the things that God had done among the Gentiles through his ministry.

> *de*
>   v 20a   They, having heard it, glorified God
>
> *te*
>   v 20b   said to him , ...

(b)   The use of *kai* in 27:19 is surprising mainly because the sentence begins with a transitional temporal expression (sec. 1.11). Apart from that, the content of the sentences so linked is similar enough for the two to be associated naturally into a single DU. They both have the same subject "they" (or the more inclusive "we" in v 19, according to some manuscripts). In addition, the content is similar; both are acts of jettisoning in order to lighten the ship:

---

de (variant *te*)

27:18   As we were being violently storm-tossed, they began next day to throw the cargo overboard;

v 19   *kai* the third day they cast out with their own hands the tackle of the ship.

---

de

v 20   When neither sun nor stars appeared for many a day , . . . all hope of our being saved was at last abandoned.

The use of *kai* in v 19 suggests that this part of the narrative does not develop with respect to the passage of time. Rather, it develops with respect to different stages of response to the storm. First, precautionary measures are taken (vv 16–17). Then occurs the more desperate measure of jettisoning all that they could (vv 18–19). Finally, total despair reigns (v 20).

(c)   Although the speech of 10:15, which is introduced by *kai*, occurs at the end of an exchange, its function cannot be explained in terms of the principle of sec. 1.221. Rather, it may be related to the fact that the exchange occurred three times (v 16a) and remained unresolved (see Part One, sec. 1.252a). Peter's refusal (v 14) and the divine insistence (v 15) appear to have been grouped into a single DU, to underline the fact that the issue remained unresolved throughout the repetitions of the exchange:

---

de

10:14   Peter said, "No, Lord; for I have never eaten anything that is common or unclean."

v 15   *kai* the voice came to him again a second time, "What God has cleansed you must not call common."

---

de

v 16   This happened three times . . .

1.3   Conclusion

Except for a very small residue of passages, all the examples in which *kai* associates distinctive elements in Acts can be explained in terms of the following general principles (see the sections indicated for the details):

(a)   At the beginning of an incident, *kai* links distinctive elements when the sum total of the information conveyed is necessary for the story to develop, as it affects the interaction of a central character with another major participant. Similarly, it links distinctive elements when the events described are preliminary, setting the stage for the interaction (sec. 1.21).

(b)   Elsewhere in an incident, *kai* introduces a sentence which presents distinctive information, because the following events do not build on the particular event concerned. Alternatively, Luke is concerned, not with the subject of the event, but with the reaction of a third party and his subsequent interaction with the central character whose action led to the event concerned (sec. 1.22).

In addition, *kai* may associate the series of events which conclude an exchange, if that exchange is a sub-unit of a larger incident (sec. 1.223).

Thus, *kai* is used for two different but related reasons in Acts. First, it introduces sentences in which nothing distinctive (sec. 1.15) is presented. Second, it associates distinctive elements, when the information conveyed does not in fact develop the story. This may be because the material is preliminary to the nucleus of the story. It may be because only as distinctive elements are grouped together is the interaction of a central character with other participants possible. It may be because the information is not the specific lead-in to the further development of the story. It may be because the description of a larger incident awaits completion. Whatever its function, the appearance of *kai* is not arbitrary, but relates to the overall structure and purpose of the book of Acts.

CHAPTER TWO

TE SOLITARIUM

Grammarians approach the analysis of *te* solitarium in two different ways. On the one hand, Hermann differentiates *te* from *kai* on the grounds that "*kai* conjungit, *te* adjungit."[1] Similarly, Winer claims that the elements linked by *te* are not "homogeneous," in the sense that they are not of equal importance. On the other hand, Abbot-Smith talks of *te* solitarium "denoting a closer affinity than *kai* between words and sentences which it connects."[2]

Although both the above assertions are sometimes true, in specific circumstances one of them is to the fore, and the other may or may not be valid. When *te* links consecutive speech acts performed by the same speaker, for instance, a "close affinity" between the events is evident. However, in some such passages (e.g., 8:31a,b), it is not at all obvious that one speech act is to be viewed as more important than the other (see sec. 2.1). Similarly, following an event which was introduced by *kai* because it was not the specific "lead-in" to subsequent events (sec. 1.222), the event linked to it by *te* is more prominent. In such circumstances, the fact that the two events may also enjoy a close affinity does not appear to be significant (e.g., in 9:28–29 [sec. 2.31], and see especially the examples of sec. 2.32).

The most basic claim for *te* follows naturally from the assertions of the grammarians: *te* links elements within the same DU. This is a natural corollary if *te* links similar events with the same basic subject (sec. 2.1), or if it introduces an additional statement about the same event (sec. 2.2). A sentence cannot at the same time present something distinctive and something similar. Similarly, the information is not to be viewed as new or distinct if it refers to the same event as before.

As to the distinction between *te* and *kai*, *te* is chosen for two reasons, one or both of which may be valid for any passage:

---

[1] Cited by Winer, *Treatise on the Grammar of NT Greek*, 542.
[2] Abbott-Smith, *Manual Greek Lexicon of the NT*, 441; citing Blass, *Grammar of NT Greek*, sec. 77.8. See also Robertson, *Grammar of the Greek NT*, 1178.

(a) it indicates a "close affinity" between the sentences it links (because the events described are similar [sec. 2.1] or even the same [sec. 2.2]);

(b) it indicates that the sentences which it links are of unequal importance.

In connection with reason (b), when the previous sentence is of a preliminary nature, then *te* gives prominence to the statement which follows, because that statement provides the specific lead-in to a nuclear interaction (sec. 2.3). In other passages also, it is not uncommon for a sentence introduced by *te* to seem more important than the one which preceded it, as far as its relevance to the following events is concerned. However, to insist that function (b) always hold requires too much to be read into some passages. Rather, the presence of *te* is motivated by either of the above reasons, though both may be valid in particular passages.

In the presentation of examples involving *te*, the sentence Y which is introduced by *te* is separated from the previous sentences of the DU by a broken line. For example:

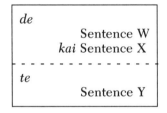

This presentation indicates that (a) Y pertains to the same DU as W and X, but (b) the relationship of Y to the other elements is different from that between elements linked by *kai*. In particular, *te* does not conjoin elements of equal importance. Rather, it adjoins an additional sentence, which may well be more or less important than the previous element of the DU.

This monograph does not discuss correlative *te* in the combinations *te* (. . .) *kai* and *te* . . . *te*, linking words or subordinate clauses which correspond to each other.[3] This

---

[3] This list of examples of *te* solitarium is much more inclusive than that of Moulton, Geden and Moulton, *Concordance to the Greek NT*, 935.

The correlation *te* (. . .) *kai* is recognized only 46 times by the present author, whereas N. Turner ("Syntax," 339) finds it on 60 occasions. The reason for the discrepancy is mainly that no passage has been included here in which the proposed correlation would be linking sentences.

Blass, Debrunner and Funk state that "Correlative *te* comes as a rule after the first word of the pair that is to be correlated. Exception: it follows a preposition which precedes and governs both of the words to be connected" (*Greek Grammar*,

correlation is traditionally translated "both . . . and," "not only . . . but also," and "joins words which have between themselves a close or logical affinity."[4] "An all-inclusiveness is conveyed" by the correlation. The two parts so linked "are drawn into a conscious whole."[5]

The correlation *te* . . . *de* (e.g., in 15:39–40 [not D], 19:18–19) is interpreted as a combination of *te* solitarium and *de* in connection with a change of subject (factor 2 of sec. 1.15).

In a large number of passages of Acts, *te* has a variant *de* or vice versa. This chapter is based only on the 47 sentences of the narrative which begin with *te* solitarium, for which Nestle and Aland (1975) give no variants.

The existence of a large number of variants tends to confirm the conclusions of this chapter. This is because the pertinent circumstances often place the passage concerned on the borderline between, for instance, two events being viewed as similar (*te*) or distinctive (*de*).

Regarding the variants, it seems likely that, in some passages, atticizing editors have added *te*.[6] In others, they have probably reduced the frequency of *te* because Luke was considered to have overused it.[7] Consequently, the textual editor of Acts is constantly faced with the task of distinguishing between Lukan usages of *te* which editors may have changed, and later introductions of the particle. By defining the implications of the use of *te* in specific contexts, the present study should provide an additional tool of value to future editors.

2.1 *Te* Links Different Events Involving the Same Basic Subject, to Bring Out a Similarity Between Them

Passages in which *te* links events X and Y, both of which have the same basic subject and are similar in nature or import, illustrate

---

sec. 444[5]). On this basis, *te* is not linking nouns in 8:3b, 18:4b or 26:30. However, *te* could still be correlative in 14:21 and 15:32; plus 22:23 (variant *de*). The problem with interpreting *te* as correlative in these passages, linking noun phrases or subordinate clauses, is that no sentence conjunction would then occur. Complete asyndeton is very rare in the narrative of Acts. Furthermore, it is usually equivalent to the presence of *de* (see sec. 4.3). *Te* is therefore treated in these passages as solitarium.

[4] N. Turner, "Syntax," 339. See also Winer, *Treatise on the Grammar of NT Greek*, 547–48; Blass, Debrunner and Funk, *Greek Grammar*, sec. 444.

[5] Levinsohn, "Four Narrative Connectives," 10; J. Callow, Review of Levinsohn, "Four Narrative Connectives," 27.

[6] N. Turner, "Syntax," 338.

[7] G.D. Kilpatrick, personal communication.

the claim that *te* indicates "rather close connection and relationship."[8]

"Similarity" is a subjective notion. The outlook of the speaker or writer determines whether or not two events are viewed as similar. Lakoff comments concerning coordinate conjunctions in English,

> a common topic is necessary. This may be overtly present in the superficial structure of the sentence, or may be derivable by more or less complex combinations of presuppositions + deductions.[9]

Similar events usually are drawn from the same semantic domain. At their most unambiguous, they are both speech acts, or perceptions, or journeys, etc. In addition, the verbs employed often come from the same semantic field.

In 12:17, for instance, both X and Y describe speech acts, and both of the independent clauses employ speech verbs:

| *de* |
| 12:17a (X) Motioning to them with his hand to be silent, Peter described to them how the Lord had brought him out of the prison. |
| - |
| *te* |
| v 17b (Y) he said, "Tell this to James and to the brethren." |

This function of *te* may be compared with the use of "in addition" or similar expressions in English.[10] Its effect is to indicate that something similar has been added to the last statement.

As with "in addition," it is not obligatory to link similar events with *te*. One can say, "he described to them how the Lord had brought him out of prison, *and* he said, 'Tell this to James and to the brethren'" (12:17 RSV). Alternatively, the two reported speeches can be linked with "then went onto," thus appending the additional comment to the first speech act. Similarly, the description of two speech acts can be linked with *kai* (e.g., 16:32). However, the use of *te* in Acts to link similar events appears to be more extensive than the use of "in addition" (etc.) in English.

In fact, 16:32 is the only occasion on which *kai* links consecutive speech acts by the same subject. This example occurs at the

---

[8] Blass, Debrunner and Funk, *Greek Grammar*, sec. 443(3).

[9] Lakoff, "If's, And's, and But's about Conjunction," 148.

[10] J. Callow (personal communication) suggests "then went on to . . ." for some narrative passages.

beginning of the series of sentences linked by *kai* which characterizes the end of the sub-incident of vv 25–34 (the presence of *te* in v 34 is discussed below). It is likely that Luke's desire to hurry through the remaining events of the incident (see sec. 1.223) leads him to use *kai* rather than *de* or *te* in vv 32–33.

If *te* is used to append a similar event Y to X, then it follows that Y is not viewed as distinctive information which would warrant the use of *de*. This is confirmed by the nature of X and Y. With very few exceptions, both deal with the same overall topic. Furthermore, Y does not introduce anything which, according to the factors of sec. 1.15, might be construed as distinctive.[11]

The similarity between two events may be due, however, not to the nature of the events themselves, but to the context in which they occur. This is illustrated in 5:41–42:

de
5:40 . . . when they had called in the apostles, having beaten them, they charged them not to speak in the name of Jesus, and let them go.

men oun
v 41 (X) They left the presence of the council, rejoicing that they were counted worthy to suffer dishonor . . .
te
v 42 (Y) every day in the temple and at home they did not cease teaching and preaching Jesus as the Christ.

Verse 40 brings together the beating of the apostles and the charge that they not speak in the name of Jesus. Once associated in this way, the responses to these respective actions, both being of the same type (viz., contrary to the intentions of the authorities), become "similar." They may then be associated with *te*.

Two similar events may be linked by *te*, even though a change of subject occurs between the sentences, provided the subject of the first sentence is affected in a similar way by both events. The one condition is that the additional point parallels the first predicate, rather than being an addition to the first subject.

This is seen by contrasting 21:18b (not D) and 21:16. In the first case, the elders (v 18b) are additional leaders to James, who was the goal of Paul's visit of v 18a. Paul (subject of v 18a) thus meets James plus (*te*) the elders:

---

[11] For this reason, *de* seems an inappropriate conjunction in 10:48 for linking Peter's two speeches (variants are *te* and *tote*).

> *de* (variant *te*)
>   21:18a   (X) On the following day Paul went in with us to James,
> -
> *te*
>   v 18b   (Y) all the elders were present.

In contrast, in v 16, the disciples were additional travellers to "us," the subject of v 15. In other words, "we" plus (*kai*) the disciples went to Jerusalem:

> *de*
>   21:15   (X) We . . . went up to Jerusalem

> *de*
>   v 16   (Y) *kai* some disciples from Caesarea went with us.

In summary, following the description of event X, *te* appends an event Y which is performed by the same subject as X, if X and Y are considered to be similar events. In addition, if the subject of X, though not also the subject of Y, is affected in a similar way by both events, then *te* is used. However, if the subject of Y performs a similar action to the subject of X (i.e., he is an additional subject who acts similarly), then *de* is used plus *kai* introducing the new subject.[12]

In 16:34, *te* introduces, not a single sentence, but a pair of sentences linked by *kai*. In this passage, the similarity conveyed by *te* is with the previous pair of sentences. The first sentence of the pair, in both v 33 and v 34, concerns the welfare of Paul and Silas, whereas the second deals with responses to Christianity on the part of the jailer and his household:

>   16:33   (X) taking them the same hour of the night he washed their wounds,
>   *kai* he was baptized at once, with all his family.
> -
> *te*
>   v 34   (Y) bringing them up into his house, he set food before them,
>   *kai* he rejoiced with all his household having believed in God.

Thus, *te* may be used also to convey similarity between a pair of events. This is particularly appropriate in a situation in which Luke is associating distinctive events, in order to move quickly

---

[12] For *de* plus *kai* linking events performed by the same subject, see 9:24b (variant *te*) and 16:1 (variant *de*; see sec. 1.141).

from the sub-incident to the conclusion of the overall incident (see sec. 1.223).

2.2   *Te* Introduces an Additional Statement About the Same Event

On occasion *te* appends an additional statement Y about the same action X (e.g., 20:7 below) or journey X (e.g., 27:5). Y concentrates on a specific aspect of X. This aspect may or may not be of particular relevance to the outcome of the following events.

In 20:7, v 7b refers to the event described in v 7a (Paul's address), and deals with a specific aspect of it, viz., its duration:

de
20:7a   (X) . . . Paul was talking with them, intending to depart on the morrow
te
v 7b   (Y) he prolonged his speech until midnight.

Verse 7b provides the specific reason for the accident which is described in v 9 (Eutychus "sank into a deep sleep as Paul talked still longer" and fell from the window where he was sitting). Consequently, the use of *te* may also reflect the unequal importance of the sentences it links.

In 18:4 (not D), however, it is not evident that either sentence is of particular significance. (Verse 4b deals with a specific aspect of the event described in v 4a, viz., the nature of Paul's audience.)

de
18:4a   (X) Paul was arguing in the synagogue every sabbath
te
v 4b   (Y) he was persuading Jews and Greeks.

In the above examples, the second sentence omits some of the information of the first, while concentrating on some detail about the same event.[13] *Kai* does not link sentences which are related in such a way. Rather, it links either separate events or *comparable* aspects of the same event. For example, in 2:14 (*epēren tēn phōnēn autou kai apephthegxato*, "he lifted up his voice and spoke out"), both clauses refer to the act and manner of speaking. *Kai* may therefore be an inappropriate conjunction to link many of the sentences of this section.

---

[13] It is a "contraction-amplification paraphrase" (Longacre, *Anatomy of Speech Notions*, 136–38).

Te is also used to append a second sentence about the journey described in the previous sentence (unless other factors require the presence of *de*). In 27:4–5, for instance, v 4 begins the description of the voyage from Sidon to the next port. The voyage is not completed until v 5, so *te* is used to append a second statement about the journey, viz., its completion:

---

de
27:4   (X) Putting to sea from there we sailed under the lee of Cyprus, because the winds were against us;

- -

te
v 5   (Y) having sailed across the sea which is off Cilicia and Pamphylia, we came to Myra . . .

See also 27:8. In neither example is it likely that the sentences linked by *te* are of unequal importance. However, in 8:25, part of the reason why *te* introduces the description of what the apostles did as they were returning to Jerusalem may be to give prominence to the part that the apostles had "in winning Samaria for the gospel."[14] Similarly, the use of *te* and the forefronting of *philanthrōpōs* in 27:3b suggests that prominence was being given to Julius' act of kindness.

In narrative, the dividing line between the use of *te* to append an additional point about event X, and the presence of *de* to introduce a background comment about X, is very fine. However, an additional point appended to X by *te* generally does not provide an explanation for X (see 8:11, 16b; 12:9c). Furthermore, if it relates to an event, an event verb is used (see 8:9; 12:3b; 13:5b; 19:7, 14; 20:8; 21:9; 23:13; 27:37). This is not usually the case when *de* introduces a background comment (cf. the examples of sec. 1.133).

If *te* introduces an additional point about the event described in the previous sentence, then the *te* of 17:14b should be so interpreted:

---

de (not D)
17:14a   (X) Immediately then the brethren sent Paul off on his way to the sea;

- -

te
v 14b   (Y) Silas and Timothy remained there.

---

[14] Lenski, *Interpretation of Acts*, 334. See the forefronted phrase "many villages of the Samaritans."

Several English versions translate *te* in v 14b by "but" (e.g., AV, RSV), as though the conjunction were *de*, and Luke's intention were to contrast what happened to Paul with what Silas and Timothy did. Such an interpretation of *te* finds no confirmation elsewhere. Furthermore, v 14b may be treated as an additional point about the same event as v 14a. Verse 14 begins *eutheōs de tote* (not D), which might well be rendered "so immediately, right then."[15] Verse 14b then contributes further to the point being made, "and (not only that,) Silas and Timothy remained there." The urgency of Paul's departure was such that Silas and Timothy had to be left behind. (*Te* is appropriate also because the statements are of unequal importance. The following events are concerned with Paul, rather than with Silas and Timothy; v 14b is therefore somewhat incidental to the development of the story.)

> Note: if v 14b were intended only to provide background information of relevance to the next DU (cf. v 15b), then *de* should have been used (factor 5 of sec 1.15).

2.3 *Te* Introduces the Specific Lead-in to a Significant Development

In secs. 2.1 and 2.2, *te* brought out the similarity between the events it linked, or introduced a further aspect of the same event. In some passages, the events it linked appeared to be of unequal importance. In others, their relative importance was unclear and probably irrelevant.

Under certain circumstances, *te* is chosen primarily to indicate that the events it links *are* of unequal importance. In particular, it may give prominence to the statement it introduces, marking this event as the specific lead-in to a significant development in the story. One such circumstance is when the last event was introduced by *kai* (sec. 2.31; cf. sec. 1.222b). Another is when the information presented in the previous sentence was of a preliminary nature (sec. 2.32).

In both the above cases, *de* would have been an inappropriate alternative to *te*. The sentence introduced by *te* did not present distinctive information. Alternatively, it set the stage for the nuclear interaction of an incident (sec. 1.212). However, when *te* introduces a response (sec. 2.33), *de* would have been the expected conjunction. Under such circumstances, the presence of *te* is

---

[15] Lenski, (*Interpretation of Acts*, 704) comments, "At once and without waiting for night to come the brethren hurried Paul off."

interpreted by analogy with the examples of secs. 2.31–32, as introducing the specific lead-in to a significant development.

2.31 The Previous Sentence is Not the Specific Lead-in to the Following Events

In the passages considered in sec. 1.222b, *te* introduced the event Y which formed the specific lead-in to the following incident, over against the previous event X which was introduced by *kai*.

In 9:28–29, for example, Saul's act of speaking against the Hellenists (v 29a; *te*) is the specific event which stimulates them to oppose him (v 29b). This stands over against the more general "he (Saul) was going in and out among them (the apostles), speaking boldly in the name of the Lord" (v 28; introduced by *kai*). Moreover, v 29a is not a different event from v 28. Rather, it is a specific aspect of "speaking boldly in the name of the Lord."[16] Consequently, *de* is not warranted.

This is seen also in 6:12–7:1:

```
┌ - - - - - - - - - - - - - - - - - - - - - - - - - - - - - - - - - ┐
│ te (variant de)                                                   │
│      6:12a  They stirred up the people and the elders . . .       │
│                                                                   │
│      v 12b  (X) kai, coming upon him, seized him and brought him  │
│      before the council                                           │
├ - - - - - - - - - - - - - - - - - - - - - - - - - - - - - - - - - ┤
│ te                                                                │
│      v 13   (Y) set up false witnesses who said, . . .            │
└                                                                   ┘
```

```
┌                                                                   ┐
│ de                                                                │
│      7:1   (Z) The high priest said, "Are these things so?"       │
└                                                                   ┘
```

In this passage, the activities of Stephen's opponents follow a natural chain of events, which also is specified in the context. Prior to taking him to the council (v 12b), they had already suborned men to testify against him (v 11), so that the introduction of these witnesses was the natural next step in their attack. Consequently, nothing distinctive is introduced by v 13 (see factor 3 of sec. 1.15),

---

[16] Winer (*Treatise on the Grammar of NT Greek*, 542) makes a similar point about *te* in Hebrews 9:1.

In 3:10, *te* seems preferable to *de*, because recognition of the lame man (Y) would seem to follow naturally from seeing him (X). Furthermore, this leads to the people moving to where Peter and John were standing (Z; v 11).

and *de* is not warranted. *Te* is used, rather than *kai*, because it is specifically the testimony of these witnesses that provides the lead-in to the nuclear interaction between Stephen and the council.

In several passages, it is the initial participial clause which describes an action Y referring to the same event as that of the previous sentence X (e.g., 12:12), or leading naturally from the previous event X (e.g., 14:21). The following independent clause then presents a new development which forms the specific lead-in to the following incident or nuclear interaction Z. (The nuclear interaction is usually described in the next DU. However, in 14:21 below, it appears to begin in the final NPC[s] of the same sentence.)[17]

In 12:12, for instance, *synidōn,* "realizing," probably refers to the same event as v 11.[18] The following independent clause provides the specific lead-in to the incident Z of vv 13–17:

---

de
  21:10 . . .
  v 11 (X) *kai* Peter came to himself, and said, "Now I am sure that the Lord has sent his angel and rescued me . . . "

- -

te
  v 12 (Y) *synidōn* "realizing,"
  he went to the house of Mary, . . . where many were gathered together and were praying.

---

de
  v 13 (Z) When he had knocked at the door of the gateway, a maid named Rhoda came to answer . . .

In 14:21, the initial NPCs described Paul and Barnabas' activities in Derbe. In the light of their reported activities elsewhere, these would appear to be a natural consequence of their going to the city (v 20b). The following independent clause describes their return to the scene of the last nuclear events (see sec. 1.222b). The final NPCs begin the description of their interaction with the Christians, once back there:

---

[17] For a similar phenomenon in connection with *men oun,* see 17:30.
[18] See AV, RSV, NIV. However, Lenski (*Interpretation of Acts,* 475) considers that it introduces something else which Peter realized; see sec. 2.1.

de
> 14:20a   When the disciples gathered about Paul, he rose up and entered the city (of Lystra);
>
> v 20b   (X) *kai* on the next day he went on with Barnabas to Derbe.
> -
> *te*
> v 21   (Y) Having preached the gospel to that city and made many disciples, they returned to Lystra and to Iconium and to Antioch,
>
> v 22   (Z) strengthening the souls of the disciples, exhorting them to continue in the faith, and saying that through many tribulations we must enter the kingdom of God.

In summary, *te* is used rather than *de* because nothing distinctive has been presented in the clause introduced by *te*. *Te* is used rather than *kai* to give prominence to the specified lead-in Y to the following incident or nuclear interaction Z, over against the previous event(s) X.

2.32   The Previous Sentence is of a Preliminary Nature

In the passages considered in sec. 2.31 above, *kai* introduced the events X which led from one incident to the specific lead-in Y to the next. However, it is not necessary for two incidents to be so linked by a continuous chain of events. Often a change of spatio-temporal setting isolates the previous incident from the events which lead up to the new one. Under such circumstances, it may well not be the first event X described following the change of setting which specifically stimulates or leads to the nuclear interaction. Rather, X may be of a preliminary nature. In that case, *te* introduces the further event Y which does provide the specific lead-in to the development of the incident.

This is illustrated in 15:4–6. The initial NPC "having arrived in Jerusalem" establishes a new spatio-temporal setting. Within this new setting, the continuing subjects, Paul and Barnabas, are no longer in contact with the participants with whom they had been interacting in v 3. The independent clause of v 4a introduces the new participants with whom they will interact. However, it is the next sentence again which describes the specific event from which the following incident develops, since it is this declaration which stimulates the challenge of v 5. (Also, v 4a is of a preliminary nature, since Paul and Barnabas are cast in a non-initiating role; see below.)

> *men oun*
> 15:3 ... they passed through both Phoenicia and Samaria reporting the conversion of the Gentiles and they gave great joy to all the brethren.

> *de*
> v 4a (X) Having arrived in Jerusalem, they were welcomed by the church and the apostles and the elders
> -
> *te*
> v 4b (Y) they declared all that God had done with them.

> *de*
> v 5 (Z) Some believers who belonged to the party of the Pharisees stood up, saying, "It is necessary to circumcise them ... " (the converts mentioned in the report of v 4b)

In the above passage (and also in 21:37 and 16:13 below), the central character is in a non-initiating role in the sentence X which precedes the one introduced by *te*. Such sentences are natural settings for events in which the central character is active (see 15:4 above).

The same is true of sentences which take the central character to the location of the following incident, but do not bring him into contact with other participants (see sec. 1.212a). Since the book of Acts consists mainly of interactions between participants, sentences which only move the central character from one location to another tend to form the background to the interactions.

See, for example, 9:3. Verse 3a is of a preliminary nature, with respect to the nuclear interaction between Saul and the voice from heaven (vv 4–6), as it describes only the location of that interaction. Verse 3b provides the specific lead-in to the exchange:

> *de*
> 9:3a (X) As he journeyed, he approached Damascus
> -
> *te*
> v 3b (Y) suddenly a light from heaven flashed abut him.

Other passages in which *te* introduces the specific lead-in to a nuclear interaction, over against the previous sentence, include:

13:4a–b (not D; the nuclear interaction of vv 6–12 occurs in Cyprus)

25:1–2   (the interaction between the Jewish leaders and
Festus in Jerusalem is preliminary to the nuclear interaction
in Caesarea which involves Paul)

28:1–2   (the nuclear interaction of vv 3–6 which leads from
the natives' act of v 2 [*te*] involves Paul and the snake).[19]

According to the principles of sec. 1.21, in none of the above
passages which occur at the beginning of a new incident would *de*
have been expected. *Te* is used, rather than *kai*, to introduce the
specific lead-in to the following nuclear interaction. In more
general terms, because *te* links sentences of unequal importance
and the first sentence is of a preliminary nature only, it gives
prominence to the sentence that it introduces.[20]

On the basis of the principle exemplified in this section, the
presence of *te* in 21:37 may be interpreted as making v 37, over
against vv 35–36, the specific lead-in to the incident involving Paul
and the tribune. Paul is cast in a non-initiating role in v 35 (X), but
takes the initiative in v 37 (Y; see 15:4 above):

---

de

   21:35   (X) When he came onto the steps, he was actually carried by
   the soldiers because of the violence of the crowd . . .

- -

te*

   v 37a   (Y) as Paul was about to be brought into the barracks, he said
   to the tribune, "May I say something to you?"

(*An explanatory comment separates v 37 from v 35. However, rather than employing *de* to mark the return to the
main events of the story (factor 4 of sec. 1.15), *te* is used to
mark both sentences as preliminary events to a following
nuclear interaction. See also 21:30, 7:26.)

The above interpretation does not correspond to the standard
analysis of the passage, which introduces a paragraph break
following vv 35–36. However, since Paul's motivation in speaking
to the tribune is to ask to be allowed to address the crowd (v 39b),
it is not inappropriate to view the description of the crowd's
attitude of vv 35–36 as setting the scene for 21:37–22:29. Further-

[19] In 8:28a, *te* is to be preferred to its variant *de* because (a) both events are
preliminary to the nuclear interaction (see sec. 1.212); (b) the second event
provides the specific lead-in to the following incident. A further variant is
asyndeton.
[20] In 11:26 (not D), 19:12 and 20:11, *te* links subordinate clauses, the second of
which appears to be of particular significance. See also 21:11 (some manuscripts
link the second and third NPCs with *te*).

more, when Paul does seek to address them, their response ("there was a great hush") then stands in sharp contrast to their previous attitude.

2.33 *Te* Introduces a Response

Occasionally, *te* introduces a response. This is a situation involving a change of subject and therefore one in which *de* would be the expected conjunction. (The passages concerned do not meet the conditions of sec. 1.22 for introducing a response with *kai*.) However, throughout secs. 2.1–2.32, sentences linked by *te* have pertained to the same DU. It is therefore likely that *te* has the same characteristic, when introducing a response. In other words, *te* is associating into a single DU an event X and its response Y.

Typically, when *te* introduces a response, the Christian leader or other major participant is more actively involved in the response than in the event which produced it. For example, in the report of Paul's trial in chapter 24, *te* introduces Paul's defense (vv 10–21). This follows the description of the case against him (vv 2–9), during which he was only an observer:

---

de
   24:2   When Paul was called, Tertullus began to accuse him, saying,
   . . .

---

de
   v 9   (X) *kai* The Jews joined in the charge, affirming that all this was so.

- -

te
   v 10   (Y) Paul replied, when the governor had motioned to him to speak . . .

---

de
   v 22   (Y) Felix . . . put them off, saying, "When Lysias the tribune comes down, I will decide your case," giving orders to the centurion that Paul should be kept in custody but should have some liberty, and that none of his friends should be prevented from attending to his needs.

It is likely that, as in the examples of sec. 2.32, the events linked by *te* are of unequal importance. The event preceding the response would then be of less consequence than the response itself. This is reasonable, since Paul is active in the response, and the response itself leads to a significant development (viz., governor Felix's decision of v 22, which furthers Luke's purpose of showing that the Roman authorities took a basically favorable view of Christianity).[21]

Other passages which confirm this view include:

13:45–46   (when the Jews revile Paul [v 45], *te* introduces his decision to turn to the Gentiles [vv 46–47], which leads to their enthusiastic response [vv 48–49])

21:30   (when the Asian Jews call on the crowds to deal with Paul [vv 27–28], *te* introduces the ensuing riot [v 30], which leads directly to the intervention of the Roman tribune [v 31], a development of crucial importance to the history of Paul's life).

Thus, when *te* introduces a response, the effect is to give prominence to the response, over against the event which produced it. The response then provides the lead-in to a significant development in the story.

2.4   Summary

Two basic claims have been made concerning the function of *te*:

(a)   sentences linked by *te* pertain to the same DU;

(b)   the presence of *te* is motivated by two factors, one or both of which may be valid for any passage:

(i)   *te* indicates a "close affinity" between sentences, which manifests itself in:

similar events with the same basic subject (sec. 2.1);
statements about the same event (sec. 2.2);

(ii)   *te* indicates that the sentences it links are of unequal importance.

In the examples of sec. 2.1, this second function of *te*, if valid at all, is probably overshadowed by the first. In these passages, the similarity or the association of the two elements is of primary significance. However, in sec. 2.3 (and to a lesser extent in sec. 2.2), the second function comes to the fore. Since the sentence introduced by *te* provides the specific lead-in to the next significant development in the story, *te* gives prominence to this sentence, over against the previous sentence, which is of a more general or preliminary nature.

---

[21] See Bruce, *The Book of Acts*, 20–24, 471.

CHAPTER THREE

OUN AND *MEN OUN*

This chapter describes how *oun* and *men oun* contribute to the development of the narrative of Acts.

Winer defines *oun* as a consequential and syllogistic particle.[1] In the reported speeches of Acts, it is used most commonly to introduce a new assertion or exhortation which is to be inferred from the last premise. See, for example, 13:37–40:

> (13:37) But he whom God raised up saw no corruption.
>
> (v 38) *oun* let it be known to you, brethren, that through this man forgiveness of sins is proclaimed to you, (39) and by him every one who believes is freed from everything from which you could not be freed by the law of Moses.
>
> (v 40) *oun* beware lest there come upon you what is said in the prophets

Oun as a particle by itself occurs so infrequently in the narrative framework of Acts that its specific function in narrative cannot be determined with any certainty. It seems most likely that it is a marked form of *de*, indicating a close consequential relationship between the elements it links (sec. 3.1).

In Classical Greek, "The particle *oun* is indicative rather of continuation and retrospect than of inference: and, in general, it should be rendered rather 'accordingly,' ... than 'therefore'...."[2] In connection with *men, oun* always indicates "continuation" with respect to the last event which featured the participants concerned (sec. 3:21). In particular, "retrospective and transitional *oun*" occurs "with prospective *men*."[3]

Such a claim is at variance with the analyses of many NT Greek scholars, who do not consider that *men* is always prospective.

---

[1] Winer, *Treatise on the Grammar of NT Greek*, 555.

[2] Winer, *Treatise on the Grammar of NT Greek*, 555, n. 4, citing Donaldson, *Grammar*, 596.

[3] Denniston, *The Greek Particles*, 470.

Instead, they divide the examples of *men oun* into two types, according to a difference in the function of *men*. Winer, for example, states:

> The examples of *men oun* are of two different kinds. (1) *Men* is in correspondence with *de*—so that here we have merely a combination of *oun* with the distributive formula *men* . . . *de*. . . . Sometimes however—as in the cases of the simple *men*—the second member is not expressed in strict form . . . . (2) *Oun* in its proper sense is combined with the confirmative *men*. . . .[4]

Sec. 3.22 claims that all the examples of *men oun* found in Acts fall into Winer's first category. In the majority of passages, two statements relate to *oun*, one introduced by *men*, the other by *de*. Even when the second is implicit, the context indicates the nature of the corresponding assertion which follows from the presence of *men*.[5]

Finally, the function of the *men oun* . . . *de* correlation is compared with that of *kai* . . . *te* and other series of conjunctions. The events linked by *men oun* . . . *de* are distinctive (sec. 3.23). The correlation groups DUs together, to bring out the opposition or "correspondence"[6] between the events so associated.

3.1   The Function of Simple *Oun* in the Narrative of Acts

Oun occurs without *men* not more than eight times in the narrative sections of Acts. In 25:23 it is the undisputed reading in Nestle and Aland (1975). In 10:23 and 22:29, it is the preferred reading; D has *tote*. In 25:1 it is also the preferred reading, with *de* as a variant. In 15:2; 16:10, 11; and 20:4 (D), it is a variant to *de*.

The basic question to be asked concerning the function of *oun* in the narrative of Acts is why it should be present at all. Unfortunately, with only four passages in which *oun* is the undisputed or preferred reading, it is not possible adequately to substantiate any answer. Consequently, this section seeks only to offer an analysis which satisfactorily explains the examples which do occur and fits neatly into an overall theory of the structure of the narrative of Acts.

In the passages in which *oun* is the preferred reading, its function is consistent with that found in the reported speeches. In every case, the event it introduces is in conformity with the

---

[4] Winer, *Treatise on the Grammar of NT Greek*, 556. See also Blass, *Grammar of NT Greek*, 263, 267, 273.

[5] See also Page, *Acts of the Apostles*, 94.

[6] Winer, *Treatise on the Grammar of NT Greek*, 551.

demands or implications of the act which stimulated it. See, for instance, 10:22–23 (not D):

> (10:22) the messengers said, "Cornelius, a centurion, . . . was directed by a holy angel to send for you to come to his house, and to hear what you have to say."
>
> (v 23) *oun* calling them in, he lodged them, and (*de*) the next day he rose and went off with them.

However, in most passages in which a speech is followed by a corresponding response, *de* introduces the response. See, for example, 13:15–16:

> (13:15) . . . the rulers of the synagogue sent to them, saying, "Brethren, if you have any word of exhortation for the people, say it."
>
> (v 16) *de* Paul, standing up and motioning with his hand, said . . . .

Why is *oun* sometimes used under these circumstances, instead of *de*? *Oun* appears in narrative to make explicit the close consequential relationship that exists between the elements it links. The second event is the direct result of the first, and closely conforms with its demands and implications.

The presence of *oun* is motivated particularly if it is not obvious from the context that such a relationship exists. For example, in some passages, it might not be obvious to the reader that in fact the second event did conform with the intentions of the first.

In 10:22–23, for instance, the messengers ask Peter to go with them to Caesarea. Peter's immediate response is to call them into his house and give them lodging. Since he had previously refused to obey an order which was contrary to his Jewish upbringing (v 14), the use of *de* would not have made it clear whether Peter's provision of lodging was a counter to their request or was in conformity with it. *Oun* makes the consequential relationship explicit, and tells the reader that Peter is acting in conformity with the divine instruction to "accompany them" (v 20).

In 25:23, *oun* makes explicit the close consequential relationship between Festus' reply to king Agrippa, "Tomorrow you shall hear Paul" (v 22b), and the elaborate ceremonial described in the GAs of v 23. In other words, the whole ceremony was put on specifically to fulfill Festus' promise. It was not, for instance, something which would have happened anyway, and Paul's appearance was now fitted into the program. The assembly was the direct result of the decision:

> (25:22b) "Tomorrow," said he, "you shall hear him."
>
> (v 23) *oun* on the morrow, when Agrippa and Bernice had come with great pomp, when they had entered the audience hall with the military tribunes and the prominent men of the city, and when Festus had commanded, Paul was brought in.

Similarly, in 22:29 (not D), *oun* makes explicit the close consequential relationship between the conversation that established that Paul was a Roman citizen (vv 27–28) and the withdrawal of his torturers:

> (22:28b) Paul said, "But I was born a Roman citizen."
>
> (v 29a) *oun* immediately those who were about to examine him withdrew from him.

The reader unfamiliar with the rights of Roman citizens might well have failed to see the consequential relationship between these two acts, were it not made explicit by the use of *oun*. The use of *de* would have left open the possibility that the withdrawal of the soldiers occurred only on the orders of the tribune. In fact, the soldiers responded directly to the assurance that Paul was a Roman citizen. This is confirmed by the following statement, "and the tribune *also* was afraid, realizing that Paul was a Roman citizen and that he had bound him" (v 29b).

The use of *oun* in 25:1 is open to several interpretations:

---

de
24:27a When two years had elapsed, Felix was succeeded by Porcius Festus

- -

te
v 27b Desiring to do the Jews a favor, Felix left Paul in prison.

---

oun (variant *de*)
25:1 When Festus had come into his province, after three days he went up to Jerusalem from Caesarea

- -

te
v 2 The chief priests and the principal men of the Jews informed him against Paul, . . . (3) asking as a favour to have him sent to Jerusalem, planning an ambush to kill him on the way.

It could be argued that *oun* in 25:1 is resumptive.[7] Luke is taking up the topic of Festus, having alluded to him in 24:27a. However, there is no evidence that simple *oun* is ever used in this way in Acts.

Secondly, *oun* could be used specifically to indicate that Festus' visit to Jerusalem was a direct result of his having just become governor.[8] However, it is difficult to see why it would be of importance to Luke to specify the relationship.

The real significance of the presence of *oun* emerges on taking into account the function of *te* in the development of the narrative (see sec. 2.32). In 24:27b, *te* indicates that Felix's action provides the specific lead-in to the following incident. In other words, his act of leaving Paul in prison is of particular significance to the outcome of the following events. *Oun* then introduces the next DU, which again consists of a preliminary event, followed by one introduced by *te*. It is between the second part of these two DUs that the close consequential relationship exists. As a direct result of Felix having left Paul in prison, the religious leaders take up Paul's case, as soon as the new governor arrives in Jerusalem.

Thus, in the narrative sections of Acts, a possible motivation for the use of *oun* rather than *de* is to make explicit the close consequential relationship that exists between the elements it links. It indicates that the event it introduces is the direct result of the previous event, and closely conforms with its demands and implications.

3.2 *Men Oun* in the Narrative of Acts

This section shows that Denniston's analysis of *men oun* in Classical Greek is equally valid for Acts. In particular, *men* is always prospective (sec. 3.22). In the narrative sections of the book, a correlative *de* is usually present. Furthermore, as in Classical Greek, *oun* indicates "continuation" with respect to the last event involving the participant concerned (sec. 3.21). As such, its function is not inconsistent with that of simple *oun* (sec. 3.1 above). However, the actions which it introduces do not always conform completely with the demands or implications of the previous event.

3.21 *Oun* in Connection with *Men*

Whenever *men oun* introduces a sentence whose subject was involved in or affected by the last event described, the *oun* indicates "continuation."[9]

---

[7] Blass, Debrunner and Funk, *Greek Grammar*, sec. 451 (1).
[8] Bruce, *The Book of Acts*, 475.
[9] Donaldson, *Grammar*, 596.

For an action to be in continuation with respect to the last event(s), it must follow naturally from that event. In particular, it must not be in opposition to its intentions (see particularly 25:4 below). (This is a weaker claim than that made for simple *oun*; see sec. 3.1.)

In many of the 21 passages in which *men oun* is the undisputed reading in the narrative of Acts, *oun* introduces a response which, as in sec. 3.1, is in complete conformity with the intention of the person whose action produced the response (e.g., 23:18). In other passages, it introduces a further action by the same participant (17:17) or by a sub-group of the previous subject (17:12), when this action follows naturally from his last one. In other passages again, it introduces a state which results naturally from the outcome of the previous incident as a whole (e.g., 9:31).[10] In 1:6, the apostles' query leads naturally from Jesus' statement of vv 4–5.[11] In 5:41–42, the response of the apostles to the directive of the authorities is in conformity with their stated position in vv 29–32 (though not with that of the authorities!). In 8:25, the return of the apostles to Jerusalem is a natural result of the completion of their work in Samaria. As for 14:3, both Knowling and Meyer claim that *oun* is "marking a result from the events of the two previous verses."[12]

One passage in which many commentators consider *men oun* to introduce a response which is in opposition to the event which produced it is 25:4:

> (25:2) the chief priests . . informed Festus against Paul; and they urged him (3) asking as a favor to have the man sent to Jerusalem, planning an ambush to kill him on the way.
>
> (v 4) *men oun* Festus replied that Paul was being kept at Caesarea, and that he himself intended to go there shortly. (5) "So," said he, "let the men of authority among you go down with me, and if there is anything wrong about the man, let them accuse him."

Lenski is practically alone in translating *men oun* "accordingly."[13] Others see in Festus' reply a rejection of the request

---

[10] Knowling, "Acts of the Apostles," 244; Meyer, *Critical and Exegetical Handbook*, 1.260. Jackson and Lake (*Beginnings of Christianity*, 4.107) dispute this, however.

[11] Bruce, *The Book of Acts*, 38.

[12] Knowling, "Acts of the Apostles," 382; Meyer, *Critical and Exegetical Handbook*, 2.38.

[13] Lenski, *Interpretation of Acts*, 990.

made in v 3.[14] However, the fact that Festus later asks Paul whether he is willing to go to Jerusalem to be tried (v 9) suggests that v 4 is not an outright refusal of the request. Rather, he may have thought that he was expediting it. Being unaware of the plot, he indicates to the Jews that the easiest way for the matter to be handled would be for them to accompany him to Caesarea, since he was going there anyway *en tachei*, "in speed." Thus Festus' reply does not have to be seen as a refusal. Rather, it offers a better alternative, and as such represents "continuation" from the last event.

In a few passages, *men oun* occurs in connection with the reintroduction of a participant, rather than with a response. In 11:19, for instance, it is used when *hoi . . . disasparentes* (last mentioned in 8:4) are reintroduced. Verse 19 provides a transition between this last reference to the group and the introduction in the following sentence of a sub-group, in connection with correlative *de*:[15]

> (11:19) *men oun* those who were scattered because of the persecution that arose over Stephen travelled as far as Phoenicia and Cyprus and Antioch, speaking the word to none except Jews.
>
> (v 20) *de* there were some of them . . . who on coming to Antioch spoke to the Greeks also, preaching the Lord Jesus.

See also 8:4, 19:32, 28:5.

However, in these passages also, the statement introduced by *men oun* follows naturally from the last mention of the participants concerned. For example, in 11:19, the last reference to *hoi . . . diasparentes* states that they "went about preaching the word" (8:4). The function of *oun* is therefore still that of indicating "continuation," albeit not with the immediately preceding events. (In 28:5, the RSV incorrectly contrasts Paul's action with the reaction of the bystanders in v 4. *Oun* indicates that his action is a natural continuation from the event of v 3.)

3.22   *Men* is Always Prospective, in Connection with *Oun*

This section argues that in Acts, as in Classical Greek, "*men* is in correspondence with *de*," or at least with an implied second member. In other words, its function is always prospective. This

---

[14] For example, "howbeit" (Bruce, *The Book of Acts*, 475), "however" (Jackson and Lake, *Beginnings of Christianity*, 4.307).

[15] "*men oun* introduces a general statement, whilst *de* (v 20) marks a particular instance" (Knowling, "Acts of the Apostles," 266).

means that, in the majority of cases which Moulton et al. classify as solitarium,[16] a corresponding *de* is to be found.

It is most common in the narrative sections of Acts for *men* to occur in connection with an initial response to the last event recorded. The presence of *men* anticipates a second response by the same subject (e.g., 15:3–4 below), or by the addressee of the initial response (e.g., 23:18–19). Furthermore, if the event which led to the initial response had a stated or implied goal, *men* anticipates the realization of that goal in the later response.

This is illustrated in 15:3. In v 2 the Christians at Antioch appoint Paul, Barnabas and some others to go up to Jerusalem to discuss a doctrinal issue with the leaders there. Their response is in two stages. *Men* introduces the journey to Jerusalem and the activities en route (v 3). This journey is a necessary part of their assignment (hence *oun*). However, it does not fulfill the goal of v 2. It is the DU of v 4 (introduced with *de*) which brings them into the presence of the people with whom they are to confer:

---

de

    15:2 . . . Paul and Barnabas and some of the others were appointed to go up to Jerusalem to the apostles and the elders about this question.

---

men oun

    v 3 Being sent on their way by the church,[17] they passed through both Phoenicia and Samaria, reporting the conversion of the Gentiles, and they gave great joy to all the brethren.

---

de

    v 4 Having arrived in Jerusalem, they were welcomed by the church and the apostles and the elders. . . .

(Verses 5–21 present the resulting debate.)

In the above passage, both v 3 (*men*) and v 4 (*de*) are in accordance (*oun*) with the commission of v 2. The correlation associates the two parts of the response together, with *men* indicating that a second and in this case more important element is to follow. *Men* is therefore prospective in v 3.[18]

---

[16] Moulton, Geden and Moulton, *Concordance to the Greek NT*, 626.

[17] As Lenski notes (*Interpretation of Acts*, 28), "there is ambiguity with regard to the participles as to whether they are to be substantivized," e.g., "those who had been sent . . ," or whether they should be regarded as modifiers. Lenski prefers the latter interpretation; Kilpatrick argues for the former (personal communication). The conclusions of this section are not affected by the interpretation chosen.

[18] Rendall ("Appendix on *men oun*," 161) considers that the correlation contrasts

See also 13:4 (v 6 [*de*] brings Barnabas and Saul to the scene of the first incident of their assignment),[19] and 23:31 (the commission was to take Paul to Caesarea [vv 32–33; *de*]). In 25:4–12, Festus' response to the Jews is in two parts: vv 4–5 (*men*) and v 6 (*de*).[20] Similarly, the response of Peter's audience in chapter 2 is two-fold: v 41 (*men*) and v 42 (*de*). Likewise, Judas and Silas fulfill the assignment of 15:22 in v 30 (*men*) plus the second part of the DU of vv 31–32.

In the case of 23:18–19, Paul's goal, in asking the centurion to take his nephew to the tribune to inform him of some matter (v 17), needs two stages to be realized. The centurion must act in accordance with the request (v 18; *men*). The tribune must then give the youth an opportunity to speak to him (v 19; *de*). The presence of *men* in v 18 thus anticipates the full realization of Paul's goal.

In 1:4–6, the disciples' initial response to Jesus' charge not to depart from Jerusalem, but to wait for the promise of the Father (v 4), does not conform to his goal in giving the directive. The use of *men* in v 6 both indicates this and anticipates their compliance. It is clear from 1:12–2:1 that the disciples did comply. However, there is no specific sentence, introduced by *de*, which spells it out. (A similar problem probably arises in 17:16–22 and 5:41–42.)

The correlation *men . . . de*, in connection with continuative *oun*, also links conflicting responses or reactions by different participants to the same event(s).

In 28:5–6, for instance, the correlation occurs after a description of the activities of two separate groups of participants: Paul and the snake (v 3), and the bystanders (v 4). *Oun*, "accordingly," introduces the reaction, first of Paul (v 5; *men*), then of the bystanders (v 6; *de*). These reactions are both to the situation of v 3:

---

de
28:3   . . . a viper . . . fastened on Paul's hand.

---

de
v 4   When the natives saw the creature hanging from his hand, they said to one another, ". . . justice has not allowed him to live."

---

the reception given to Paul and Barnabas by Phoenicia and Samaria (*men*) and the church in Jerusalem (*de*).
[19] Page, *Acts of the Apostles*, 161.
[20] Page, *Acts of the Apostles*, 249.

men oun
v 5   He shook off the creature into the fire and suffered no harm.

de
v 6   They were waiting, expecting him to swell up or suddenly fall down dead.

See also 12:5, 14:3–4, 17:12–13.

The *men . . . de* correlation is used at the beginning of an incident. *Men* occurs in connection with background information which forms the transition from an earlier incident. *De* introduces the events of the incident proper.

This is particularly clear in 11:19–20 (see sec. 3.21). The statement introduced by *men oun* reintroduces participants last referred to in 8:4, and provides the transition from that reference to them. In turn, this transitional statement serves as the ground for a contrastive statement about a sub-group, in connection with correlative *de*. (See also 8:4–5, 19:32–33.)

The same principle applies also to passages in which *men oun* introduces a natural conclusion to the last incident recorded, and the statement associated with *de* concerns a different topic. The sentence featuring *men* provides the transition to the new incident, and presents the general background for it. *De* then introduces the incident proper.

In 8:25–26, for instance, v 25 is a natural conclusion to the incident of vv 14–24 (hence *oun*). However, it also provides the general background for the events of vv 26–39, in that it removes the central characters (Peter and John) from the scene. The reader then knows that attention is to be fixed on Philip (v 26):

men oun
8:25   When Peter and John had testified and spoken the word of the Lord, they returned to Jerusalem. . . .

de
v 26   An angel of the Lord said to Philip, "Rise and go toward the south . . ."

See also 9:31–32[21] and 16:5–6.[22]

[21] Jackson and Lake (*Beginnings of Christianity*, 4.107) comment, "More probably the *men oun* implies that this verse is the introduction to the story of Peter's work in Lydda and Joppa."

[22] Rackham (*The Acts of the Apostles*) begins his fourth major section of the book at v 5.

(Note: The above analysis is in conflict with the proposal, e.g., of C. H. Turner, that 9:31 and 16:5 *terminate* major sections of the book of Acts.[23] It is more accurate to say that such verses provide the *transition* between the different incidents or sections.[24] The function of *men* elsewhere then leads to the claim that its presence in these verses in fact associates the transitional statement with the *following* incident or section, rather than the preceding one.)

3.23 Conclusions concerning *Men Oun*

Previous sections have claimed that *men oun* is always to be viewed in Acts as a combination of continuative *oun* and prospective *men*. *Men* is either in correspondence with a following *de*, or at least implies the corresponding assertion. This section describes how the function of this combination differs from that of comparable conjunctions and correlations. It also considers the role of the correlation in connection with DUs.

The function of the *men oun* . . . *de* correlation (a) may be compared usefully with that of *te*, since both *te* and *men* anticipate a new development in the story. The role of the correlation (b) may also be contrasted with that of a simple *de* . . . *de* series contrasting the actions of different subjects. This leads to the conclusion (c) that the role of the correlation is to associate corresponding DUs together, without playing down the distinctiveness of the separate units.

(a)   The use of the *men oun* . . . *de* correlation linking responses X and Y to a previous event W may be compared with the use of *kai* introducing X and *te* linking X and Y (sec. 2.31).

The difference between the two correlations is two-fold:
> (i) Most basic is the difference in the relation between X and Y:
>> When *men oun* . . . *de* is used, X and Y are distinctive elements.
>> When *kai* . . . *te* is used, X and Y are not distinctive elements.
> (ii) In addition, when *men oun* . . . *de* is used, *oun* relates to both X and Y. Both result from the previous event W, *oun* indicating that they are a continuation from W. This means that, where appropriate, Y fulfills the goal of W.
>> When *kai* . . . *te* is used, no such continuation with W is conveyed. In particular, Y is never a stated or implied goal of W.

---

[23] C. H. Turner, "Chronology of the New Testament" 421. See also Blood and Blood, "Overview of Acts," 3.
[24] See Cadbury, "The Summaries in Acts," 5.395.

These differences are exemplified in 15:2–4 (*men oun . . . de*) and 9:27–28 (*kai . . . te*).

In 15:2–4, v 3 and v 4 are distinctive elements, involving interactions with different participants (sec. 1.131). In addition, they are both in conformity with the intention of v 2, and v 4 begins to fulfill the specific goal of v 2:

---

de

15:2 (W) . . . Paul and Barnabas and some of the others were appointed to go up to Jerusalem to the apostles and the elders about this question.

---

men oun

v 3 (X) Being sent on their way by the church, they passed through both Phoenicia and Samaria, reporting the conversion of the Gentiles, and they gave great joy to all the brethren.

---

de

v 4 (Y) Having arrived in Jerusalem, they were welcomed by the church and the apostles and the elders. . . .

In 9:27–28, v 28 and v 29 are not distinctive elements (see sec. 2.31). In addition, only the first part of v 28 directly conforms with the goal of v 27, which was to enable Paul to join the Christians in Jerusalem (see v 26a):

---

de

9:27 (W) Barnabas, taking Paul, brought him to the apostles and declared to them how on the road he had seen the Lord, who spoke to him, and how at Damascus he had preached boldly in the name of Jesus.

v 28 (X) *kai* he went in and out among them at Jerusalem, preaching boldly in the name of the Lord.

- -

te

v 29 (Y) he was speaking and disputing against the Hellenists.

The use of the *men oun . . . de* correlation to introduce sentences X and Y when beginning a new incident may be compared with the use of *te* to introduce the specific lead-in Y to the following nuclear events, following a preliminary event X (sec. 2.32).

The basic difference is again in the relation between X and Y. When *men oun . . . de* is used, X and Y are distinctive elements with different subjects, and are not in sequence with each other

(Part One, sec. 1.11). Often they are in contrast (11:18–19, 19:32–33), or involve different participants and locations (8:25–26, 9:31–32, 16:5–6).

When *te* is used, X and Y occur in the same spatio-temporal setting and are in sequence with each other. They involve the same participants (e.g., 15:4a–b), though Y may introduce a second participant into the presence of the first (e.g., 9:3a–b).

(b) The *men oun . . . de* correlation may be compared with the use of *de . . . de* to introduce contrasting actions performed by different participants. When *men . . . de* is used, the conflicting statements are grouped together,[25] to bring out their contradictory nature. For example, in 12:5–6, *men oun . . . de* links "Peter was kept in prison" and "earnest prayer for him was made to God by the church." Lenski comments, "The two imperfect tenses describe the situation and ask the reader to visualize and to dwell on it. Which will be the stronger, the dungeon and its guards or the prayers of the church?"[26] In other words, the conflicting forces both seek to resolve the situation in different ways. See also 14:3–4, 17:12–13, 28:5–6. (In this last passage, the bystanders are eventually forced to change their opinion [v 6b].)

When the *men . . . de* correlation is not used to associate contrastive statements about different participants, the conflict is never brought to a head in succeeding sentences. Instead, the paths of the two participants simply diverge and their differences remain unresolved (e.g., 13:13b–14). Alternatively, the action of the second participant itself overrules that of the first (e.g., 27:42–43).

(c) It follows from the above comparison that, like the simple *men . . . de* correlation, *men oun . . . de* groups together distinctive events. This distinctiveness is not played down by the use of *kai*. (Contrast sec. 1.211; *kai* would be an inappropriate way of linking a two-part response, for instance, because the second part builds on the first.) Instead, the events linked by the correlation are treated as distinctive, yet at the same time are grouped together.

The *men oun . . . de* correlation is therefore a means of grouping together two DUs. As such, its function complements that of the combination of *de* and *kai* in a single clause (see sec. 2.1). This combination normally brings out the similarity between events performed by different subjects. For its part, *men oun . . . de*

---

[25] Winer, *Treatise on the Grammar of NT Greek*, 551.
[26] Lenski, *Interpretation of Acts*, 471.

indicates correspondence or even opposition between the events it introduces.

In summary, the *men oun . . . de* correlation groups together corresponding or opposing events expressed in different DUs. The presence of the *oun* indicates continuation with respect to the last event which involved the subject concerned. The *men. . . de* part of the correlation indicates that the events are in correspondence or opposition. In the absence of the second member of the correlation, the *men* is still prospective, implying that the assertion which corresponds with the one it introduces holds true.

CHAPTER FOUR

OTHER SENTENCE CONJUNCTIONS AND ASYNDETON

"The connective is retained on the whole in narrative,"[1] and examples of complete asyndeton are extremely rare in the narrative of Acts. However, a number of sentences are linked by other means than the standard conjunctions *de, kai, (men) oun, te. Tote* is used as a conjunction at least 15 times (sec. 4.1). A demonstrative pronoun occurs without a conjunction in eight or more passages (sec. 4.2). A few examples of *eti, meta* and *houtōs* are found without conjunctions, as is complete asyndeton between an event and its response. These are discussed in sec. 4.3, together with three occurrences of *alla*.

This chapter is concerned with the relationship of these means of linkage to the more common conjunctions and to the DU. *Tote* and *alla* are marked forms of *de*. The instances of *eti* and of *meta* also occur at the beginning of DUs. However, the demonstrative pronoun is often the equivalent of a relative pronoun.

4.1 *Tote*

Tote is the undisputed reading on 18 occasions in Acts (1:12; 4:8; 5:26; 6:11; 7:4; 8:17; 10:48b; 13:3,12; 15:22; 21:26,33; 23:3; 25:12; 26:1b; 27:21,32; 28:1). In addition, it is the preferred reading in 10:46b (variant *de*; D), 17:14a (*men oun*; D) and 21:13 (*de*; D). (It is also a frequent variant to *de* in D.) Except in 11:26 (D), 17:14, 27:21 and 28:1, no conjunction concurs with *tote*. In other words, it is "a connective particle to introduce a subsequent event."[2]

As a conjunction, *tote* occurs when *de* would be expected. Normally, it introduces a sentence whose (underlying) subject is different from that of the previous sentence (factor 2 of sec. 1.15). 6:11 is an exception. *Tote* introduces a new initiative on the part of

---

[1] Blass, Debrunner and Funk, *Greek Grammar*, sec. 462(1).
[2] Blass, Debrunner and Funk, *Greek Grammar*, sec. 459(2).

the same subject, but this initiative is in response to the last event, and the subject was the undergoer of the other participant's action. ("They could not withstand the wisdom and the Spirit with which Stephen spoke. *Tote* they secretly instigated men, who said, . . .") There is therefore no doubt that this initiative also is a new development such as would warrant the use of *de*.

When *tote* introduces a subsequent event, it is "not one taking place at a definite time ('thereupon,' not 'at that time')."[3] "Thereupon" or "forthwith" is a very satisfactory rendering in the vast majority, if not all, of the examples of connective *tote* in Acts. It indicates that the event it introduces is in "close chronological sequence" with the event that led up to it. This means that no *unnecessary* action, delay or debate separates them. The event introduced by *tote* occurs without further argument or prevarication.[4]

In many passages, the context seems to demand this meaning. In others, it gives a very satisfactory interpretation. In 4:8, for instance, when Peter and John are asked, "By what power or by what name did you do this?" (v 7), Peter's reply goes straight to the point; "*tote* Peter . . . said, ". . . be it known to you all . . . that by the name of Jesus Christ of Nazareth, whom *you* crucified . . . this man is standing before you well" (v 10). Similarly, in 25:12, after Paul has appealed to Caesar (v 11), the force of "*tote* Festus . . . answered, '. . . to Caesar you shall go' " is that his decision was not separated from the appeal by further efforts to reach a compromise; the decision was taken "forthwith."

Only in 10:48b is there some doubt as to *why* Luke should wish to indicate that the response was without delay:

> (10:48) Peter commanded the new Gentile Christians to be baptized in the name of Jesus Christ.
>
> *Tote* they asked him to remain for some days.

A reason for using *tote* is possibly found in Lenski's comment:

> The aorist tenses imply that Peter gladly remained "for some days." But this means a great deal, as 11:3* indicates. Peter had not only entered a Gentile's house and thus defiled himself according to Jewish mores, he remained and

---

[3] Blass, Debrunner and Funk, *Greek Grammar*, sec. 459(2).

[4] In Luke's Gospel, *tote* is used in a much greater variety of ways (e.g., following *kai* [6:42], or a clause subordinated by *hotan* [5:35]). As a conjunction, however, it still indicates close chronological sequence between events. See especially Luke 11:26, 13:26, 14:21b, 23:30, 24:45.

lodged in the home of Cornelius, ate his Gentile host's food which was anything but kosher.[5]

(* "When Peter went up to Jerusalem, the circumcision party criticized him, saying, 'Why did you go to uncircumcised men *and eat with them?*' " [11:2–3].)

In other words, what Luke had in mind may have been not so much the invitation to remain per se, as Peter's ready response to it, when it was given.

The evidence of the other passages is strong enough to conclude that Luke uses *tote* as a conjunction to indicate that the event it introduces occurred "forthwith," with no unnecessary action separating it from the event which led up to it.

4.2 Demonstrative Pronouns

In the narrative sections of Acts, a demonstrative pronoun without a conjunction begins a sentence on eight occasions: 1:4; 8:26b; 9:36b; 13:7b; 14:9; 16:3,17; plus 18:25 (variant; *hos*). (In 20:5, asyndeton is a variant to the preferred reading *de*; see below.) In contrast, a conjunction accompanies the demonstrative pronoun in 17:11, 18:26, and 21:9. (See also 10:16; 19:10,17; and 28:9, in connection with *touto/tauta*.)

The absence of a conjunction in the majority of the above passages may be explained as a result of the application of a "flexible constraint"[6] on the use of a relative clause following a relative clause. Winer notes,

> After a relative sentence where we might expect a repetition of *hos* or a continuance of the relative construction, Greek writers not unfrequently, indeed almost regularly ... change the structure of the sentence and substitute *kai autos* (*houtos*).[7]

The presence of the demonstrative pronoun *houtos* is probably a product of this constraint in 9:36b; 13:7b; 14:9; 16:3,17; and 17:11. Since *houtos* is considered to have replaced *hos*, no conjunction would normally be expected. The sentence introduced by *houtos* effectively continues the previous one. (In 17:11, *de* is present because the behaviour of the subject is contrasted with that of an earlier subject.)

A similar constraint may apply to the remaining passages. All of

---

[5] Lenski, *Interpretation of Acts*, 435–36.
[6] Hockett, *State of the Art*, 60.
[7] Winer, *Treatise on the Grammar of NT Greek*, 186.

them could be viewed as the equivalent of appositional relative clauses. The constraining factor would be the amount of descriptive information conveyed in the previous sentence. *Houtoi pantes* (1:14), for instance, has as its referent a list of eleven names.

Even if the above explanation is valid, however, an unresolved question remains.Why does Luke sometimes express parenthetical information in appositional form, using a relative or demonstrative pronoun and no conjunction, and at other times present similar information as a background comment introduced by *de*? For example, why is 21:9 (*toutō de ēsan thygateres ... prophēteuousai*, "Now this man had ... daughters who were prophetesses") not in the form of a relative clause?

4.3   Complete Asyndeton

This section considers passages in which no conjunction begins the sentence. In the narrative sections of Acts, this occurs once when *eti*, "still," opens the sentence (10:44), once with *meta tauta*, "after these things" (18:1; not D), twice with *houtōs*, "thus" (17:33, 19:20), and three times in connection with a response (1:7 [variants: *de*, *kai*], 8:1c [variants: *de*, *te*], 25:22b [variant *de*]).

(a)   In 10:44, the sentence begins with *eti lalountos tou Petrou*, "while Peter was still speaking." There are no contrasting examples with a conjunction. Blass, Debrunner and Funk note that "*eti* . . . [is] likely to be used without *de*."[8]

When *meta touton/tauta*, "after him/these things," begins an incident of narrative (18:1; not D), or a new point in reasoned argument (5:37), then no connective is used. (If a point of argument is continuing, however, *kai* is used preceding *meta tauta*. See 7:7 and 13:20.)[9]

In both 10:44 and 18:1, *de* would be the expected conjunction, since the information is distinctive (factors 2 and 1 of sec. 1.15 respectively).

(b)   In 27:44b and 28:14, *kai houtōs* introduces the natural result of the previous event.[10] See 27:43–44, for example:

---

[8] Blass, Debrunner and Funk, *Greek Grammar*, sec. 459(4).

[9] Winer (*Treatise on the Grammar of NT Greek*, 677) calls *meta touton/tauta* a connective. It would then be treated like *tote* (sec. 4.1).

[10] Winer (*Treatise on the Grammar of NT Greek*, 678) comments, "the design is to give prominence to the apodosis; *houtōs*, in particular, alludes again to the circumstances expressed in the protasis."

(27:43b) The centurion ordered those who could swim to throw themselves overboard first and make for the land, (44) and the rest on planks or on pieces of the ship.

(v 44b) *kai houtōs* it was that all escaped to land.

In 17:33 and 19:20, however, *kai* is not used, and *houtōs* alone begins the sentence. In these passages, the circumstances to which *houtōs* alludes are not expressed in the immediately preceding sentence alone, but are spread over two or more. Lenski writes concerning "*houtōs* the word of the Lord was growing and prevailing mightily" (19:20), "*houtōs*, 'thus,' extends back over the entire previous account concerning the work in Ephesus."[11] In 17:33, J. B. Phillips renders *houtōs* "so with this mixed reception" (referring back to the different reactions of v 32).[12]

Kai is therefore not used in 17:33 and 19:20, because its presence would limit the referent of *houtōs* to the last sentence. Asyndeton is still to be interpreted as the equivalent of *kai* rather than *de* in these passages, however. This is because the sentences, in summarizing the previous events, do not introduce distinctive information.

(c)   Possible examples of complete asyndeton in the narrative of Acts are found in 1:7, 8:1c and 25:22b. In each case, the sentence concerned is a response by the undergoer of the last event, so that *de* is the expected conjunction. *De* is in fact a variant in every passage (*kai* is an additional variant in 1:7, and *te* in 8:1c).

The absence of *de* is significant in 1:7, coming as it does in a chapter which is preliminary to the nucleus of the book (see sec. 1.213). Furthermore, the element which corresponds to the *men oun* of v 6 is not v 7 (sec. 3.22). It is therefore probable that Luke deliberately omitted *de* in v 7. (See also chapter 1, n. 28.)

In 25:22b, the reported speech begins before the quotation margin (*phēsin*) which pertains to it. Consequently, it would be unclear whether any conjunction which might occur should belong to the reported speech or to the margin (but see 26:25):

(25:22b) *(ho de) aurion, phēsin, akouse autou.*

" 'Tomorrow,' he says,[13] 'you shall hear him.' "

---

[11] Lenski, *Interpretation of Acts*, 798.

[12] See Newman and Nida, *Translator's Handbook*, 344.

[13] N. Turner (*Syntax*, 340–41) observes a preference for asyndeton with the historic present of speech verbs.

No motivation is discerned for the absence of a conjunction in 8:1c.

(d) *Alla*

Alla is found three times outside the reported speeches of Acts. In each case, "it appears . . . as the contrary to a preceding *ou*."[14] For example:

> (18:20) When they asked him to stay for a longer period, Paul declined (*ouk epeneusen*);
>
> (v 21) *alla* having taken leave of them and said, "I will return to you if God wills," he set sail from Ephesus.

See also 4:32c and 5:13b (both within descriptive material).

These passages should probably be interpreted as examples of a particular form of "negated antonym paraphrase."[15] The first element states what did not happen, and the second describes the corresponding event which did take place. For *de* used "in the sense of *alla*"[16] (e.g., 8:16b; 12:9c,14b), see sec. 1.133.

In the above narrative passages, *alla* introduces distinctive information (sec. 1.133). It is perhaps, therefore, a marked form of *de* linking opposing statements.

---

[14] Blass, Debrunner and Funk, *Greek Grammar*, sec. 448(1).
[15] Longacre, *Anatomy of Speech Notions*, 134–35.
[16] Blass, Debrunner and Funk, *Greek Grammar*, sec. 447(1).

CHAPTER FIVE

CONCLUSIONS

The basic functions of the conjunctions discussed in previous chapters are now related to each other and to the DU.

Chapter 1 introduced the concept of "development units" (DUs), each new DU being introduced by *de*. The elements of the DU were linked by *kai*.

Each of the conjunctions considered in subsequent chapters may also be related to the DU. Their distribution is as follows (see secs. 4.2–3 for the distribution of the individual forms of connection associated with asyndeton):

non-developmental conjunctions (*within DUs*)	developmental conjunctions (*linking DUs*)
kai	alla
te	de
	oun
	tote

In addition to these conjunctions, prospective *men* is employed in connection with *oun* to group together corresponding DUs.

The introduction of background material has still to be fitted into the above scheme. It clearly does not always represent further development of the narrative. This is confirmed by the use of *te* following a comment. The DU begun before the comment continues, after its completion.

See, for instance, 21:35–37:

de
> 21:35   When Paul came onto the steps, he was actually carried by the soldiers because of the violence of the crowd;
>
> (v 36   *gar* the mob of the people followed, crying, "Away with him!")

- -

te
> v 37   As Paul was about to be brought into the barracks, he said to the tribune, . . .

See also 21:27–30.

Nevertheless, the story may build directly on a background statement introduced by *gar* or *de*. In 19:24, for instance, *gar* introduces an exposition of the statement of v 23, "About that time there arose no little stir concerning the Way." The subsequent DUs build, not on v 23, but on the initial DU which extends to v 27. Similarly, the events of 4:36–5:11 do not develop from the statement "great grace was upon them all" (v 33b). Rather, they develop from the description of the custom of selling property and giving the proceeds to the apostles for distribution (vv 34–35), which is introduced with *gar*.

There is considerable variation in the relevance to further events of sentences introduced by *de* which describe a state rather than an action ("non-event" sentences). Some give information of no relevance to further events (e.g., at the end of the incident of 19:1–6, "There were [*ēsan-de*] about twelve of them in all" [v 7]). Others provide background information for the events described (e.g., "they were [*ēsan-de*] days of Unleavened Bread" [12:3b], explaining why Peter was kept in prison, rather than executed immediately).[1] Others again introduce an item of significance for the direction of development of the story ("there were [*ēsan-de*] many lights in the upper chamber where we were gathered" [20:8], helping to explain why Eutychus fell asleep [v 9]). They may even introduce new major participants (e.g., 2:5, 9:10), with the following events developing directly from them.

In reality, when introducing a background comment, the function of *de* is not basically different from when it marks a switch of attention to a different subject in a different location, thus beginning a new incident. (See, for example, the switch from Philip [8:40] to Saul in 9:1.) In the latter case, following DUs develop a different topic from the previous ones:

[1] Bruce, *The Book of Acts*, 248.

Diagram 5A

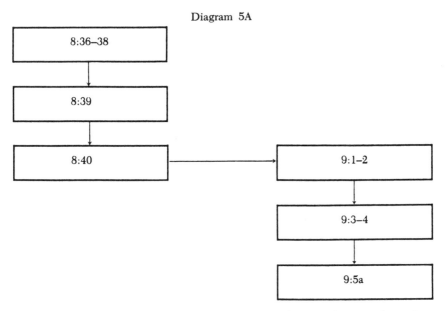

(Each box represents a DU. Lower DUs build directly on higher DUs [e.g., they are responses]. The horizontal arrow represents a switch of attention away from the topic which was being followed.)

When introducing a non-event sentence or background comment, *de* again indicates a switch of attention away from the main events which were being followed. Only the following DUs determine whether a new direction is to be pursued, or whether the sentence is treated as a "digression"[2] from the previous main event line, which is then resumed.

In 9:10–19, the following DUs build on the non-event sentence "Now there was a disciple at Damascus named Ananias" (v 10a):

Diagram 5B

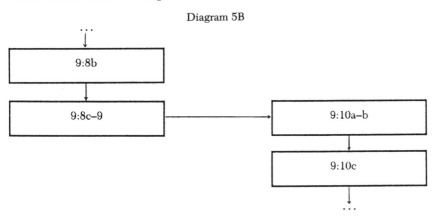

[2] Levinsohn, "Progression and Digression," 138–44.

In 20:7–12, however, the following DUs build, not on the non-event sentence of v 8 about the many lights, but on the previous DU:

Diagram 6A

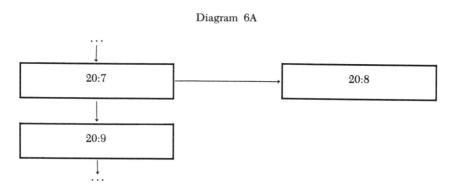

In the case of the explanatory sentence of 21:36, a further element of the same DU follows. (Only the sense of the context determines whether the sentence introduced by *te* pertains to the explanation or to the previous DU.)

Diagram 6B

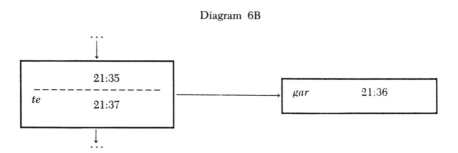

Thus, it would be misleading to classify *gar* and *de* as "non-developmental," when introducing background material. These conjunctions may still be considered to link DUs. The following DUs determine whether they in fact mark digression from the main event line, or whether they set the scene for further progression.[3]

In summary, DUs in Acts are usually linked together in an unmarked way by *de*, as the narrative develops. However, it is possible to specify the following particular relationships between them: opposition (*alla*), close consequential sequence (*oun*), close chronological sequence (*tote*), explanation (*gar*; see sec. 1.133),

---

[3] Levinsohn, "Progression and Digression," 123–31.

and correspondence (*men*). (There is no reason to suppose that the relevant forms of connection associated with asyndeton [secs. 4.3a,c] are marked with respect to *de*.) As for the internal elements of DUs, they are linked in an unmarked way by *kai*. Alternatively, an element may be added to a DU by using *te*, the elements so linked potentially being of unequal importance.

APPENDIX 1 TO PART ONE
TABLE OF FOREFRONTED SUBJECTS/THEMES IN THE NARRATIVE OF ACTS

The following table indicates the section(s) to which each example of a forefronted subject/theme relates.

Column 1: If two or more sentences occur in one verse, they are labelled "a, b . . . ." However, in the body of the text, "a" is usually omitted, when the reference is to the first sentence of a verse.

Column 2 indicates if the clause concerned is not an independent clause or NPC. The abbreviations used are as follows:

GA—genitive absolute

gar, hina, hōste, hoti—a clause introduced by the element indicated

infin—an infinitival clause subordinated to *egeneto*

Obl—the subject/theme is in an oblique case

rel—relative clause

T—transitional temporal clause

?—there are variant word orders; in some manuscripts, the subject/theme precedes the verb; in others, it does not.

Column 3 indicates the section(s) in which the example is discussed, or to which it relates. All the sections are in Part One.

1	2	3	1	2	3
Ref	*Clause*	*Section*	3:1		1.111
1:1	Obl	1.244	3:2		1.111, 1.243
1:6		1.26	3:5		1.26
1:9b		1.23	3:6	?	1.26
1:10		chap. 1, n. 2; 1.23	4:4a		1.111, 1.3
2:4b	rel	1.111	4:8		1.252a
2:12	final NPC	1.21	4:19		1.252a
2:13		1.252b	4:21a		1.252a
2:38		1.252b	4:21b	hoti	1.3
2:41a		1.26	4:22	gar/Obl	1.111
2:43b		1.111, 1.3	4:24		1.26
2:44		1.111, 1.3	4:32a	Obl	1.111
2:47b		1.111	4:32b		1.3

1	2	3		1	2	3
4:33b		1.111		10:23c		1.243
4:34a	gar	1.3		10:24b		1.111
4:34b	gar	1.112		10:26		1.252b
4:36		1.21		10:30		1.251
5:1		1.111, 1.243		11:19		1.111, 1.244
5:7b		1.24		11:21b		1.3
5:8b, 9		1.252a		11:29	Obl	1.26
5:12b	Obl	1.111		12:5a		1.244
5:13a		1.111, 1.3		12:5b		1.111
5:15	hina	1.3		12:6b		1.111
5:19		1.23		12:7a		chap. 1, n. 2
5:22		1.23		12:7b		1.111
5:33		1.22		12:11		1.111
5:41		1.26		12:15a, b, c		1.252a
6:7a		1.111		12:16a		1.111
6:7c		1.21, 1.3		12:19		1.111
6:8		1.111		12:21		1.242
7:2		1.252a		12:22		1.252b
7:58b		1.21		12:24		1.111
8:1a		1.111		12:25		1.111
8:1c		1.3		13:4		1.26
8:3		1.111		13:6	rel	1.111
8:4		1.111, 1.244		13:9		1.24
8:5		1.111		13:13b		1.21
8:7a	gar	1.21, 1.3		13:14		1.111
8:7b		1.111, 1.3		13:44		1.3
8:9		1.243		13:50		1.111
8:13		1.111		13:51		1.241
8:20		1.251		13:52		1.111
8:25		1.244		14:2		1.21
8:26a		1.111		14:4b		1.21
8:27b		chap. 1, n. 2		14:4c		1.111
8:31		1.252b		14:8		1.111, 1.243
8:32		1.111		14:11		1.22
8:39a		1.23		14:12	rel	1.111
8:40		1.111		14:13		1.22
9:1		1.111		15:1		1.111, 1.243
9:3a	infin	1.242		15:3		1.26
9:5b		1.252b		15:7	GA	1.3
9:7		1.111		15:30		1.26
9:10c, 11		1.251		15:32		1.21
9:22		1.111		15:35		1.111
9:26b		1.3		15:37		1.252a, 1.22
9:27		1.111		15:38		1.252a
9:29b		1.22		15:39	hōste	1.21
9:31		1.244		15:40		1.111
9:32	infin	1.111		16:1b		chap. 1, n. 2; 1.243
9:36		1.243		16:5		1.244
9:38		1.23		16:9a		1.23
9:40c		1.26		16:9b		1.111
10:1		1.111, 1.243		16:14a		1.21
10:4a		1.251		16:4b	rel	1.23
10:14		1.252a, 1.253b		16:16	infin	1.243
10:15		1.252a		16:22b		1.111
10:17		chap. 1, n. 2		16:25a		1.242
10:19	GA	1.111		16:26a		1.23
10:22		1.251		16:26c	Obl	1.111, 1.3

1	2	3	1	2	3
16:31		1.252b	21:34a		1.252a
16:35	GA	2.14	21:37b		1.251
16:37		1.252a	21:40a		1.26
17:4		1.21	21:40b	GA	1.3, 1.26
17:10		1.23	22:27b		1.252b
17:12		1.21, 1.3	22:28b		1.252b
17:14a	Obl	1.241	22:29b		1.111
17:15		1.23	23:2, 3, 4		1.251
17:18a		1.111	23:8a	gar	1.112, 1.21
17:18b		1.21	23:8b		1.111
17:18c		1.252b	23:10	GA	1.3
17:21		1.111	23:18		1.26
17:32b		1.21	23:22, 31		1.26
17:32c		1.111	25:1		1.111
17:33		1.241	25:4		1.252b, 1.253b
17:34		1.111	25:8	GA	1.251, 1.253b
18:7	rel	1.111	25:9		1.22, 1.251
18:8a		1.111, 1.243	25:12		1.26
18:8b		1.111, 1.3	25:13	GA	2.14
18:12	GA	1.111, 1.243	25:13		1.243, 1.26
18:17b	Obl	1.3	25:14		1.26
18:18		1.111	25:22a		1.251, 1.26
18:19b	Obl	1.21	25:22b	?	1.251, 1.26
18:19c		1.111	26:1a, b		1.252a
18:24		1.111, 1.243	26:24, 25, 28, 29		1.252a
19:1	infin	1.111	26:32		1.252a
19:2b		1.251	27:3b		1.21
19:3a	?	1.251, chap. 1, n. 15	27:9a	GA	1.3
19:3b		1.251	27:11		1.111
19:9	T	1.21	27:12	GA	1.111
19:10	hōste	1.3	27:12		1.22
19:11	Obl	1.111	27:20a	GA	1.3
19:12c	hōste	1.111	27:20b	GA	1.111
19:18		1.111, 1.3	27:21	GA	1.3
19:19		1.21, 1.3	27:27	T	2.14
19:20		1.111	27:30	GA	1.22
19:24	gar	1.112	27:33	T/?	2.14
19:30	GA	1.22	27:39	T	2.14
19:31		1.111, 1.243	27:39a	Obl	1.21
19:32a		1.111, 1.244	27:39b	Obl	1.111
19:32c		1.21	27:41b		1.21
19:33a	Obl	1.111	27:41c		1.111
19:33b		1.22	27:42	Obl	1.21, 1.3
19:34b		1.3	27:43		1.111
20:6		1.111	27:44c	infin	1.3
20:7		1.242	28:2		1.111
20:13a		1.111	28:3		1.23
20:37		1.3	28:5		1.244
21:3c	gar	1.112	28:6a		1.111, 1.22
21:6c		1.111	28:6b	GA	1.22
21:7		1.111	28:8	infin	1.111, 1.243, 1.26
21:9	Obl	1.111	28:8	rel	1.26
21:18b		1.111, 1.3	28:9		1.26
21:20		1.26	28:15a		1.243
21:26		1.22	28:21		1.252b
21:27	?	1.22	28:24		1.21
21:32b		1.26	28:25a		1.111

APPENDIX 2 TO PART TWO

SENTENCE CONJUNCTIONS IN THE NARRATIVE OF ACTS

The following table records the conjunction used to introduce each sentence in the narrative sections of Acts, together with the section which refers to the sentence concerned.

The following sentences are not included:
(a) those introduced by *gar*;
(b) those introduced by *kai* which have the same subject as the previous sentence and which begin with an independent clause.

The sentence references "a, b . . ." correspond with those used in Appendix 1, where relevant. If a reference is given in brackets (e.g., [15:39b]), this indicates that the variant reading produces an additional sentence.

If conjunction variants occur for a particular sentence, then the "preferred" reading is given first, and alternative readings noted in Nestle and Aland or suggested by G. D. Kilpatrick (proposed changes) are placed in brackets. "[rel.]" means that the variant is a relative clause. The "preferred" reading is usually that given in the text of Nestle and Aland. Occasionally, however, a different variant is substituted, in which case their textual reading is italicized.

In the case of sentences with conjunction variants, the section to which the preferred variant would pertain is noted in brackets in the "Section" column.

Ref.	Conjunction	Section	Ref.	Conjunction	Section
1:4	kai	1.213	1:10	kai	1.213
1:6	men oun	3.21, 3.22	1:12	tote	4.1
1:7	Ø [de, kai]	[4.3c], chap. 1,	1:13	kai	1.213
		n. 21;	1:14	houtoi	4.2
		[1.213]	1:15a	kai	1.213
1:9a	kai	1.213	1:15b	de [te]	[1.213]
1:9b	kai	1.213	1:23	kai	1.213

Ref.	Conjunction	Section	Ref.	Conjunction	Section
1:24	kai	1.213	4:32b	kai	1.12
1:26b	kai	1.213	4:32c	alla	4.3d
1:26c	kai	1.12	4:33a	kai	1.222a
2:1	kai	1.213	4:33b	te	2.31
2:2a	kai	1.213	4:35b	de	1.12, 1.222a
2:3a	kai	1.213	4:36	de	1.12
2:4a	kai	1.12	5:1	de	1.12
2:5	de	1.12	5:2b	kai	[1.12], 1.131
2:6a	de	1.12	5:3	de	1.12
2:7a	de	1.134	5:5a	de	1.12, 1.221
2:12a	de	1.132, 1.141	5:5b	kai	1.222a
2:12b	kai	1.141	5:6a	de	1.12
2:13	de	1.12	5:6b	kai	1.134
2:14a	de [tote]	[1.12]	5:7a	de	1.141
2:37a	de [tote]	[1.12]	5:7b	kai	1.141, 1.12
2:37b	te [kai]	[2.2]	5:8a	de	1.12
2:38	de	1.12	5:8b	de	1.12
2:40a	te	2.1	5:9	de	1.12
2:41a	men oun	3.21, 3.22	5:10a	de	1.12, 1.221
2:42	de	1.11	5:10c	de	1.12
2:43a	de	1.12	5:10d	kai	1.134
2:43b	de [te]	[1.12]	5:11	kai	1.222a
2:44a	de [kai de]	[1.12]	5:12a	de [te]	[1.12]
2:46	te [de]	[2.1]	5:12b	kai	1.12
2:47b	de	1.12	5:13a	de [kai]	[1.12]
3:1	de	1.12	5:13b	alla	4.3d
3:2	kai	1.211	5:14	de	1.12
3:4	de	1.12	5:16	de kai	1.12, 2.1
3:5	de	1.12	5:17	de [kai]	[1.12]
3:6	de	1.12	5:19a	de [tote]	[1.12], 1.211b
3:7a	kai	1.134	5:19b	te [de]	[2.32]
3:7b	de	1.12, 1.221	5:21a	de	1.12
3:8a	kai	1.12	5:21c	de	1.12
3:9	kai	1.222b	5:22a	de	1.12
3:10a	te [de]	[2.31], chap. 2, n. 16	5:22b	de	1.131
			5:24	de	1.11
3:11	de [te]	[1.11]	5:25	de	1.12
3:12	de	1.12	5:26	tote	4.1
4:1	de	1.11, 1.211	5:27a	de	1.132
4:4a	de	1.12	5:27b	kai	1.211a
4:4b	kai	1.12	5:29	de	1.12
4:5	de	1.11	5:33a	de	1.12
4:7	kai	1.211a	5:34	de	1.12
4:8	tote	4.1	5:35	te	2.1
4:13a	de	1.12	5:40a	de	1.12, 1.221
4:13b	te [de]	[2.1]	5:40b	kai	1.131
4:14	te	2.1	5:41	men oun	3.21, 3.22
4:15	de	1.131	5:42	te	2.1
4:18	kai	1.131	6:1	de	1.11
4:19	de	1.12	6:2	de	1.12
4:21	de	1.12	6:5a	kai	1.221, 1.223
4:23a	de	1.12	6:5b	kai	1.12, [1.223]
4:24a	de	1.12	6:6b	kai [rel.]	[1.223]
4:31a	kai	1.222a	6:7a	kai	1.223
4:31b	kai	1.12	6:7b	kai	1.223
4:32a	de	1.12	6:7c	te	2.2

Ref.	Conjunction	Section	Ref.	Conjunction	Section
6:8	de	1.12	8:36a	de	1.11
6:9	de	1.12, 1.211	8:36b	kai	1.12, 1.142
6:11	tote	4.1	8:38b	kai	1.12
6:12a	te [de]	[2.1]	8:38c	kai	1.12
6:12b	kai	1.222b	8:39a	de	1.11
6:13	te	2.31	8:39b	kai	1.222a
6:15	kai	1.222a	8:40a	de	1.12
7:1	de	1.12	8:40b	kai	1.131
7:2	de	1.12	9:1	de	1.12
7:54a	de	1.12	9:3a	de	1.11
7:55	de	1.12	9:3b	te	2.32
7:57a	de	1.12	9:4	kai	1.211b
7:58a	kai	1.134	9:5a	de	1.12
7:58b	kai	1.222a	9:5b	de	1.12
7:59	kai	1.12	9:7	de	1.12
7:60a	de	1.12	9:8a	de	1.12
7:60b	kai	1.222a	9:8b	de [∅]	[1.11]
8:1a	de	1.12	9:8c	de	1.12
8:1b	de	1.11	9:9a	kai	1.222a
8:1c	de[∅, te]	[1.12] [4.3c]	9:10a	de	1.12
8:2a	de	1.12	9:10b	kai	1.211b
8:3a	de	1.12	9:10c	de	1.12
8:3b	te	2.2	9:11	de	1.12
8:4	men oun	3.21, 3.22	9:13	de	1.12
8:5	de [te]	[1.12]	9:15	de	1.12
8:6	de [te]	[1.12]	9:17a	de [tote]	[1.12]
8:7b	de	1.12	9:17b	kai	[1.223]
8:8	kai [de]	[1.12]	9:17c	kai	1.223
8:9	de	1.12	9:18a	kai	1.223
8:11	de	1.133	9:18b	te	2.2
8:12	de	1.11	9:18c	kai	1.223
8:13a	de . . . kai	1.12, 2.1	9:19a	kai	1.223
8:13b	kai	1.134	9:19b	de	1.141
8:13c	te	2.2	9:20	kai	1.141
8:14	de	1.12	9:21a	de	1.12
8:16b	de	1.12	9:22a	de	1.12
8:17a	tote	4.1	9:23	de	1.11
8:17b	kai	1.222a	9:24a	de	1.12
8:18	de	1.12	9:24b	de kai [te]	chap. 2, n. 12
8:20	de	1.12	9:25	de	1.12
8:24	de	1.12	9:26a	de	1.12
8:25a	men oun	3.21, 3.22	9:26b	kai	1.212b
8:25b	te	2.2	9:27a	de	1.12
8:26a	de	1.12, 1.211b	9:28	kai	1.222b
8:26b	hautē	4.2	9:29a	te	2.31
8:27a	kai	1.212a	9:29c	de	1.12
8:27b	kai idou	1.212a	9:30a	de	1.12
8:28a	te/∅ [de]	[2.32], chap. 2, n. 19	9:31a	men oun	3.21, 3.22
			9:32	de	1.12
8:29	de	1.12, 1.211b	9:33	de	1.131
8:30a	de	1.12	9:34a	kai	1.223
8:31a	de	1.12	9:34b	kai	1.223
8:31b	te	2.1	9:35	kai	1.223
8:32	de	1.12	9:36a	de	1.12
8:34	de	1.12	9:36b	hautē	4.2
8:35	de	1.12	9:37a	de	1.11

Ref.	Conjunction	Section	Ref.	Conjunction	Section
9:37b	de	1.12	11:22a	de	1.12
9:38	de	1.12	11:22b	kai	1.12
9:39a	de	1.12	11:24b	kai	1.221
9:39b	kai	1.222a	11:25	de	1.12
9:40a	de	1.12	11:26a	kai	1.131
9:40b	kai	1.134	11:26b	de [rel.]	[1.12]
9:40c	de	1.12	11:27	de	1.11
9:40d	kai	1.131	11·28a	de	1.12
9:41a	de [te]	[1.12]	11:29	de	1.12
9:41b	de	1.131	12:1	de	1.11
9:42a	de	1.12, 1.222a	12:2	de	1.134
9:42b	kai	1.12	12:3a	de [kai]	[1.134]
9:43	de	1.12, 1.222a	12:3b	de	1.12
10:1	de	1.12	12:5a	men oun	3.21, 3.22
10:4a	de	1.12	12:5b	de	1.12
10:4b	de	1.12	12:6a	de	1.11
10:7	de	1.11	12:6b	te	2.1
10:9	de	1.11	12:7a	kai idou	1.211
10:10a	de	1.134	12:7b	kai	1.222a
10:10c	de	1.11	12:7c	de	1.12
10:11	kai	1.12, 1.142	12:7d	kai	1.12
10:13	kai	1.211b	12:8a	de [te]	[1.12]
10:14	de	1.12	12:8b	de	1.12, 1.142
10:15	kai	1.224c	12:8c	kai	1.142, 1.223
10:16a	de	1.141	12:9a	kai	1.223
10:16b	kai	1.141, 1.12	12:9c	de	1.133
10:17	de	1.11	12:10a	de	1.12
10:18	kai	1.131	12:10b	kai	1.223
10:19	de	1.11	12:10c	kai	1.223
10:21	de	1.12	12:11	kai	1.212b, 1.223
10:22	de	1.12	12:12	te	2.31
10:23a	oun [tote]	[3.1]	12:13	de	1.11
10:23b	de	1.11	12:14a	kai	1.134
10:23c	kai	1.222a	12:14b	de	1.131
10:24a	de [kai]	[1.11]	12:15a	de	1.12
10:24b	de	1.12	12:15b	de	1.12
10:25	de	1.11	12:15c	de	1.12
10:26	de	1.12	12:16a	de	1.12
10:27a	kai	1.222b	12:16b	de	1.12
10:27b	kai	1.142	12:17a	de	1.12
10:28	te	2.31	12:17b	te	2.1
10:30	kai	1.224a	12:17c	kai	1.131
10:34	de	1.12	12:18	de	1.11
10:44	∅	4.3a	12:19a	de	1.12
10:45	kai	1.222a	12:19b	kai	1.131
10:46b	tote [de]	[4.1]	12:20a	de	1.131
10:48a	te [de, tote]	[2.1], chap. 2, n. 11	12:20b	de	1.12
			12:20c	kai	1.134
10:48b	tote	4.1	12:21	de	1.11
11:1	de	1.12	12:22	de	1.12
11:2	de [kai, men oun]	[1.11]	12:23a	de	1.12
			12:23b	kai	1.222a
11:4	de	1.12	12:24a	de	1.12
11:18a	de	1.12, 1.222a	12:25	de	1.12
11:19	men oun	3.21, 3.22	13:1	de	1.12
11:20	de	1.12	13:2	de	1.11, 1.211b
11:21a	kai	1.222a	13:3	tote	4.1
11:21b	te	2.33	13:4a	men oun	3.21, 3.22

Ref.	Conjunction	Section	Ref.	Conjunction	Section
13:4b	te [not D]	2.32, 1.135	15:4b	te	2.32
13:5a	kai	1.135	15:5	de	1.12, 1.211
13:5b	de kai	1.133, 2.1	15:6	te [de]	[2.33]
13:6	de	1.131	15:7	de	1.11
13:7b	houtos	4.2	15:12a	de	1.12
13:8	de	1.12	15:13	de	1.11
13:9	de	1.12	15:22	tote	4.1
13:11b	de [te, kai]	[1.12]	15:30a	men oun	3.21, 3.22
13:11c	kai	1.12	15:30b	kai	1.211a
13:12	tote	4.1	15:31	de	1.12
13:13a	de	1.12	15:32	te	2.1
13:13b	de	1.12	15:33	de	1.11
13:14a	de	1.12	15:35	de	1.12
13:14b	kai	1.135	15:36	de	1.11
13:15	de	1.11	15:37	de	1.12
13:16	de	1.12	15:38	de	1.12
13:42	de	1.11	15:39a	de	1.12
13:43	de	1.11	[15:39b]	infin [tote]	—
13:44	de [te]	[1.11]	15:40	de	1.12
13:45a	de	1.12	15:41	de	1.135
13:46	te	2.33	16:1a	de kai/de	1.141, chap. 2,
13:48a	de	1.12, 1.222a			n. 12
13:48c	kai	1.12	16:1b	kai idou	1.141, 1.211
13:49	de	1.12, 1.222a	16:3a	touton	4.2
13:50a	de	1.12	16:3b	kai	1.134
13:51	de	1.12	16:4	de	1.11
13:52	te [de]	[2.2]	16:5a	men oun	3.21, 3.22
14:1	de	1.12	16:6	de	1.12
14:2a	de	1.12	16:7a	de	1.135
14:3	men oun	3.21, 3.22	16:7b	kai	1.211b
14:4a	de	1.12	16:8	de	1.12
14:4b	kai · · · men	1.12	16:9	kai	1.211b
14:4c	de	1.12	16:10	de [oun]	[1.11]
14:5	de	1.11	16:11a	de [oun]	[1.134]
14:7	kai	1.135	16:11b	de [te, kai]	[1.11]
14:8	kai	1.211	16:12a	kai [te]	[1.135]
14:9	houtos	4.2	16:12b	de	1.12
14:10b	kai	1.221	16:13a	te	2.32
14:11	te [de]	[2.33]	16:13b	kai	1.134
14:12	te	2.2	16:14	kai	1.211
14:13	te [de]	[2.1]	16:15a	de	1.11
14:14	de	1.12	16:16	de	1.11
14:18	kai	1.222a	16:17	hautē	4.2
14:19a	de	1.12, 1.211	16:18a	de	1.133, 1.141
14:19b	kai	1.134	16:18b	de	1.12
14:20a	de	1.11	16:18c	kai	1.221
14:20b	kai	1.222b	16:19	de [kai, te]	[1.12]
14:21	te	2.31	16:20	kai	1.223
14:23	de	1.131	16:22a	kai	1.223
14:24	kai	1.131	16:22b	kai	1.222b, 1.223
14:25a	kai	1.135	16:23	te [de]	[2.31]
14:25b	kai	1.135	16:25a	de	1.11
14:27	de	1.131	16:25b	de	1.12
14:28	de	1.141	16:26a	de	1.12, 1.211b
15:1	kai	1.141, 1.211	16:26b	de [te]	[1.12]
15:2	de [oun]	[1.11]	16:26c	kai	1.222a
15:3a	men oun	3.21, 3.22	16:27	de	1.12
15:4a	de	1.131	16:28	de	1.12

Ref.	Conjunction	Section	Ref.	Conjunction	Section
16:29a	de	1.12	18:12	de	1.11, 1.211a
16:29b	kai	1.134	18:14	de	1.11
16:30	kai	1.134	18:17a	de	1.12
16:31	de	1.12	18:17b	kai	1.12
16:32	kai	[1.223]	18:18	de	1.12
16:33a	kai	1.223	18:19a	de	1.12
16:33b	kai	[1.223]	18:19b	kai	1.222a
16:34a	te	2.1	18:19c	de	1.12
16:35	de	1.11	18:20	de	1.11
16:36	de	[1.12]	18:21	alla	4.3d
16:37	de	1.12	18:22	kai	1.223
16:38a	de [te]	[1.12]	18:23	kai	1.223
16:38b	de [kai]	[1.12]	18:24	de	1.12
16:39a	kai	1.131	18:25a	houtos [rel.]	[4.2]
16:39b	kai	1.134	18:25b	kai	1.222b
16:40a	de	1.12, 1.221	18:26a	te	2.31
16:40b	kai	1.131, 1.134	18:26b	de	1.12
17:1	de	1.135	18:27	de	1.11
17:2a	de	1.12	19:1	de	1.11
17:4a	kai	1.221	19:2a	te	2.31
17:5a	de	1.12	19:2b	de	1.12
17:5b	kai [te]	[1.131]	19:3a	de [te]	[1.12]
17:6	de	1.134	19:3b	de	1.12
17:8	de	1.12, 1.134	19:4	de	1.12
17:9	kai	1.12	19:5	de	1.12, 1.221
17:10	de	1.12	19:6a	kai	1.223
17:11	de	1.12	19:6b	te	2.2
17:12	men oun	3.21, 3.22	19:7	de	1.133
17:13	de	1.11	19:8	de	1.12
17:14a	de [men oun]	[1.12]	19:9	de [men oun]	[1.11]
17:14b	te	2.2	19:10	de	1.12, 1.141
17:15a	de	1.12	19:11	te	2.32
17:15b	kai [de]	1.221	19:13	de kai	1.12
17:16	de	1.12, 1.11	19:14	de [rel.]	[1.133]
17:17	men oun	3.21, 3.22	19:15	de [tote]	[1.12]
17:18a	de kai	1.12, 2.1	19:16	kai	1.12
17:18b	kai	1.12	19:17a	de	1.12
17:18c	de	1.12	19:17b	kai	1.222b
17:19	de [te]	[1.131]	19:17c	kai	1.222b
17:21	de	1.12	19:18	te	2.31
17:22	de	1.12	19:19a	de	1.12
17:32a	de	1.12	19:20	∅	4.3b
17:32b	de	1.12	19:21	de [tote]	[1.11]
17:33	∅	4.3b	19:22	de	1.131
17:34	de	1.12	19:23	de	1.11
18:1	∅ [de]	[4.3a]	19:28	de	1.12, 1.221
18:2	kai	1.212b	19:29a	kai	1.222b
18:3b	kai	1.12	19:29b	te	2.31
18:4a	de	1.12	19:30	de	1.12
18:4b	te [not D]	[2.2] [1.133]	19:31	de kai	1.12, 2.1
18:5	de	1.11	19:32a	men oun	3.21, 3.22
18:6	de	1.11	19:32b	kai	1.12
18:7	kai [de]	[1.131]	19:33a	de	1.12
18:8a	de	1.12	19:33b	de	1.12
18:8b	kai	1.222a	19:34	de	1.12
18:9	de	1.12, 1.211b	19:35	de	1.12
18:11	de [te, kai]	[1.12]	19:41	kai	1.222a

Ref.	Conjunction	Section	Ref.	Conjunction	Section
20:1	de	1.11	21:30d	kai	1.222a
20:2	de	1.135	21:31	te [de]	[2.31]
20:3	te	2.32	21:32b	de	1.12
20:4	de [oun]	[1.12]	21:33a	tote	4.1
20:5	de [∅]	[1.132]	21:34a	de	1.12
20:6a	de	1.12	21:34b	de	1.12
20:7a	de	1.11	21:35	de	1.11
20:7b	te	2.2	21:37a	te	2.32
20:8	de	1.12	21:37b	de	1.12
20:9a	de	1.12	21:39	de	1.12
20:10a	de	1.12	21:40a	de	1.11
20:10b	kai	1.134	21:40b	de	1.11
20:11	de	1.131	22:2a	de	1.12, 1.142
20:12a	de	1.12	22:2b	kai	1.141
20:13	de	1.12	22:22a	de	1.12, 1.141
20:14	de	1.11	22:22b	kai	1.141
20:15a	kai	1.135	22:23	te [de]	[2.31]
20:15b	de	1.11	22:25	de	1.11
20:15c	de [kai]	[1.11]	22:26	de	1.12
20:17	de	1.132	22:27a	de [tote]	[1.12]
20:18	de	1.11	22:27b	de	1.12
20:36	kai	1.222a	22:28a	de [te, kai]	[1.12]
20:37a	de	1.12	22:28b	de	1.12
20:37b	kai	1.134	22:29a	oun [tote]	[3.1]
20:38b	de	1.134	22:29b	kai … de	1.12, 2.1
21:1a	de [kai]	[1.11]	22:30a	de	1.11
21:1b	de	1.11	22:30c	kai	1.212b
21:1c	kai	1.135	23:1	de	1.12
21:2	kai	1.135	23:2	de	1.12
21:3a	de	1.135	23:3	tote	4.1
21:4	de [kai]	[1.12]	23:4	de	1.12
21:5a	de	1.11	23:5	te	2.33
21:5b	kai	1.134	23:6	de	1.134
21:6c	de	1.12	23:7	de	1.11
21:7a	de	1.12	23:8b	de	1.12
21:7b	kai	1.222a	23:9a	de	1.12, 1.141
21:8a	de	1.11	23:9b	kai	1.12, 1.141
21:8b	kai	1.135	23:10	de	1.11
21:9	de	1.12	23:11	de	1.11, 1.211b
21:10	de	1.11	23:12	de [te]	[1.11]
21:11	kai [de]	[1.135]	23:13	de	1.133
21:12	de	1.11	23:16	de	1.12
21:13	tote [de]	[4.1]	23:17	de	1.12
21:14	de	1.11	23:18a	men oun	3.21, 3.22
21:15	de	1.11	23:18b	kai	1.142
21:16	de kai	1.12, 2.1	23:19	de	1.12
21:17	de [kai]	[1.11] [1.135]	23:20	de	1.12
21:18a	de [te]	[1.11]	23:22	men oun	3.21, 3.22
21:18b	te [not D]	[2.1] [1.12]	23:23	kai	1.211a
21:19	kai [rel.]	[1.224a]	23:31	men oun	3.21, 3.22
21:20a	de	1.12	23:32	de	1.11
21:20b	te [NPC]	[2.1]	23:34	de	1.12
21:26	tote	4.1	24:1	de	1.11
21:27a	de	1.11	24:2	de	1.11
21:30a	te	2.33	24:9	de kai	1.12, 2.1
21:30b	kai	1.131	24:10	te	2.33
21:30c	kai	1.134	24:22	de	1.12

Ref.	Conjunction	Section	Ref.	Conjunction	Section
24:24a	de	1.11	27:28a	kai	1.134
24:25	de	1.11	27:28b	de	1.135
24:27a	de	1.11	27:29	te [de]	[2.31]
24:27b	te [de]	[2.32]	27:30	de	1.11
25:1	oun [de]	[3.1]	27:32a	tote	4.1
25:2a	te	2.32	27:33	de	1.11
25:4	men oun	3.21, 3.22	27:35a	de	1.222a
25:6	de	1.11	27:35b	kai	1.134
25:7	de	1.11	27:36	de . . . kai	1.12, 2.1
25:9	de	1.12	27:37	de	1.12
25:10	de	1.12	27:38	de	1.12
25:12	tote	4.1	27:39a	de	1.11
25:13	de	1.11	27:39b	de	1.12
25:14	de	1.11	27:40a	kai	1.134
25:22a	de	1.12	27:40b	kai	1.134
25:22b	∅ [de]	[4.3b]	27:41a	de	1.135
25:23	oun	3.1	27:41b	kai · · · men	1.12
25:24	kai	1.212b, 1.142	27:41c	de	1.12
26:1a	de	1.12	27:42	de	1.12
26:1b	tote	4.1	27:43a	de	1.12
26:24	de	1.11	27:43b	te	2.2
26:25	de	1.12	27:44b	kai	1.12
26:28	de	1.12	28:1	kai	1.222b
26:29	de	1.12	28:2	te	2.32
26:30	te [kai]	[2.33]	28:3	de	1.11
26:31	kai	1.134	28:4	de	1.11
26:32	de	1.12	28:5	men oun	3.21, 3.22
27:1	de [kai]	[1.11]	28:6a	de	1.12
27:2	de	1.12	28:6b	de	1.11
27:3a	te	2.2	28:7	de	1.12
27:3b	te	2.2	28:8	de	1.12, 1.211a
27:4	kai	1.135	28:9a	de . . . kai	1.11, 2.1
27:5	te	2.2	28:10b	kai	1.222a
27:6	kai	1.135	28:11	de	1.11
27:7	de	1.135	28:12	kai	1.212a
27:8	te	2.2	28:13b	kai	1.212a
27:9	de	1.12	28:14b	kai	1.212a
27:11	de	1.12	28:15	kai	1.135, 1.212a
27:12	de	1.12	28:16	de	1.11
27:13	de	1.11	28:17a	de	1.11
27:14	de	1.11	28:17b	de	1.11
27:15	de	1.11	28:21	de	1.12
27:16	de	1.135	28:23	de	1.11
27:17b	te [de]	[2.1]	28:24	kai · · · men	1.12
27:18	de [te]	[1.11]	28:25a	de	1.12
27:19	kai	1.224b	28:25b	te [de]	[2.31]
27:20	de	1.11	28:30a	de	1.141
27:21	te	2.1, 2.31	28:30b	kai	1.141
27:27	de	1.11			

APPENDIX 3

DEVELOPMENT UNITS IN THE GOSPEL OF LUKE[1]

In many narrative sections of Luke's Gospel, *de* and *kai* are used in exactly the same way as in Acts. *De* introduces DUs, the sentences of which are linked by *kai*. *Kai* both introduces sentences in which nothing distinctive is presented, and associates into a single DU sentences which present distinctive information, for the same reasons as those described in Part Two, sec. 1.2.

The parable of the Prodigal Son (Luke 15:11–32) exemplifies this. Every sentence in which *de* is used presents distinctive information (see sec. 1.15). From v 23 onwards, every sentence introduced by *kai* is non-distinctive. *Kai* is also used, in at least vv 12a,12b (variant *de*), 13a,14b,15b,16a, in connection with distinctive information. This is because the events described in these sentences are treated as preliminary to the main events of vv 17–32 (see sec. 1.21).

The nature of Acts hides an important feature about the distribution of *de* and *kai*. DUs must develop *from* some other unit. In the body of the narrative of Acts, every DU develops from the immediately preceding DU, or else begins the development of a further train of thought within the overall purpose of the book. This continuity of development is not a feature of all narratives. In particular, it is not a feature of Luke's Gospel.

In contrast with Acts, *kai* often introduces the first sentence(s) of an incident or sub-incident in the Gospel of Luke. In general terms, the presence of *kai* in these circumstances signifies that the event(s) concerned do not represent a further development from the immediately preceding one(s). This may be true in two or three distinct situations.

(a) Most commonly, *kai* introduces the first sentence(s) of a new incident because the events concerned are *transitional*. They are

---

[1] For a more extensive discussion of this topic, see Levinsohn, "Notes on the Distribution of *de* and *kai* in the Narrative Framework of Luke's Gospel."

intermediate acts which must occur before the next significant development in the story can take place.

This use of *kai* can be seen from a comparison of the different ways in which Luke reports the movement of Jesus between the scenes of his trials. He faces first the Jewish council (22:66–71), then Pilate (23:1–7), Herod (23:8–12), and finally Pilate again (23:13–25). The movement to the last two of these scenes is expressed at the close of the previous incident (23:7,11). However, the initial journey to Pilate (23:1) is described in the opening sentence of the incident itself (if the traditional analysis into paragraphs is followed) and is introduced with *kai*.

The rationale behind the use of *kai* in 23:1 is that the transfer of Jesus to Pilate in itself does not represent a significant development in the story. Rather, it is a necessary prerequisite to the next development, viz., the presentation of charges against Jesus before the Roman authority:

---

de

22:71　　They said, "What further testimony do we need? . . . "

(paragraph break)

23:1　　*kai* rising up, the whole company of them brought him before Pilate.

---

de

v 2　　They began to accuse him, saying, . . .

Contrast:

---

de

23:6　　Pilate, hearing this, asked whether the man was a Galilean

v 7　　*kai*, having learned that he belonged to Herod's jurisdiction, he sent him over to Herod . . .

(paragraph break)

---

de

v 8　　Herod, seeing Jesus, was very glad . . .

In transitions from one incident to another in Acts, the final events of the first incident were linked by *kai*, following which *te solitarium* introduced the specific lead-in to the first significant development of the next incident (see secs. 1.222b, 2.31). *Te solitarium* is not used in Luke's Gospel. A possible equivalent of *te* in the Gospel is *kai egeneto*, when followed immediately by a transitional temporal expression which relates to the last events presented.

See, for example, Luke 1:23. The temporal clause which follows *kai egeneto* refers to the completion of the period during which the events of the previous verses took place:

---

de

1:22a   Coming out, Zechariah could not speak to them,

v 22b   *kai* they perceived that he had seen a vision in the temple;

v 22c   *kai* he made signs to them

v 22d   *kai* remained dumb.

- -

v 23   *kai egeneto* when his time of service was ended, he went to his home.

---

de

v 24   After these days his wife Elizabeth conceived . . .

Kai is used exclusively throughout a number of incidents in Luke's Gospel, e.g., the events surrounding Jesus' circumcision and dedication (2:21–39). This feature may reflect Semitic influence.[2] Alternatively, the whole incident may be viewed as transitional. In other words, it does no more than describe the events that preceded the next significant development in the story.

If such an interpretation is followed in the case of 2:21–39, the next significant development after the events concerned with Jesus' birth (vv 1–20) would be the detail of v 40 about Jesus' growth as a child. The intervening events would simply form a bridge to that statement.

(b)   Although the presence of *kai* at the beginning of an incident is usually due to the transitional nature of the event(s) concerned, it is used also if the incident does not develop from the immediately preceding topic or interaction.

In Luke 22:58, 59, for instance, *kai* introduces the second and third exchanges which produced Peter's denials. This implies that Luke did not consider them to develop from the previous exchange. In other words, according to Luke, Peter denied his Lord on three separate and independent occasions:

---

[2] N. Turner discusses the relative frequency of *de* and *kai* in different sections of Luke's Gospel, and suggests that Luke may consciously have imitated the Septuagint (*Style*, 56–58).

> *de*
> 22:56   (Exchange 1) A maid, seeing Peter as he sat in the light and gazing at him, said "This man also was with him."

> *de*
>   v 57   He denied it, saying, "Woman, I do not know him."

> v 58a   (Exchange 2) *kai* a little later some one else, seeing him, said, "You also are one of them."

> *de*
>   v 58b   Peter said, "Man, I am not."

> v 59   (Exchange 3) *kai* after an interval of about an hour still another said emphatically, "Certainly this man also was with him . . . "

> *de*
>   v 60a   Peter said, "Man, I do not know what you are saying."

Sometimes, the presence of *kai* at the beginning of an incident may indicate on a much larger scale that the incident is unrelated to the previous material. This is particularly the case when the passage begins with *kai egeneto* plus a temporal expression apparently unrelated to the setting of the immediately preceding events.

For example, 17:11 (*Kai egeneto en tō poreuesthai eis Ierousalēm, kai autos diērcheto dia meson Samareias kai Galilaias*, "It happed that, on the way to Jerusalem, he was passing along between Samaria and Galilee") begins an incident of the major section "Progress towards Jerusalem" (9:51 to 19:10 or 19:27).[3] However, this incident must be placed "at the very beginning of the journey by way of Perea."[4] It is probably therefore neither in chronological sequence with the last events presented nor otherwise a development from them.

(c)   Other differences in the organizational structure and purpose of the Gospel of Luke and the book of Acts may also be identified, which influence the use of *kai*. For example, with the exception of

---

[3] Marshall, *The Gospel of Luke*, 400, 650.

[4] Circumstances tend to confirm Hendriksen's view that, while the events of 9:51-19:10 (or 27) all relate to the same single journey to Jerusalem, "Luke never planned to compose a strictly chronological account of the journey" (*The Gospel of Luke*, 542–43).

parts of the first three chapters of the Gospel, Jesus is the sole central character. The story develops as he interacts with others. Consequently, interactions which do not involve Jesus personally tend not to be segmented into DUs unless particular events represent significant developments affecting him.

For example, the interaction of 18:37–38 between the crowds and the blind man is expressed in a single DU. Only as the man's shouts reach Jesus (v 39b) is a new DU begun:

de
18:36   Hearing a multitude going by, he inquired what this meant.

de
v 37   They told him, "Jesus of Nazareth is passing by."
v 38   *kai* he cried, "Jesus, Son of David, have mercy on me!"
v 39a   *kai* those who were in front rebuked him, telling him to be silent.

de
v 39b   He cried out all the more, "Son of David, have mercy on me!"

de
v 40a   Jesus, stopping, commanded him to be brought to him.

Similarly, if Jesus is the sole initiator in a passage, all his acts tend to be linked by *kai*, especially if they are followed immediately by an incident in which he interacts with others. In the Garden of Gethsemane, for instance, Jesus is the sole initiator, and *kai* alone is used (22:40–46; not Textus Receptus). In the following incident, however, in which Jesus interacts with Judas and his company, *de* reappears.

Further study is needed, to define in detail these and other factors affecting the use of *kai* in Luke's Gospel. However, to quote N. Turner, "one thing is certain, . . . the final editor [of Luke-Acts] has been able to impose his own style upon all the material."[5] In particular, a single set of principles accounts for the function of *de* and *kai*, not only in the book of Acts, but also in extensive sections of the Gospel of Luke.

---

[5] N. Turner, *Style*, 56–57.

GLOSSARY

apodosis—"consequent clause of conditional sentence" (*The Concise Oxford Dictionary of Current English* [Oxford, Clarendon Press, 1976]).

asyndeton—"omission of conjunction" (*Oxford*).

background comment—explanatory or parenthetical comment (see Part Two, sec. 1.133).

background information—"supportive material that does not itself narrate the main events" (Hopper, "Aspect and Forefronting in Discourse," 213), e.g., explanations and parenthetical comments.

basis—part of a sentence which indicates the primary relationship of the sentence to its context—see also: replacement basis.

cast—group of characters present during an incident.

central character—participant about whom the story (or a section of it) is primarily concerned. The central characters of Acts are Christian leaders (see Part One, sec. 1.52).

circumstantial participial clauses—cover term for anarthrous participial clauses in the nominative case (NPCs) and genitives absolute (GAs) which precede the independent clause to which they are subordinate in Acts (see Part One, sec. 4.2).

close chronological sequence—relationship between two events such that no unnecessary action, delay or debate separates them (see Part Two, sec. 4.1).

closed conversation—reported conversation such that each successive speaker and addressee was a speaker or addressee of a previous speech (see Part One, sec. 1.25).

continuing utterance (CU)—any non-initial speech of a reported conversation which fails to bring the conversation to a satisfactory conclusion (see Part One, secs. 1.251–52).

continuity of situation—relationship between two independent clauses such that, apart from modifications described in any participial clause which precedes the second independent clause, the setting of the events described in the independent clauses remains unchanged, as do the participants involved (see Part One, sec. 4.2).

development unit (DU)—one or more sentences of narrative, introduced by a developmental conjunction (e.g., *de*) and associated by *kai* or *te*, which presents a new development in the story (see Introduction to Part Two).

distinctive information—change of setting or subject, or switch between the story line of the narrative and a background comment (see Part One, sec. 1.15).

existential-locative clause—clause whose verb is *einai*, which posits the existence in a location of a person, group or object.

forefronted (elements)—sentence elements which precede their verb (see Introduction to Part One).

in sequence—see: sequence, in.

incident—interaction between two or more people or groups, together with any preliminary events (q.v.) that set the scene for the interaction.

initiating utterance (IU)—speech which opens a reported conversation (see Part One, sec. 1.251).

initiator—participant who performs an action or series of actions.

intermediate step—speech or act which potentially leads to the goal of an interaction, but is not itself the goal (see Part One, secs. 1.25–26).

lead-in—in contrast with a previous preliminary event, the specific event from which the next interaction develops (see Part Two, secs. 1.222b, 2.3).

main line events—the actual story line of the narrative, as distinct from background information (q.v.).

major participant—see: participant, major.

marked, unmarked—the presence or absence of a particular linguistic feature. Note: "unmarked" does *not* imply the opposite of the feature. For example, *alla* is marked for "opposition" (Part Two, sec. 4.3d), whereas *de* is unmarked for this feature. This does not imply that *de* means "not in opposition." Rather, *de* indicates nothing about opposition.

minor participant—see: participant, minor.

narrative—material whose overall framework is chronological and which is concerned with actions performed by specific people or groups.

non-event sentences—sentences which describe a state rather than an action.

nucleus, nuclear events—the central interaction(s) of an incident or story, in contrast with the preliminary events (q.v.) and any background information (see Part Two, sec. 1.21).

participant, major—person or group involved in a series of events, usually introduced by name and further identified (see Part One, sec. 1.2).

participant, minor—person or group, usually not introduced formally, who is involved in an event and then disappears from the story (see Part One, sec. 1.2).

preliminary events—events which set the scene for the central interaction(s) of an incident or story (see Part Two, sec. 1.21).

protasis—"clause expressing condition in conditional sentence" (*Oxford*).

replacement basis—forefronted element (q.v.) which indicates that the sentence concerned is to be related to its context primarily by contrast with or replacement of a corresponding element of the last events described (see Part One, chap. 4).

resolving utterance (RU)—final speech of a reported conversation, by means of which one of the participants persuades the other to perform a particular action (see Part One, sec. 1.251).

rheme—in this monograph, not distinguished from the comment about the topic or theme of a sentence (see Introduction).

sentence—single independent clause, together with those clauses which are subordinated to it (see Introduction).

sequence, in—chronological relationship between two events such that the second event occurs either after or before the first.

sequence, not in—either the second event occurs at the same time as the first, or no chronological relationship between the events is indicated.

setting—"where, when and under what circumstances actions take place" (Grimes, *Thread of Discourse*, 51).

setting, spatio-temporal—where (spatial) and when (temporal) actions take place.

temporal clauses—cover term for circumstantial participial clauses (q.v.) and adverbial clauses of time subordinated by *hote* or *hōs*.

temporary focus—momentary attention to an element of a sentence (usually the subject), in anticipation of a change of attention and initiative (see Part One, sec. 1.2).

theme—topic of a sentence (see Introduction).

tight-knit—relationship between reported speeches such that each successive speaker continues to develop the topic of the previous speech (see Part One, sec. 1.253b).

transitional temporal phrases—term used by Blass, Debrunner and Funk (*Greek Grammar*, sec. 472[3]); references to a point in time (see Part One, sec. 2.1).

undergoer—person or object who experiences or otherwise is affected by an action.

unmarked—see: marked.

BIBLIOGRAPHY

1. Texts and Commentaries of Acts and Luke's Gospel

Blood, D. L., and Blood, D. E. "Overview of Acts." *Notes on Translation* 74 (1979) 1–36.

Bruce, F. F. *The Book of Acts.* Grand Rapids: Eerdmans, 1954.

Cadbury, H. J. "The Summaries in Acts." In Jackson and Lake. *Beginnings of Christianity.* Vol. 5.

Hendriksen, W. *The Gospel of Luke. New Testament Commentary.* Edinburgh: The Banner of Truth Trust, 1978.

Jackson, F. J. F. and Lake, K. *The Beginnings of Christianity. Part I. The Acts of the Apostles.* 5 vols. London: Macmillan, 1926.

Jamieson, R.; Fausset, A. R.; and Brown, D. *Commentary on the Whole Bible.* Grand Rapids: Zondervan, 1961.

Knowling, R. J. "The Acts of the Apostles," *The Expositor's Greek Testament.* London: Hodder & Stoughton, 1901.

Lenski, R. C. H. *The Interpretation of the Acts of the Apostles.* Minneapolis: Augsburg Publishing House, 1961.

Marshall, I. H. *The Gospel of Luke: A Commentary on the Greek Text.* New International Greek Testament Commentary, No. 3. Grand Rapids: Eerdmans, 1978.

Meyer, H. A. W. *Critical and Exegetical Handbook to the Acts of the Apostles.* 2 vols. Edinburgh: T. & T. Clark, 1883.

Moulton, H. K. *The Acts of the Apostles: Introduction and Commentary.* Madras: Christian Literature Society, 1957.

Neil, W. "The Acts of the Apostles," *New Century Bible.* London: Oliphants, 1973.

Nestle, E., and Aland, K. *Novum Testamentum Graece.* 25th edition. London: United Bible Societies, 1975.

Newman, B. M., and Nida, E. A. *A Translator's Handbook on the Acts of the Apostles.* London: United Bible Societies, 1972.

Noorda, S. J. "Scene and Summary. A Proposal for Reading Acts 4,32–5,16." In *Les Actes des Apôtres: Traditions, rédaction, théologie,* edited by J. Kremer. Bibliotheca Ephemeridum

Theologicarum Lovaniensium 48. Leuven: Leuven University Press, 1979.

Page, T. E. *The Acts of the Apostles*. London: Macmillan, 1886.

Rackham, R. B. *The Acts of the Apostles*. London: Methuen, 1901.

Rendall, F. *The Acts of the Apostles in Greek and English*. London: Macmillan, 1897.

Turner, C. H. "Chronology of the New Testament." In *Dictionary of the Bible*, edited by James Hastings. Vol. 1. Edinburgh: T. & T. Clark, 1898.

de Zwaan, J. "Was the Book of Acts a Posthumous Edition?" *Harvard Theological Review* 17 (1924) 95–153.

2.   Works concerned with the Grammar of Greek

Abbott-Smith, G. *A Manual Greek Lexicon of the New Testament*. Edinburgh: T. & T. Clark, 1937.

Bauer, W.; Arndt, W. F.; and Gingrich, F. W. *A Greek-English Lexicon of the New Testament and other early Christian Literature*. Chicago: University of Chicago Press, 1957.

Blass, F. *Grammar of New Testament Greek*. London: Macmillan, 1898.

Blass, F.; Debrunner, A.; and Funk, R. W. *A Greek Grammar of the New Testament*. Chicago: University of Chicago Press, 1961.

Callow, J. C. Review. *Notes on Translation*. Dallas: Summer Institute of Linguistics, 1/1979. Pp. 20–36.

Davies, D. P. "The Position of Adverbs in Luke." In *Studies in New Testament Language and Text*, edited by J. K. Elliott. Supplement to Novum Testamentum 44. Leiden: E. J. Brill, 1976.

Denniston, J. D. *Greek Prose Style*. Oxford: Clarendon Press, 1952.

Denniston, J. D. *The Greek Particles*. Oxford: Clarendon Press, 1959.

Donaldson, J., *Modern Greek Grammar for the Use of Classical Students*. Edinburgh: A. & C. Black, 1853.

Dover, K. J. *Greek Word Order*. Cambridge: Cambridge University Press, 1960.

Funk, R. W. *A Beginning-Intermediate Grammar of Hellenistic Greek. Part II: Syntax*. Missoula, MT: Scholars Press, 1973.

Goddard, J. "Some Thoughts on *De* and *Kai* in Acts 5:1–8:1a." Dallas: Summer Institute of Linguistics, 1977. Manuscript.

Goodwin, W. W. *A Greek Grammar*. London: Macmillan, 1894.

Greenlee, J. H. *A Concise Exegetical Grammar of New Testament Greek.* Grand Rapids: Eerdmans, 1963.

Healey, P., and Healey, A. "The "Genitive Absolute" and Other Circumstantial Participial Clauses in the New Testament." Dallas: Summer Institute of Linguistics, 1979. Manuscript.

Kahn, C. H. "The Greek Verb "To Be" and the Concept of Being," *Foundations of Language* 2 (1966) 245–265.

Kilpatrick, G. D. "The Historic Present in the Gospels and Acts," *Zeitschrift für die neutestementliche Wissenschaft* 68 (1977) 258–262.

Kilpatrick, G. D. "List of Proposed Changes from Nestle and Aland's Text." 1979. Manuscript.

Levinsohn, S. H. "Four Narrative Connectives in the Book of Acts," *Notes on Translation.* Dallas: Summer Institute of Linguistics, 1/1979. Pp. 1–20.

Levinsohn, S. H. "Notes on the Distribution of *De* and *Kai* in the Narrative Framework of Luke's Gospel," *Selected Technical Articles Related to Translation* 5 (1981) 39–53.

Moorhouse, A. C. *Studies in the Greek Negatives.* Cardiff: University of Wales, 1959.

Moulton, W. F.; Geden, A. S.; and Moulton, H. K. *Concordance to the Greek Testament.* Edinburgh: T. & T. Clark, 1978.

Robertson, A. T. *A Grammar of the Greek New Testament in the Light of Historical Research.* London: Hodder & Stoughton, undated.

Smyth, H. W. *Greek Grammar.* Revised by G. M. Messing. Cambridge: Harvard University Press, 1956.

Thrall, M. E. *Greek Particles in the New Testament: Linguistic and Exegetical Studies.* Leiden: E.J. Brill, 1962.

Turner, N. *Syntax.* In *A Grammar of New Testament Greek,* edited by J. H. Moulton. Vol. 3. Edinburgh: T. & T. Clark, 1963.

Turner, N. *Style,* In *A Grammar of New Testament Greek,* edited by J. H. Moulton. Vol. 4. Edinburgh: T. & T. Clark, 1976.

Winer, G. B. *A Treatise on the Grammar of New Testament Greek.* Edinburgh: T. & T. Clark, 1882.

3.   Linguistic Works on other than Greek

Beneš, E. "Die Verbstellung im Deutschen, von der Mitteilungs-perspektive her betrachtet." *Philologica Pragensia* 5 (1962) 6–19.

Callow, K. *Discourse Considerations in Translating the Word of God.* Grand Rapids: Zondervan, 1974.

Chafe, W. L. *Meaning and the Structure of Language*. Chicago: University of Chicago Press, 1970.

Chafe, W. L. "Language and Consciousness," *Language* 50 (1974) 111–123.

van Dijk, T. A. *Some Aspects of Text Grammars*. The Hague: Mouton, 1972.

Dressler, W. U., ed. *Current Trends in Textlinguistics*. Berlin: Walter de Gruyter, 1978.

Firbas, J. "On Defining the Theme in Functional Sentence Analysis," *Travaux de Cercle Linguistique de Prague* 1 (1966) 267–280.

Firbas, J. "On the Prosodic Features of the Modern English Finite Verb as Means of Functional Sentence Perspective," *BRNO Studies in English* 7 (1968) 11–47.

Firbas, J. Review of O. Dahl (*Topic and Comment: A Study in Russian and General Transformational Grammar*. Göteburg: Slavica Gothburgensia, 1969) *Journal of Linguistics* 7 (1969) 91–101.

Firth, J. R. *The Tongues of Men and Speech*. Oxford: Oxford University Press, 1964.

Forster, D. K. "The Narrative Folklore Discourse in Border Cuna." In *Discourse Grammar: Studies in Indigenous Languages of Colombia, Panama, and Ecuador*, edited by R. E. Longacre. Vol. 2. Dallas: Summer Institute of Linguistics, 1976.

Garvin, P. E. "Czechoslovakia." In *Current Trends in Linguistics*, edited by T. A. Seboek. Vol. 1. The Hague: Mouton, 1963.

Gindin, S. I. "Contributions to Textlinguistics in the Soviet Union." In Dressler, ed. *Current Trends in Textlinguistics*.

Grimes, J. E. *The Thread of Discourse*. The Hague: Mouton, 1975.

Hale, A., ed. *Clause, Sentence and Discourse Patterns in Selected Languages of Nepal*. 2 parts. Norman: Summer Institute of Linguistics, 1973.

Halliday, M. A. K. "Notes on Transitivity and Theme in English," *Journal of Linguistics* 3 (1967) 37–81, 199–244; 4 (1968) 179–215.

Halliday, M. A. K. "Language Structure and Language Function." In *New Horizons in Linguistics*, edited by J. Lyons. Pelican, 1970.

Halliday, M. A. K., and Hasan, R. *Cohesion in English*. London: Longman, 1976.

Hockett, C. F. *A Course in Modern Linguistics.* New York: Macmillan, 1958.

Hockett, C. F. *The State of the Art.* The Hague: Mouton, 1968.

Hopper, P. J. "Aspect and Forefronting in Discourse." In *Syntax and Semantics: Discourse and Syntax,* edited by T. Givon. New York: Academic Press, 1979.

Hutchins, W. J. "Subjects, Themes and Case Grammars," *Lingua* 35 (1975) 101–133.

Kiefer, F. "On the Problem of Word Order." In *Progress in Linguistics,* edited by M. Bierwisch and K. E. Heidolph. The Hague: Mouton, 1970.

Kirkwood, H. W. "Aspects of Word Order and its Communicative Function in English and German," *Journal of Linguistics* 5 (1969) 85–107.

Lakoff, R. "If's, And's, and But's about Conjunction." In *Studies in Linguistic Semantics,* edited by C.J. Fillmore and D.T. Langendoen. New York: Holt, Rinehart & Winston, 1971.

Levinsohn, S. H. "Progression and Digression in Inga (Quechuan) Discourse," *Forum Linguisticum* 1 (1976) 122–147.

Levinsohn, S. H. "Participant Reference in Inga Narrative Discourse." In *Anaphora in Discourse,* edited by J. Hinds. Edmonton: Linguistic Research Inc., 1978.

Levinsohn, S. H. "Initial Elements in a Clause or Sentence in the Narrative of Acts," *Selected Technical Articles Related to Translation* 4 (1981) 1–28.

Longacre, R. E. *Discourse, Paragraph and Sentence Structure in Selected Philippine Languages.* Vol. 1. U.S. Dept. of Health, Education & Welfare, 1968.

Longacre, R. E. *An Anatomy of Speech Notions.* Lisse: Peter de Ridder Press, 1976.

Longacre, R. E., and Levinsohn, S. H. "Field Analysis of Discourse." In Dressler, ed. *Current Trends in Textlinguistics.*

Lyons, J. *Introduction to Theoretical Linguistics.* Cambridge: Cambridge University Press, 1968.

Lyons, J. *Semantics 2.* Cambridge: Cambridge University Press, 1977.

Mathesius, V. "On Some Problems of the Systematic Analysis of Grammar." In *A Prague School Reader in Linguistics,* edited by J. Vachek. Bloomington: Indiana University Press, 1966.

Vachek, J. *The Linguistic School of Prague.* Bloomington: Indiana University Press, 1966.